Applied Linguistics and Language Study

General Editor: C. N. Candlin

Computers in English Language Teaching and Research

Selected papers from the 1984 Lancaster Symposium 'Computers in English Language Education and Research'

Edited by

Geoffrey Leech and Christopher N. Candlin

Longman

London and New York

Longman Group Limited
Longman House, Burnt Mill, Harlow,
Essex CM20 2JE, England
and Associated Companies throughout the world.

Published in the United States of America by
Longman Inc., New York

First published 1986

ISBN 0 582 55069 6

BRITISH LIBRARY CATALOGUING IN PUBLICATION DATA
Computers in English language teaching and research.
  1. English language – Study and teaching –
Foreign speakers   2. English language – Computer
assisted instruction
  I. Leech, Geoffrey   II. Candlin, Christopher N.
  428.2'4'07   PE1128.A2

LIBRARY OF CONGRESS CATALOGING IN PUBLICATION DATA
Computers in English language teaching and research.
  (Applied linguistics and language study)
  Bibliography: p.
  Includes indexes.
  1. English language–Study and teaching – Data
processing. 2. Computer-assisted instruction – Congresses.
  3. English language – Research – Data
processing – Congresses. I. Leech, Geoffrey.
  II. Candlin, Christopher. III. Series.
  PE1066.C574   1986   428'.0028'54   85-17405

Set in 10/12pt Linotron 202 Erhardt
Printed in Great Britain
by Mackays of Chatham Ltd

The Contributors

J. Charles Alderson
University of Lancaster

Eric Atwell
University of Leeds

Graham Davies
Ealing College of Higher Education

John Higgins
The British Council

Gerry Knowles
University of Lancaster

Geoffrey Leech
University of Lancaster

Robert Lewis
University of Lancaster

Annette Odell

Martin Phillips
The British Council

Geoffrey Sampson
University of Leeds

John Sinclair
University of Birmingham

Jenny Thomas
University of Lancaster

Scott Windeatt
University of Lancaster

Contents

Preface

The contents of this latest volume in the *Applied Linguistics and Language Study* series have already had a 'dry run' at a British Council Special Course* held at the University of Lancaster in September 1984, which was attended by teachers and educators from many parts of the world. Those closely involved in the organization and teaching of this course agreed that the experience was a remarkable one. There was an almost inspirational feeling of being engaged, as a small but growing community of enthusiasts, in the opening of doors to new and exciting educational opportunities, and the contacts made on the course have already led to more than one international meeting. The enthusiasm exemplified in that course seems to be found wherever teachers are finding or being given the chance to harness their imaginations to the power of computers. But it needs to be combined with a healthy practicality and realism – perhaps with a dash of scepticism – if it is to produce the best results. Above all, innovations in CALL (computer-assisted language learning) need to be firmly set within a curriculum framework, advancing rather than setting back developments in modern language teaching and learning, gained with difficulty over the last decade.

Specifically within the context of other volumes in the *ALLS* series, the collection of papers presented here continues the theme of inter-relating theory and practice. It does so by exploring common interests between CALL and computer-based language research. In the immediate future, both hardware and software developments are likely to bring these two areas of inquiry and practice together, so that, for example, 'intelligent' text processing systems developed in research can be adapted for the more powerful micros where they can in turn be used for CALL. In the same way, no doubt, networking will lead

---

*Course 458: 'Computers in English Language Education and Research'

to the availability for educational use of text databases such as those developed for purposes of research.

Geoffrey Leech and Christopher Candlin highlight this convergence as well as giving attention, through the papers, to other educational applications of the computer: for example, in language learning databases and computer-based language testing. In all of these areas, the purpose of the collection is to further the concerns of applied linguistics, especially in demonstrating how the interests of the practitioner and the researcher are less compartmentalized than they are frequently held to be.

Christopher N. Candlin
General Editor

Lancaster
1985

Introduction

From the list of this book's contents, it will be seen that the topics of contributors 'fan out' from a concentrated focus on CALL (computer-assisted language learning) represented by the first seven contributions, to a more general educational perspective, and finally to a broader context including computational research on English, seen as a background to the educational applications.

Some readers will perhaps feel (at least initially) that the book would have been more useful if we had focused more directly on the computer as a tool for the classroom. It is no doubt true that CALL is the lure which has attracted the ELT professions to the computer, and equally CALL will be the most immediate interest in computing for a large proportion of our readership. (Apart from anything else, many educators have had to develop rapidly some kind of limited expertise in CALL, if only to justify a decision either to invest or not to invest in educational hardware and software.) At the same time, we have to be wary of dangers which may arise from a naive or addictive enthusiasm for CALL, if it is allowed to develop without critical scrutiny. As we shall now proceed to argue, the best corrective to these dangers is to step back a pace or two in order to see how CALL fits into a more general programme of research, educational and curriculum development in the use of computers.

Our first argument is that CALL is still in an experimental stage, when the potentiality of the medium is still being explored, and software (particularly good software) is in short supply. There is therefore a danger, as has already been seen in applications of computer technology elsewhere, that the innovatory powers of the computer will be oversold, and that a backlash will follow, accompanied by the usual obfuscatory effects of controversy. Already one can sense, in overheard conversations, that the battle lines are being drawn up between technophiles and Luddites.

In this exploratory phase, it is important that many points of view should be given an airing. Our contributors on CALL therefore include not only leading pioneers and practitioners, such as Graham Davies and John Higgins, who by their commitment, skill and imagination have opened up the possibilities of this newly-fledged medium, but also those who are prepared to take a more critical or at least non-committal stance, such as Jenny Thomas and Charles Alderson. A negative point of view, however, is not for any of our contributors a blanket rejection of computers in the classroom, but rather a plea for discrimination between the good and the bad products of the micro revolution. To that end, Scott Windeatt and Annette Odell offer ways of evaluating both CALL products and CALL process in the classroom.

This need for discrimination is the keynote of our second argument, heralded by Martin Phillips's paper, which is that CALL should be seen and evaluated as only one part – if the most conspicuous part – of a computational provision for educational purposes. This is true not only for language teaching, as Robert Lewis's paper indicates, but also for other areas where there are overlaps with the use of equipment and software. One such example is their use for what has come to be known as CBELT (computer-based English language testing), the subject of Charles Alderson's paper. Further, both CALL and CBELT connect with the use of computer databases for educational and research purposes, a topic explored by Jenny Thomas. The more educational computing can be seen as multi-functional, the less persuasive will be the argument that the classroom micro, like the language laboratory which resulted from an earlier technological revolution, is a technology vainly searching for an educational justification.

Our third argument is that it is hasty to evaluate CALL at the present stage of development, when software is so limited, and when hardware is far less powerful than it is likely to become within a very short time. To say that CALL for ELT is in the 'Stephenson's Rocket' stage is in no way to decry the excellence of some work that is now being done. But if we broaden our vision to look at some current developments in computational research, this will be a better guide to what CALL materials may be possible within the next ten years than restricting one's attention to what is being produced for the present generation of educational micros (already a *past* generation for more affluent users!). Hence the last three papers of this book are concerned with relevant tools now available on mainframe computers (Eric Atwell), with tools for lexical analysis (John Sinclair), and for grammatical analysis (Geoffrey Leech). But perhaps the most direct demonstrations of the educational relevance of computational linguistic research are those provided by the papers which precede these. Geoffrey Sampson, for example, explains the need to incorporate advanced language-processing models, in particular augmented transition networks, into educational software. A comparable research background informs Gerry Knowles's paper on the computer in phonetics teaching. These are just two examples of many developing interconnections between research and the classroom.

We have been stressing the need to see how CALL fits into a general programme of research and development in the use of computers. We have also warned that any developments in CALL should be set within a curriculum framework. It is now time to bring these desiderata more closely together.

Any curriculum for language teaching and learning (one might say, any curriculum), whether viewed from the macro end of state or institutional policy or from the micro end of classroom management, is a compromise forged against a background of learner needs and abilities, teacher resources and society's requirements. A complex juggling act takes place, in which a number of distinct but relatable balls are in play: *data* (or texts to be worked upon and transmitted), *information* (or tools needed to access and make accessible those data), *process* (or tasks and means whereby the accessing and the making accessible of data take place), and, finally, *procedure* (or the classroom scenarios drawn up by teachers, learners and authorities in their various roles, within which all the balls combine).

Broadly speaking, two perspectives have traditionally been taken on the execution of this act. On the one hand, the components (now leaving the juggling metaphor) may be locked tightly together so that their interdependence is, as it were, prescribed for the benefit of learners on their behalf. On the other hand, the process of artfully combining and recombining the components in response to classroom eventuality and learner/teacher need may be seen as the way in which the curriculum itself is created in the procedures of teaching and learning.

In terms of *language* teaching and learning, a number of recent papers (Breen, Candlin and Waters 1979; Breen 1983, 1984; Candlin 1984) have set out the alternatives and have argued, on linguistic, psycholinguistic and educational terms, for the latter course. In a prescriptive and product-oriented curriculum, data are typically selected or manufactured, as language texts, in order to highlight aspects of linguistic information, whether phonological, lexico-syntactic, semantic, or (more rarely) discoursal and pragmatic. Alternatively, data are introduced and particular items of linguistic information are deemed to be notable and learn-worthy for whole classes of learners. Yet again, whatever data are selected and whatever information highlighted, certain processes of accessing and making accessible those data, aided by the given information, become valued as the most effective aids and means to learning. All this, as we say, is done prescriptively on behalf of unfamiliar learners. In a negotiated and process-oriented curriculum, on the other hand, the modes of combination are not pre-set. Data to be worked upon and made accessible arise from classroom decision, as does the information needed by teacher and learners in the class. Range, speed and user-friendliness of such access to information is what is important. Moreover, given the extreme variability among learners, in terms of a host of criteria, what is needed in process terms is a bank of authentic and interactive tasks, available to be accessed by learners at different levels of competence and with different learning styles and strategies in the accomplishment of problem-solving activities. In this model, judgements about the curriculum are made within the process of teaching and learning, very much as an expert system guides a set of procedures. Here instruction is negotiative within a framework of curriculum guidelines, not transmissive on the basis of a set of regulations.

Returning now to CALL, what options are available in the light of these broad curriculum alternatives? The papers in this volume indicate both a present position and a future possibility, the achievement of which depends, of course, in part on software and hardware availability, but even more on the orientation of the computer-assisted curriculum. Crudely, we can remain where many individuals, institutions and publishers stand at present, offering teachers and learners software designed for a curriculum of the first type: packages in which data, information and practice material are presented as a system to be followed and within which there is little or no opportunity for flexibility, let alone user contribution. The self-containedness of the software encourages a transmissive view of the educational process. At one or two removes from this most convergent practice is the use of authoring systems and templates which allow users choices of content and information; the use of database systems with which learners can organize and manage all kinds of information and data relevant to their learning interests; and the use of open-ended packages which, in particular, permit the storage of new kinds of content. As soon as we can make the educational shift to the more divergent and process-oriented curriculum, however, three immediate consequences will derive for our view of CALL, and, incidentally, for our view of the link between CALL and computer-based language research. Firstly, we will take a different view of the relationship between computer, teacher and learner. The computer will take on a function of mediating social interaction within the classroom, becoming neither (to cite John Higgins) master nor slave. It will offer the means for learners and teachers to design their own curricula by providing access to data, information and process in relation to their specific and changing demands. In short, it will offer conditions whereby the cognitive, social and communicative aims of the language classroom can be satisfied. Secondly, we will alter our perception of the economy of language learning and teaching. Rather than requiring teachers and institutions constantly to meet the fresh costs of packaged software (a cost already too high to bear in programming time for all except the professional, and in end-cost for all except the most affluent), the combinability of the curriculum components will allow us, in computing terms, to separate programs which can generate learner-tasks from files which provide texts upon which the tasks can operate. Such a system will, like the curriculum model it emulates, consist of an augmentable text bank on file, a suite of programs designed to generate tasks, and a control program to effect the variable co-selection of task and text. The economy will derive from the reusability of these tasks on new texts. What of the third consequence? No paper on CALL is without its futuristic appeal. Hopes are pinned on a judicious combination of hardware development, software innovation, and changes in user behaviour. Currently, interest is focused on interactive video, speech synthesis and recognition, multi-tasking and networking and the possibility of access to ever-larger and more specific databases greatly enhanced by the deployment of optical character readers. Many of these developments are already in experimental and laboratory use. To deliver these and other futures to the language learning classroom will require, however, more than merely an increase of resource; it will need, on the one hand, an interdependence between CALL and computer-based language research and on the other hand, especially, a curriculum framework appropriate and ready to receive them.

To conclude, we might, speculatively enough, indicate what such a curriculum for CALL ought to be requiring, if it is to be more proactive and less reactive to software and hardware possibilities. In the world of *data*, we will need a range of texts, interactively available in audio-visual and hardcopy modes, utilizing computers and videoplayers for classroom access. Furthermore, we will need the competence and resources in the classroom to create such texts and augment those already available. We need, in short, comprehensible input tailored to our learners' needs and abilities, deliverable to them in a user-friendly fashion. Looking farther ahead, perhaps, we need in the world of *information*, classroom access to language databases, lexicographic and grammatical corpora, oriented to learners' interlanguages and displayed in terms that learners (not only lexicographers and grammarians) can understand. Such corpora could, in principle, be augmented by speech analysers and synthesizers, focusing especially on the problems of supra-segmental patterning, and by pragmatic databases with their inventories of sociolinguistically specified forms of use. To these could be added a collection of discourse types, as a kind of text typology, covering a range of spoken and written activities. There is no doubt, too, that learners would find it useful to have access to diaries of the learning processes of other learners like themselves, routes through the problems of second language learning, if you like, displayed in the form of tried and tested learning procedures. What of the *process* tasks to be made available as problem-solving exercises for learners to apply to text? Two characteristics will predominate: they will have to involve learners in solving problems and experimenting with language learning, and they will need to be differentiated in terms of offering alternative routes, varying levels of demand and attainment, and alternative possibilities of solution. In short, they will need to mirror the cognitive requirements of language learning. More than that, however, since language learning is a social endeavour, such process tasks ought to encourage co-operation and negotiation among learners, and with the machine. Finally, what are the demands on *procedure*? We will need software which matches what we already know from research into second language learning; it will need to be reliable, able to be amended after evaluation, centrally cataloguable and easily accessible. Above all we need teacher and learner involvement in development. In hardware, we will need compatibility and the possibility of gradual augmentation in line with use and a marketing policy set at a price which educational establishments in a range of countries and systems can afford. Perhaps most important of all, however, we will need a shift in teacher attitude and competence through extended in-service education and training. Given that, CALL can move away from a hobbyist purism towards an attitude which will encourage utilization and adaptation of a whole range of presently existing software not specifically designed for language learning, but which can meet the criteria we have outlined. Central to the encouragement of that process of change, however, is the need to keep open lines of communication between practice and research, and the need to begin from a curriculum base. Both of these desiderata, as we have said above, underpin this collection of papers.

Geoffrey Leech   *University of Lancaster*
Christopher Candlin

Introduction to Chapter 1

Innovations in educational technology, especially those, like CALL, which offer challenges not only to the established roles of teachers and learners, the nature of materials and the organization of classrooms, but indeed to the language curriculum as a whole, need to be provided with an educational rationale if they are not to become fashionable instruments of a self-promotive *avant garde*. In short, they need to be critically examined for their educational potential, their classroom costs and benefits. In the first paper in this collection, Martin Phillips offers just such a salutary critique. He does so by posing a series of questions for debate, selecting as his topic what he terms 'the boundaries of what is educationally computable'. In so doing, his paper sets the scene for the book as a whole, looking at CALL and computer-assisted language research as mutually influencing, but always within the framework of the professional context of the curriculum.

1 CALL in its educational context

Martin Phillips

What can be appropriately done in a paper such as this, in my view, is to try to provide some context for the activities in which practitioners of CALL, as teachers and as course participants, become engaged. In the immediacy of the appeal that interacting with computers has, it is unusually easy to lose sight of the *point* of using them, that is their educational rationale. More importantly, it is only rarely that consideration is given to when computers should *not* be used. And so a useful exercise will be to ask the kind of context-setting questions which will help stimulate debate on where the boundaries are to be drawn of what is educationally computable, if I may use the term. At this point it is usual to make the customary disclaimer to the effect that no attempt will be made to provide answers, merely to raise issues. This, of course, is a convenient evasion of responsibility which is perhaps not always entirely legitimate. And yet in this instance it is not only justified but inescapable. We simply do not have answers yet. Indeed we are only just beginning to explore what the appropriate questions are that need asking. It is important that we undertake this exploration. I believe that computers have much to offer us as English language teachers and will have more to offer in the future. But with so seductive, so powerful and so pervasive a technology it is vital to develop and maintain a continuous critique.

In one sense CALL is nothing new. We have always had educational technology of more or less sophistication. As Roe (1985) has pointed out, the original educational technology is the teacher's voice and it is still, potentially at least, the best. The first quantum leap came with a revolutionary technology for preserving the teacher's voice in writing. Chalk was invented. In the right hands it is a powerful if somewhat dusty tool! And then came ways of breaking down to some extent the barrier set up by the classroom walls between education and the world outside: tape recorders and language laboratories for sound and an increasingly sophisticated range of graphic devices from felt and magnet boards to OHTs, film strips, films and latterly videotape. All these inventions served, in principle at least, to enhance the teaching process.

Now we are faced with a new technology which promises, or perhaps threatens, to change the process. For in the educational applications of information technology, that is the convergence of computers and communications, we see the emergence of a technology which is even now an order of magnitude more powerful than any teaching aids we have been accustomed to use hitherto. And educational computing is still only in its infancy. For the first time we have the possibility of teaching materials which can adapt in real time to the needs of the individual student. This is a tremendously exciting prospect. We have a technology which some say could supplant the teacher altogether. This seems less welcome. We have a technology which could continue the process of breaking down the barrier of the classroom walls to the point that classrooms become redundant. To what extent would this be desirable?

But we are all hardened language teachers. We have heard it all before from the pundits of the new approach, whether they set themselves up as the prophets of imminent shipwreck on the rocks of structuralism or whether they were the itinerant hawkers of the latest miracle cure for all ailing language teaching methodologies. After all, was not the language laboratory, if administered in the prescribed dose, supposed to be the panacea? There is indeed cause for scepticism. There is no reason to suppose that conditioning by the computer, if that is how we chose to use it, will be any more successful than brainwashing in the language lab booth.

It is now widely recognized that a major problem with the language lab was software design. More resources were poured into the development of the hardware than ever went into the design of language lab materials. And the same problem is currently being faced by computer-assisted language learning. We are busy pouring old methodological wine into the bottles of the new technology. In some cases, the wine is so old that it has turned to vinegar and when we try it it leaves a sour taste in the mouth. Much of the current CALL software is trivial and apparently untouched by the advances in communicative methodology of the seventies. Its origins can be traced to programmed learning and the behaviourist psychology which gave rise to it. Thus we have a grave responsibility to alert ourselves to the dangers as well as to the opportunities if the computer is not simply to become a teaching machine writ large. The current level of exploitation brings to mind an anecdote about computer communications. It has been suggested that now it is commonplace to transmit data from one computer to another it cannot be long before someone invents a way of inputting and outputting speech via the computer so that we can send it over the telephone wires to each other. There is a danger that through a similar loss of perspective language teaching is busy reinventing its own telephone in the mistaken belief that this is all that is required in order to facilitate a successful CALL.

Does this mean that the computer is comparable to the language lab if it runs the same risks of trivializing the learning process? Clearly there is a danger. The computer, like the lab, is a reductionist device. Let us examine what is meant by this claim. Every time we apply the computer to the solution of some real-world problem, it has to be endowed with an internal representation of the aspect of reality that constitutes the problem and the kind of behaviour that is appropriate for its solution. In other words, the computer must be provided with a model of reality. This is normallly done by means of the program we feed into it. The program is in this sense a model of the problem. Now, whatever model of behaviour one wishes to impart to the computer, for it to be acceptable to the computer it has to be reduced to the form of effective procedures, that is, to an algorithm. This is what I mean when I say that the computer is a reductionist device. But there are no algorithmic solutions to the problems of real life, or if there are they are not apparent to me! And it is this reductionism that the computer shares with the language lab. But there is also a crucial difference. The language lab was always a specialized piece of technology with no roots in the society outside the educational system, a hothouse plant incapable of being transplanted to the environment of the world outside. This is clearly untrue of the computer. It is now part of mass consciousness and permeates social life at many different levels.

It is the computer's major function in society which suggests a first educational role for the computer. This is the reduction of inauthentic labour. I borrow this term from Kemmis's work on the evaluation of the National Development Programme in computer-assisted learning, which was an exploration in Britain of the teaching uses of computers in a number of subjects in the pre-micro years 1973–1980 (Kemmis *et al.* 1977). By inauthentic labour is meant the non-productive work generated as a side effect of the task to be accomplished. This is frequently a feature of the language classroom where exercises are often performed which bear no relation to the ways in which language is actually put to social use. As language teachers we encourage our students to write. Students, however, are often defeated by the complexities of the mechanics of the task. There is an understandable reluctance on the part of the student to revise and correct a script which has cost so much effort to produce, even imperfectly. The result is that teachers gain far more experience of proofreading than students, homework is covered in red ink and we all complain about how incredible the student's apparent blindness to his or her own mistakes is. It has been suggested that the word-processor can help with this particular problem. It is a device for reducing inauthentic labour *par excellence*. The ability of the computer to manipulate text must clearly be of interest to language teachers. And indeed, reports of experience in the British school system in the field of mother-tongue English suggest that word-processing is a powerful stimulus to creative writing (Chandler 1983).

Word-processing is one aspect of the fundamental ability of the computer to store and manipulate symbols. This suggests a more generalized educational role. Where it is possible to formalize our knowledge of the world, and the proviso is important, this 'knowledge' can be transmitted to the computer. In other words, the computer can be provided with the data that structure a learning experience, which define a given learning environment. The computer can embody an abstraction of the critical aspects of reality, an abstraction which constitutes a 'micro-world', so to speak, for the learner to explore. This may sound fanciful, but it has already been done for some subjects, most notably geometry. I refer to the way in which the Logo programming language was developed to allow children to explore intuitively some of the basic concepts of geometry (Papert 1980). Higgins has begun to investigate the application of this approach to ELT (Higgins 1983a).

These possibilities are not neutral. The computer is not, as some seem to think it is, an impartial 'delivery system', that is, simply a medium which transmits a message without affecting it. On the contrary, the new technology has profound implications for our activity. It brings into question quite fundamental notions such as the nature of the curriculum, the concept of the classroom itself, the locus of control over the learning process as well as the status of materials, the nature of language-teaching methodology, the role of the teacher and of teacher training. Let us briefly look at the sort of issues involved; I unfortunately do not have space to explore any of them in great detail.

I shall start with the relation between the computer and the curriculum. Taking the Logo example again as a convenient starting point, the essence of the Logo micro-world is that it allows children to relate geometrical concepts to their own experience. Let me offer an example. What is the definition of a circle? It could be defined as an arc subtending 360 degrees. Or alternatively, as the set of all points equidistant from a given point. Or as the limiting case of a regular polygon. All these definitions are in some sense correct and used in traditional geometry. But what of the following definition? A circle is what you get when you move forward a little and turn a little and continue repeating these actions until you arrive at the point you started at (Hayes 1984). I leave the reader to judge which definition would make most sense to the average schoolchild. Thus plane figures can be modelled by physical movement. Now Logo offers the possibility of controlling a mechanical robot called a 'turtle', or a simulation on the computer screen of the turtle. The turtle can be made to make the movements under program control and so to draw the required geometric figure. This 'turtle geometry' is in fact a new kind of geometry. The geometry commonly taught in schools, consisting of the derivation of theorems from axioms, can be called demonstrative geometry. We all remember the *Quod erat demonstrandum* of the Euclidean school proof. Logo offers a different approach which can be termed procedural or experiential geometry. The child can enact his understanding of geometric figures and thus relate the concepts of plane figures to the physical movements of his own body. Thus the nature of the task has changed and with it our standards of evaluation.

I am not entirely sure what the relevance of the Logo experience to language teaching might be. I do think, however, that it suggests an interesting question. Is there any reason to suppose that the new technology could not have the same impact on the definition of the language curriculum? Is this, for example, the kind of approach that is needed to give muscle to the notion of the procedural syllabus, which has recently been receiving some attention (Prabhu 1983)? I should, as a footnote, point out that although Logo is most commonly described in its function of enabling turtle geometry, it is in fact quite a powerful programming language for the manipulation of natural language and thus may have further relevancies for the language teacher beyond those that I have already implied may exist.

Let me now turn to the concept of the classroom. The instant and easy communications that computers offer suggest that the provision of distance learning could be revolutionized. It would no longer be necessary for students, and teachers for that matter, all to be available at the same time and in the same place. So-called computer bulletin board systems and educational databases, such as Micronet on Prestel, allow computer users to communicate with each other using the telephone system. Again, this is not fanciful. I am describing today's technology and techniques already in use amongst computer hobbyists. Thus this technology affords the prospect of the distributed classroom, and indeed the distributed university, of the future; a truly open university accessible to anyone with a personal computer. This possibility provokes my second question. With the prospect of direct student to student communications through computer networks unmediated by the teacher (perish the thought!), who will decide whether performance criteria have been achieved? Will the computer finally usher in the age of self-evaluation against the standards of efficacious outcomes in the real world? And if so, what might the implications be for examination systems and the comparability of qualifications? This naturally provokes a further question concerning the locus of control over the learning process which I propose to examine briefly.

One of the conventional rationales for the computer in language learning is the justification that it offers a powerful self-access facility. It can easily generate learner-centred, self-pacing activity. The proportion of teacher-led to learner-controlled activity can change. More importantly, it offers choice: programs can be called up by the student at will, they can be sensitive to level of proficiency and, in the future, self-adjusting in real time in response to what they 'learn' about the student (O'Shea and Self 1983). The computer offers a tool to students which allows them to assume mastery of their own learning experience. The question, then, is whether this possibility should be viewed as a liberation or as a new tyranny brought about by a twentieth century *trahison des clercs*, the abandonment to a machine of functions that should properly be performed by people and in particular by trained teachers.

Pursuing for a moment the point about self-adjusting materials, we are led to questions about the status of materials. Hitherto language-teaching materials have been passive. Nothing the student said or did could influence in any deep sense the linear progression of the content. Now, however, as I have already suggested, materials can be self-modifying to accommodate themselves to the requirements of the individual student. That is to say, materials can become interactive. If this is the case, we need to ask ourselves what the implications are of having materials that can, as it were, 'bite back'. To what extent is it desirable that more of the management of learning be embodied in the materials themselves rather than in the way they are exploited?

Let me now turn to questions of methodology. New technologies often bring about changes in the teaching methodologies of the subjects they are designed to support. For example, the introduction of video into ELT applications has stimulated novel teaching techniques. But unfortunately these changes need not always be for the good. I have already indicated that it is possible to criticize many examples of the current generation of CALL materials in this respect. All too often they appear to be methodologically retrograde and incompatible with current theories of language. This is a point which has been made most eloquently by Frank Smith at the Toronto TESOL conference in 1983 and more recently at the seminar on computer-assisted language learning held at the English-Speaking Union in June 1984. We must thus be prepared to distance ourselves from time to time from direct involvement in the development of CALL programs in order to adopt a more critical perspective. In particular, it is necessary to ask to what extent the ways in which we propose to exploit the computer lead to positive benefits in terms of their impact on methodology.

And what of the teacher? How will his or her role be affected? We have already seen that one possibility offered by the computer is that more of the management of learning can be embodied in the materials themselves. This provokes the question of how the teacher's role is thereby affected. Given the arguable advantages of the new technology for individualizing learning, does this mean that it will replace the teacher as some claim and indeed seem happy to envisage?

This is one question to which I am prepared to offer an immediate response. I do not believe this is or should be the case. The more interesting and powerful CALL programs are those which generate a task which involves inter- and intra-group negotiation for its solution. It seems to me that helping to ensure that relevant learning takes place in the course of responding to, for example, a computer-managed simulation demands teaching skills of a very high order at least commensurate with anything required by the more sophisticated techniques in communicative language teaching. An issue that could usefully be explored on courses and in collections such as this, then, is what the nature should be of the new equilibrium that will be brought about by the computer in the delicate balance among students, materials and the teacher. I say 'should be' rather than 'might be' because we must not forget that our decisions can determine what the place of the computer in the learning process is to be and at what point we draw the line and say that the province of the teacher, rather than of the machine, has been reached.

At this point, let me quote the English poet, William Blake. Blake's poem 'Auguries of Innocence' is doubtless familiar. It opens with the lines

> To see a World in a Grain of Sand
> And a Heaven in a Wild Flower,
> Hold Infinity in the palm of your hand
> And Eternity in an hour.

Here Blake is pointing to the miracle of nature, to its metaphysical and physical complexity. This is an anti-reductionist position. With that other grain of sand, however, the silicon chip, the best that we can achieve is a model of some aspect of reality from which *most of the features present in the real thing have been omitted*, as Weizenbaum (1984) has reminded us. This is in the nature of models. Thus there is no way in which in my view the computer can replace the teacher. Who else can put the model into perspective and compensate for its shortcomings?

This is not to say that the learning environment we create with the help of computers cannot become considerably more sophisticated and realistic than has been achieved in the present generation of CALL materials. The question is whether the new educational technology will merely reinforce current practice or, what would be even more sterile, fossilize outmoded methodologies, or whether in contrast it will be successfully exploited to offer fruitful opportunities for curriculum renewal. What will happen depends in part on our willingness to identify and face issues of the sort I have just outlined, in part on technical advances and in part on theoretical progress in language studies.

These are not separate problems. To exploit fully the potential of the computer for language learning, a number of currently distinct applications need to be integrated and the man-machine interface has to become considerably more natural than it is at present. Linguistic databases containing lexical and syntactic information, word-processing functions, natural language parsing, knowledge-based systems, speech synthesis, and ultimately speech recognition, need to be integrated with pedagogic programs and computer-based testing procedures if the use of the computer in language teaching is to transcend its present comparatively primitive level of development. At the same time, we must beware of claiming for computer-assisted language learning more than we know about language or about learning. Our theories of both are at present inadequate to base on them really powerful, and more importantly trustworthy, technologies. Thus CALL has to be rooted in research.

I believe there is a degree of urgency in the need to face issues of the kind I have raised. To return to the comparison with the language lab, I consider that the questions raised by the computer in its applications to language teaching are far subtler and the temptations more seductive than they ever were with the language lab. It is important that we as teachers and practitioners take control of the influence of the new technology upon our profession. Otherwise the inexorable advance of what is called technological progress will remove the power of decision making from our grasp. This is a view which is shared by many workers in the field and which in particular is endorsed by Graham Davies (p. 15, this volume) in his discussion of authoring systems.

It is thus crucial that we consider our position, prepare ourselves for the impact of the computer and absorb its implications for curriculum renewal and methodological change so that we can channel its force in the directions that we as professionals judge to be appropriate. Otherwise much of the developing world, and a large part of the developed world too, risks being littered, firstly with the hardware wreckage of ill-conceived CALL, and secondly with the aftermath of the curriculum changes that it will bring in its wake.

I shall conclude with one final question which in many ways is the most crucial of all. This is the fundamental design question that must be addressed, whether overtly or implicitly, in any development work in CALL. What sort of learning environments do we want to create by means of the computer? This is not merely a technical question, that is a matter of technique only. There is a deeper reason why it demands urgent consideration. This is because it is ultimately an ethical question. We have to be clear about the nature of the learning environments we are creating by the use of educational technology because the answer we give reveals our view of man and of what we deem proper for man to delegate to machines.

Introduction to Chapter 2

Given current enthusiasms for CALL, it is easy to overlook the fact that in a few educational centres in this country, CALL is nothing new. One such place is Ealing College of Higher Education, where, as Graham Davies points out in this contribution, work on computer-assisted language learning has been a component of the modern languages curriculum for almost a decade. What we have here, then, is a personal, practitioner's account of producing and implementing CALL courseware. The focus, however, is not intended to be only historical. Davies describes a number of authoring packages which enable courseware to be relatively quickly and imaginatively written by teachers with no knowledge of the intricacies of computer programming. He thus offers not only a forward perspective, but a double advantage: ease of access to practising CALL and a freedom for interested teachers to go beyond the often educationally-constricting world of pre-packaged software. In short, he offers them the freedom to experiment and to undertake their own CALL-based action research. More than this, however, and very usefully for teachers and curriculum developers concerned with the impact of micro-technology on institutional administration and organization, Davies also discusses the logistic and maintenance problems associated with running a microcomputer laboratory, and the associated issue of staff development and training.

2 Authoring CALL courseware: a practical approach

Graham Davies

First steps on the Prime 300

Our first tentative steps into the world of computer-assisted language learning (CALL) at Ealing College of Higher Education took place in 1977. The impetus to this initiative was a European Communities Commission document entitled 'Bringing Order out of Babel' (COM 76/705, 23/12/1976), which outlined a three-year plan for making greater use of computers for basic translation purposes. For many years Ealing College had been providing vocationally-orientated courses for students of languages, and had gained a reputation for being in the forefront of technological applications to language learning; so this document could not be ignored.

Most lecturers in the School of Language Studies were aware of the presence of a computer (a Prime 300 minicomputer) somewhere in the college, but none had actually used it and only a few had even seen a computer terminal. Nevertheless, it was decided that an approach should be made to the computing division, with a view to setting up a small multilingual terminology bank. The aim of this was to be able to offer students of languages 'hands-on' experience on a computer terminal, so that they would at least know how it 'felt' to consult an automatic dictionary. We were therefore more concerned with the provision of relevant practical training for future careers, rather than making extensive use of the computer's capacity for storing data.

A member of the computing staff was assigned the task of writing a demonstration dictionary program, according to my specifications. It was at this point that the communication gap between linguists and programmers became painfully obvious. I understood nothing about the difficulties of programming and expected the program to appear within a day or two, while the programmer understood nothing about the organization of dictionaries, and had to be convinced of the necessity for allowing for different contexts and one-to-many relationships between terms in different languages. After several weeks of intensive activity, the program finally appeared and was tried out on students. It was a primitive effort, but it worked. In spite of the hostile environment of the computer laboratory, with its complex logging-in procedures and noisy teletype terminals, students appeared to enjoy this new experience.

The original dictionary program contained 40 terms relating to economics and politics in five different languages: English, French, German, Spanish and Russian. It had to be expanded in order to be convincing, but this was easier said than done, because the programmer had not made it possible for the inexperienced computer user to enter new data. The dictionary program had been written to handle 40 terms, no more no less, a completely arbitrary figure which I thought would be a useful starting point, and it required the intervention of the programmer in order to cope with additional data. I had also realized that if the computer could be used as a look-up device it could also ask students questions about the data it contained, and I had ambitious plans for using the lists of words in the dictionary for a variety of vocabulary tests and exercises. But the programmer's time was strictly limited, and he could not be expected to keep writing new programs. I decided it might be easier in the long run to become independent, and I set about teaching myself BASIC, the language in which most programs were written on our Prime 300. In retrospect I probably made the right decision, but such a step should not be taken lightly, as learning a programming language is at least as demanding as learning a natural language, and it certainly takes just as long to become fluent.

The outcome (nearly two years later, in 1979) was an improved dictionary program entitled LEX, a flexible interactive question-answer program known as GDTEST, and a multiple-choice test program called GDMULT. LEX and GDTEST were my own creations, but GDMULT was a modified version of an existing program. These three programs had been designed in such a way that all one had to do to enter new data was call up the Prime 300's EDITOR and create a data file (Davies 1980). Essentially, I had evolved three basic 'template' programs which could read from an unlimited number of data files. The problem of creating new material had thus been reduced to a typing job, and it proved possible to produce a large range of courseware relatively quickly.

To create material for LEX it was only necessary to type each new term in a suitable context, together with a unique reference number and its foreign language equivalent(s). Material for GDTEST consisted of a few lines of explanatory notes, followed by a set of questions together with acceptable answers (including alternatives, if required), comments and 'help' notes. For GDMULT a set of introductory notes, questions, correct answers and distractors had to be provided. The computer 'shuffled' each correct answer and the distractors automatically, when they were presented to the student, so the teacher did not even have to consider this aspect. The Prime 300's EDITOR was, however, not very easy to use, and several hours' tuition was necessary in order to familiarize members of staff with the techniques of file creation. Most of the material produced in this way was aimed at *ab initio* students of German, although the programs worked equally well for students of any other language.

It was at this time that I came into contact with Rex Last, then at the University of Hull, who had been working along the same lines as myself. He had taken the principle of authoring courseware for students of foreign languages several stages further on an ICL 1904S mainframe, and had produced a package known as FAG, which bypassed the computer's editor and simplified the process of inputting and editing exercises (Last 1979). The process of authoring courseware had thus been made much easier for teachers, who did not have to be confronted with the complexities of the computer's editing facilities. FAG was, in effect, an authoring package. Students wishing to access the material created in this way used a package known as EXERCISE, which was described in a detailed instruction booklet. Newcomers to the computer could view a fifteen-minute videotape, which took them through the steps of logging-in and calling up the required exercises.

The students' programs within Rex Last's EXERCISE and my own GDTEST package could be categorized as tutorial programs. Typically, these would consist of some short introductory notes, followed by a series of questions, to which the student responded at the keyboard. Discrete comments could be built in, and error-review routines were automatic. If required, a set of 'help' notes could also be called up during the question-answer sequence, in order to assist the student who had not fully understood the point of the exercise. The results of students' attempts at each exercise were stored on the computer.

Tutorial programs were already well-established in computer-assisted language learning, so no new ground had been broken. Many programs in this category (but much more sophisticated) had already been written on the now legendary PLATO system (Chapelle and

Jamieson 1984). Most PLATO programs are created by professional programmers, who use an authoring language known as TUTOR. Unlike an authoring package, such a language cannot be learned in a matter of hours. It does, however, offer a much greater degree of flexibility and control over the tutorial material. Although authoring languages like TUTOR, or the popular PILOT, speed up the process of creating courseware, the user has to master a set of complex instructions and approach the problem with a programmer's mentality. Most PLATO programs therefore tend to be the result of collaborative efforts between programmers and subject specialists.

The essential difference between an authoring language and an authoring package is that the latter shields the user from the complexities of the logic of programming, and offers a simple framework into which the tutorial material can be slotted. Because the presence of the programmer is no longer required, once the package of authoring programs has been written, the user therefore enjoys more independence.

The disadvantage of authoring packages is that they can be restrictive and result in rather unimaginative courseware. The user is saddled with the framework set up by the creator of the authoring package, and although the tutorial material itself can be infinitely varied, the form of presentation tends to become monotonous. For example, it is difficult, though not impossible, to produce interesting screen displays with graphics or moving text. Nevertheless, authoring packages do enable courseware to be produced at an impressive rate, giving the lie to the story which programmers love to tell: that it takes from one hundred to three hundred hours to write a program to occupy the average student for one hour. When a programmer relates this story, it is probably assumed that the program will include elaborate presentation sequences and complex branching depending on the student's responses.

Programmers tend to perceive computer-assisted learning in terms of so-called 'expert' systems, that is packages of programs which assign an intelligent role to the computer, and control and guide the student to a considerable degree. Such packages take a long time to write, and it must be considered that the enormous costs involved in their development may outweigh their usefulness. If you adopt this approach to CALL, you end up with a collection of dedicated programs – dedicated in the sense that each program fulfils only one function. Last (1980) claims that this approach is 'rather like throwing away the plans of each Concorde after it is built and starting from scratch'.

Even the optimistic ratio of one hundred programming hours to one learning hour would be unacceptable to most educational institutions. Only the richest could possibly afford it. This ratio can be reduced considerably by using an authoring package, and the material can be just as pedagogically sound as that contained in a dedicated program. I estimate that I used to spend about three to five hours producing one hour of learning material for my GDTEST program on the Prime 300. This is a much more acceptable figure, making the creation of a complete set of exercises, say of about one hundred learning hours, a reality rather than a pipe dream.

The main obstacle, which seemed to be preventing this dream becoming a reality, was the Prime 300 itself. First, the machine was painfully slow. It used an inefficient time-sharing system, which could result in long delays before the computer replied to students' inputs, particularly if several students were using the same material. This is not to say that time-sharing systems are necessarily slow – PLATO is impressively fast. Second, the whole system could be shut down for a whole morning or afternoon while maintenance work was carried out, thereby inconveniencing large numbers of users. Third, the process of logging-in and accessing the necessary programs was not 'user-friendly' and caused many students to develop a fear of the machine. Finally, many students disliked the idea of the computer keeping records of their 'connect time' – the 'Big Brother' approach, as some perceived it.

Enter the microcomputer

What was required was a more hospitable environment for learning. During the course of 1979–80, I gained valuable experience with Commodore and Apple microcomputers, and produced an authoring package, known originally as *Teacher's Toolkit* and later as *Questionmaster* (Davies and Higgins 1982, Holmes 1984, Last 1984). In early 1980, Ealing College acquired a multi-user Tandberg EC10 microcomputer, which was used to create exercises for students of German and of English as a Foreign Language (Davies 1982). The EC10 was accompanied by an authoring package known as TEST/T (Last 1981), which, together with programs derived from the original GDTEST and GDMULT programs on the Prime 300, formed the basis of new courseware. So it proved possible to implement the principle of speedy courseware creation on a microcomputer. Students found the EC10 easier to use than the Prime 300, and more interest was generated amongst members of staff. The increase in interest was no doubt due in part to the fact that the microcomputer was located within the main language-teaching area of the college, so that staff and students no longer had to go across to another building and up several flights of stairs to the terminal room.

The EC10 was not ideally suited to our work. Major criticisms were its poor graphics, lack of colour, limited file-handing facilities and the difficulty of producing diacritics and special characters for foreign languages. Moreover, because the EC10 was a rare machine it was almost impossible to obtain new software for it. Consequently we found ourselves somewhat isolated. The moral of this story is that it is extremely inadvisable to choose a microcomputer which is not widely used within one's own sphere of work. We decided (in 1982) to look for a more suitable machine. The BBC micro seemed the obvious choice, as it had all the features which were missing on the EC10 and it was already being used by many schools and other educational establishments in the UK. Some CALL software was already available for the BBC micro, including a commercial translation of my own *Questionmaster* authoring package.

Over the next two years, a dozen BBC micros were bought by the School of Language Studies specifically for the use of students of languages. These machines were housed in one microcomputer laboratory in the same suite of rooms as the conventional language laboratories. The result of the setting up of this new microcomputer laboratory was an unprecedented demand for courseware. I estimated that if the microcomputer laboratory were used to its full capacity, at least one hundred hours of courseware would have to be available to students of each of five languages: French, German, Russian, Spanish and English as a Foreign Language. Although commercial CALL programs for the BBC micro are relatively cheap – typically £8 to £15 – it is unlikely that there will ever be enough of them to satisfy the demand. A good range of authoring packages, with which teachers can write their own material, is therefore implicit in the creation of a CALL software library.

Examples of CALL authoring packages

Questionmaster

This was the first authoring package to be used on the BBC micro at Ealing College. It has a number of features which are desirable in computer-assisted language learning. It can present a stimulus to the learner; accept a response, which is then checked against a range of alternative answers; highlight minor spelling errors; offer discrete clues and 'help' notes and review errors. A typical computer-student dialogue might look like this:

COMPUTER:	What fits here – 'some' or 'any'?
	He cannot go to the theatre because he hasn't . . . . . . money.
STUDENT:	some
COMPUTER:	No, that's not what I want. Note that there is a negative here. Try again!
STUDENT:	any
COMPUTER:	'any' is correct. We say 'any' because there is a negative here.

Minor spelling errors are indicated by an arrow under any offending letters, thus:

computor

If necessary, the teacher can set up the data so that the shape of the best anticipated response is shown to the student, thus:

**** *****

This indicates that a response consisting of two words, one of four and one of five letters, is anticipated.

If required, allowances can be made for missing or superfluous spaces and letters which are in lower instead of upper case – or vice versa.

Questionmaster has not found much favour amongst teachers of English as a Foreign Language, possibly because it forces the teacher into adopting a drill-and-practice approach and because it is more appropriate for routine vocabulary and grammatical exercises. It has, however, proved quite popular with teachers of German and French and, apparently, as a memory training aid for medical and law students to assist them in learning the enormous number of technical terms they have to know by heart.

Copywrite

This was the next authoring package to be introduced, and it immediately attracted a lot of interest from staff teaching English as a Foreign Language. The program was developed by myself in collaboration with John Higgins from a package originally known as *Storyboard*. *Copywrite* enables a short text to be displayed on the computer screen, and after a time the text is reduced to punctuation marks and dashes indicating the length of the missing words. The student then attempts to reconstruct the text. This seemingly impossible task is easier than it looks, because any word anywhere in the text can be chosen. Each time a correct word is entered, every occurrence of it appears on the screen.

Different strategies may be adopted. Students may begin with low-frequency content words they remember from the first reading, or high-frequency words such as articles, common verbs, prepositions, conjunctions and pronouns. A partially completed screen might look like this:

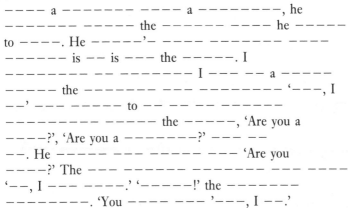

A scoring facility is provided, the maximum number of points being the number of words in the text multiplied by 10. If the student gets stuck, it is possible to call up the first letter of a word as a clue, to request the computer to fill in a whole word or to read the text again. This, however, causes points to be deducted: 5 for a letter, 10 for a word and 50 for reading the text again. The original *Storyboard* had no scoring facility, but field-testing by the publishers in various educational institutions indicated that some kind of points system provided a powerful incentive.

Our experience with *Copywrite* is that it encourages intensive reading, and gives the student valuable insight into language redundancy and the way words tend to combine and suggest what is coming next. If several students work together, it is interesting to note how much conversation the exercise generates about both the content and the language of the text.

Creating new *Copywrite* texts is simplicity itself. The teacher chooses a passage of suitable length, calls up the teacher's 'Builder' program, and just types the text line by line. The completed text is stored on a floppy disk, and can immediately be made available to students. It is therefore possible to produce a constant supply of up-to-date material; a text from the morning newspaper can be ready by lunchtime.

Teachers have also discovered that students can benefit by using the 'Builder' program. The student uses the program to create a short essay, which the teacher corrects on the computer screen. The essay is thus marked as it is actually written, and can also be used by other students as a reading exercise.

The idea of dismantling a text and then restoring it is a well-established practice in language reinforcement exercises and tests, but the *Copywrite* technique would be difficult to implement without a computer. The program's appeal is perhaps due to the fact that it makes sensible use of the computer's power.

Clozewrite and Clozemaster

Two authoring packages, my own *Clozewrite* and Chris Jones's *Cloze-master*, are used for the creation of computerized cloze exercises. *Clozewrite* uses the same 'Builder' program as *Copywrite*, and texts created for *Copywrite* are completely compatible with *Clozewrite*. The principle of making a text compatible with a number of different programs and doing different things with it, has also been incorporated into Longman's *Quartext* package. *Quartext* offers the student a choice of four different exercises centred on each text stored on the disk. Two of the exercises in *Quartext*, *Tell-Tale* and *Hopscotch*, are similar to *Copywrite* and *Clozewrite*.

The difference between *Copywrite* and *Clozewrite* (and the programs in the *Quartext* package) lies in the way the text is mutilated. In *Cloze-write*, words are deleted at chosen regular intervals and replaced by numbered blanks. The student can choose any deletion interval from 2 to 9, and also specify the deletion starting point, so that a variety of different exercises can emerge from one text. The length of each deleted word is not revealed to the student, until at least one attempt at the word has been made. A 'partial matching' routine reveals minor typing or spelling errors. At any stage, the student can ask for individual letters or whole words to make the task easier, but then points are deducted – *Clozewrite* also includes a scoring facility. *Clozemaster* works in a similar way, but permits the creation of longer texts – up to 50 lines, compared with the 18 lines allowed by *Clozewrite* – and has less elaborate error diagnostic routines. The longer texts are handled by means of a 'scrolling screen' facility, which is built into the program.

Purists will argue that *Clozewrite* and *Clozemaster* do not produce true cloze exercises, because the computer accepts only words which appear in the original texts. Ideally, the student should be able to enter any semantically and syntactically correct words in the numbered blanks. The difficulties of implementing a true cloze exercise on a computer have been highlighted in the Moray House Computer Clozentrophy Project (Cousin 1983). The main problem is that the computer is unable to recognize what words make sense in a particular context. Therefore every possible alternative has to be anticipated and built into the data. Our experience at Ealing indicates that although teachers feel that it would be wonderful if the computer could accept a range of alternative responses, scarcely anyone would be prepared to invest the necessary time in setting up the data accordingly. A *Clozewrite/Copywrite* text can be typed in about twenty minutes, but it would take much longer to prepare a text that allowed for every possible alternative rendering of every word which might be deleted.

It is also debatable to what extent students would benefit from more elaborate preparation. The computerized cloze exercise tends to be perceived by students as a sort of game. The fact that this 'game' concentrates their attention on a variety of texts, which call upon their store of linguistic knowledge and which they have to read intensively in order to 'win the game', probably justifies the 'impure' approach. Moreover, it must also be borne in mind that the ease with which the teacher can create material means that new and topical texts are constantly being produced, so that the data never goes out of date.

Gapkit

While the principle of deleting words from a text at regular intervals is useful, it is sometimes desirable in reinforcement work to present the student with a text in which specific categories of words, or even parts of words, have been deleted: for example, prepositions, phrasal verbs, or suffixes and prefixes. This principle of selective deletion is a well-established practice in language teaching and easily implemented on a computer. My own *Gapkit* authoring package speeds up the creation of exercises of this type. It is designed to make the teacher's job as easy as possible. The teacher just types the text, indicating where the gaps are to appear by placing the 'slash' character (/) at the beginning and end of each gap, thus:

I /woke up/ this morning at 8 o'clock, /got out/ of bed and /went down/ to the breakfast room.

I always /for/get people's names, but I am good at /re/membering faces.

Explanatory notes and clues can also be built into the data.

The above sentences would be presented to the student like this:

I − − − − − − this morning at 8 o'clock, − − − − − − of bed and − − − − − − − − to the breakfast room.

I always − − −get people's names, but I am good at − −membering faces.

The computer works out where the gaps are positioned on the screen, and locates the cursor in turn at the point where each gap begins. The student can then attempt to fill in the gap, ask for a clue, or make the computer fill in the gap itself. Errors are reviewed over and over again, until the student has produced a perfectly correct 'page'.

The old version of *Gapkit* always indicated the length of the anticipated response, but a new version has been developed which allows the teacher to conceal the length of each gap. This makes it possible to produce exercises which would be pointless if the student could work out the answers just by counting the dashes.

Speedread

A useful package for producing exercises to improve reading skills has been produced by Arthur Rope. This new package, known as *Speedread*, enables the teacher to create a text, interspersed with sets of multiple-choice questions to test the student's comprehension. The text can be presented to the student at specified speeds, thus providing a controlled and flexible environment for the development of rapid-reading skills.

Choicemaster

Teachers who wish to produce straightforward multiple-choice exercises and tests, can use Chris Jones's *Choicemaster* package. It offers two modes: tutorial and test. In tutorial mode, the student is given immediate feedback as each question is attempted, and offered clues or explanations when wrong answers are selected. In test mode, the student attempts the questions but is offered no feedback until the whole test has been completed. Teachers often tend to disparage multiple-choice exercises, but our experience has indicated that students perceive them as beneficial. One of the sets of multiple-choice exercises developed for the old EC10 microcomputer contains a large range of material geared towards EFL students taking the Cambridge First Certificate and Proficiency examinations. As examinations loom on the horizon each year, an enormous increase in the usage of these programs is noticeable. Teachers are generally happy with this situation, because it has led to a proportionate decrease in the demand for practice examinations.

Vocab

A completely different type of authoring package, entitled *Vocab* and also written by Chris Jones, attempts to move away from the tutorial approach to CALL by offering the teacher the facility to create files of words in suitable contexts, which are used in a variety of linguistic games. The games include *Skullman*, a variation of *Hangman*, the word guessing game; *Anagrams; Mindword*, a word game based on the 'Mastermind' principle; *Alphagame*, a game in which the student has to guess what word the computer is thinking of; *Which Word?*, a multiple-choice exercise; *Word Order*, a game in which the student has to sort a set of jumbled words into order to form a meaningful sentence.

Games

Games form an important part of available CALL software. Programs produced for English primary school children, such as Acornsoft/ESM's *Word Sequencing, Sentence Sequencing* and *Word Hunt*, have proved popular with EFL students at all levels. At present the programs are not accompanied by authoring packages, but the organization of data within them is simple enough to enable a programmer to produce new variations. ASK's *Facemaker*, another program written for primary school children, has found favour amongst EFL students. It offers an exploratory approach to learning the vocabulary of physiognomical description by allowing the user to create all manner of human faces on the computer screen.

Other programs, which were not designed primarily as educational programs, nevertheless contain enough textual material to be used as a stimulus and focus of attention by language students. These include *Yellow River Kingdom* (part of the BBC micro's 'Welcome Package') and *Classic Adventure* by Melbourne House Software. The former falls into the same category as the old 'Hammurabi' game (Ahl 1978), and the latter is a new version of the original 'adventure' game, which requires the user not only to read the imaginative texts very carefully, but also to indulge in some mind-stretching lateral thinking. Some teachers have also found primitive artificial intelligence programs, such as *Animal* and *Doctor*, useful. In the former, the computer attempts to 'learn' about the distinguishing features of different animals according to questions and answers supplied by the user – useful for training students in question formation. The latter, which is derived from Weizenbaum's original ELIZA program, casts the computer in the role of a psychoanalyst who is attempting to solve the user's 'problem'. *Animal* is listed in Ahl (1978) and *Doctor* is listed in Krutch (1981). Listings of versions of both programs appear in my book, *Talking BASIC*. At the end of this paper there is a list of software which gives more details of these and other materials, and of the types of computer required.

Organizational and maintenance problems

Setting up a microcomputer laboratory is easy compared with the day-to-day organization and maintenance of the hardware, and, more importantly, the software. Hardware presents few problems. Modern microcomputers are relatively trouble-free. They consist mainly of solid-state electronic components, which either work or fail. If they fail, they are simply replaced. The only two problem areas we have identified are the keyboards and disk drives, which are, significantly, the only components with moving parts. It goes without saying that regular maintenance checks should be carried out by a competent technician, but microcomputer laboratory hardware is generally easier to maintain than language laboratory hardware.

In Ealing College's microcomputer laboratory, each computer has its own disk drive. We rejected the ECONET system, which enables several computers to share a common disk drive, on the grounds that this offered insufficient flexibility. With ECONET, all students using the microcomputers are obliged to work on the material stored on the disks in the common drive. If individual students wish to work on material which is stored on other disks, then a member of staff has to be responsible for choosing and inserting the new disks. This assumes that a member of staff, a technician or teacher, is present all the time the laboratory is in use.

If each computer has its own disk drive, then it is easier for students to use the microcomputer laboratory on a self-access basis, but this does not rule out the possibility of the laboratory being used by groups under the supervision of a teacher. In other words, our perception of the microcomputer laboratory is similar to our long-held view of the language laboratory. Students who wish to work on their own collect a disk from the software library, use the material it contains for as long as they wish, and then return the disk to the library. Staff working with groups use the software library in exactly the same way. If several students in the group wish to work on the same program, then the teacher moves round the class, loading the chosen program from one disk into the memory of each computer. It takes no more than a few minutes to do this, even with groups of up to twelve students. It is therefore not usually necessary to make multiple copies of disks – which is expensive. Some programs, for example *Speedread*, rely on the presence of a disk in the drive while the program is being used. In such cases, sets of disks have to be provided for group work.

Ealing College already had a large audiotape library when the microcomputers were introduced, so it was not difficult to apply the principles of organizing and maintaining audiotapes to floppy disks. In many respects the media are similar. Both dislike dust, smoke, magnets, damp, heat and metal storage cabinets, so technician staff quickly appreciated many of the problems associated with handling disks. They also knew that master copies of storage media have to be locked away safely and that students' copies must be checked regularly to ensure that the material they contain is in good condition. Maintaining computer software is, however, a more complex task than maintaining audio tapes. It is therefore essential that technicians are given relevant training. A technician must know how to make backup copies of disks, test individual programs, move copies of programs and data files from one disk to another, use diagnostic software to identify and rectify faults, maintain a software reference catalogue and be on hand to offer help and advice to students and staff who are unfamiliar with computers. Ideally, a technician should also know something about programming. If possible, a fully-trained programmer should also be available to solve more difficult problems and help develop new software, but this is a luxury we have not yet been able to afford, so we rely on academic staff who are primarily linguists but also proficient programmers.

The provision of training for academic staff is of key importance. Teachers with a background in the arts are prone to fear machines and must be helped to overcome this fear. The computer is not an awesome beast in itself, but it must be regarded with a certain attitude of mind. Using a computer for the first time can be a salutary experience. The rigid discipline the computer imposes can be humiliating or frustrating, and many language teachers kick against its inflexibility. The most difficult point to get across is that the machine only does what it is programmed to do, and that it is up to the teacher to specify precisely how it should behave. A training course should therefore include an introduction to the nature of the machine and its limitations.

The essential theoretical aspects of CALL should be covered, but 'hands-on' sessions are by far the most important part of any training course. Teachers should be able to switch on the equipment, insert disks correctly in the drive and load and run the programs they wish to use. Most of the disks in the software library at Ealing College contain a 'bootstrap' program, which enables the user to get started simply by pressing two keys – the so-called 'auto-boot' facility. Thus it is not necessary to learn strange new commands. If teachers wish to author their own material, they need to be taught how to use the relevant authoring packages. But once teachers begin to create new material, additional organizational considerations arise. It is most important, for example, that technician staff are informed about any new courseware created by means of authoring packages, so that the catalogue can be updated and necessary backup copies made. Finally, it helps if teachers know something about BASIC, so that they may gain a better appreciation of what programming entails. Ideally, teachers should be offered a training course of about twenty hours to cover all these aspects of CALL.

Training students presents far fewer problems. Virtually all young people seem to have basic keyboard skills nowadays, but for those who are unfamiliar with the QWERTY keyboard, the *Keyboard* program (part of the BBC micro 'Welcome Package') has proved invaluable. This program takes newcomers on a guided tour of the keyboard, explaining the functions of the unfamiliar keys and testing the user's ability to identify keys quickly. Most students need only a brief introduction to CALL. They need to know how to switch on the equipment, insert disks and how to start a program running – using the 'auto-boot' facility. After about an hour or two, the majority of students feel quite at home with the machines. Because they tend to learn from one another, exhaustive demands are rarely made upon staff time. In the case of difficulties, students can always call upon a technician. Awareness of computers is considered important at Ealing College, so all students on our Applied Language Studies degree course have to follow a series of ten lectures on computer applications to language, as well as participating in ten one-hour practical programming sessions in BASIC. This takes place during their first year.

So far the microcomputer laboratory has run very smoothly. No equipment has been damaged or lost, and surprisingly few disks have been badly corrupted. No important software has been lost irretrievably, largely thanks to an invaluable technician who keeps tight control over the storage of master disks and ensures that backup copies of software are made at regular intervals. A judicious measure of security is, however, vital. When the microcomputer laboratory is not in use, it is kept locked. Staff and students wishing to use it must ask a technician to unlock it, and it is important that records are kept of all disks which are out on loan. Disks can only be used in the microcomputer laboratory, and cannot be taken home by students. Most of the software we use is 'home-grown', so this gives rise to few copyright problems. As for software bought in from outside, it is important that copyright is respected and that no unauthorized copies of disks are made.

All in all, the microcomputer laboratory has been a successful venture, and we look forward to increased activity in the future. In particular, we are interested in the development of audio-interactive and computer-controlled videodisc systems, but that depends on the important factors of time and money.

Software

Classic Adventure: Interactive adventure game (in English). Text only, based on original mainframe game. User explores strange world of the Colossal Caves, finding valuable treasures guarded by unfriendly creatures lurking in the darkness. Published by Melbourne House Software, 131 Trafalgar Rd, Greenwich, London SE10. Runs on the BBC micro and other popular home computers.

Choicemaster: Multiple-choice exercise/test authoring package. Teacher just types in questions, correct answers and distractors. Optional clues may be built in. Student can run program in tutorial or test mode. Published by Wida Software, 2 Nicholas Gardens, London W5 5HY. Runs on the BBC micro, Apple.

Clozemaster: Authoring package for cloze exercises/tests. Teacher just types in plain texts, which may be up to 50 lines long (circa 300 words). Word deletion is automatic and the interval can be varied by student (5–15). Includes 'scrolling screen' facility. Published by Wida Software, 2 Nicholas Gardens, London W5 5HY. Runs on the BBC micro, Apple.

Clozewrite: Authoring package for cloze exercises/tests. Teacher just types in plain texts, which may be up to 18 lines long (circa 120 words). Word deletion is automatic and the interval can be varied by student (2–9). Published by Camsoft, 10 Wheatfield Close, Maidenhead, Berks SL6 3PS. Runs on the BBC micro.

Copywrite: Authoring package for creating text reconstruction exercises. Originally known as *Storyboard*. Similar to cloze principle, but whole text is deleted and replaced by dashes and punctuation. Includes score. Published by ESM, Duke St, Wisbech, Cambs PE13 2AE. Runs on the BBC micro. Commodore computer versions available from Camsoft, 10 Wheatfield Close, Maidenhead, Berks SL6 3PS.

Facemaker: An entertaining program, which allows the user to create different human faces on the computer screen by typing in words (in English) associated with physiognomical description. Published by ASK, London House, 68 Upper Richmond Rd, London SW15 2RP. Runs on the BBC micro and Commodore computers.

Gapkit: An easy-to-use authoring package for creating gap-filling exercises. Teacher can create one page of introductory/help notes and up to three pages of exercises of up to 18 lines each. Up to 40 gaps per page can be designated. Gaps can be whole words, groups of words, suffixes, prefixes, etc., in any combination. Includes automatic review of students'errors. Published by Camsoft, 10 Wheatfield Close, Maidenhead, Berks SL6 3PS. Runs on the BBC micro, Commodore PET.

Keyboard: Part of the BBC micro 'Welcome Package'. Takes the user on a guided tour of the BBC micro keyboard. Explains functions of different keys and tests user's ability to find specified keys quickly. Published by British Broadcasting Corporation, 35 Marylebone High St, London W1M 4AA. Runs on the BBC micro.

Questionmaster. Originally known as *Teacher's Toolkit*. A universal authoring package, designed for language teachers who wish to create exercises on grammar, vocabulary, factual knowledge, etc., together with introductory tutorial material and help notes. Material is presented to student as series of questions. Allows for alternative responses, diagnoses minor typing and spelling errors. Includes automatic error-review routine. Published by Hutchinson Software, 17–21 Conway St, London W1P 6JC. Runs on the BBC micro, Apple, Commodore PET.

Sentence Sequencing: Presents groups of short sentences on the computer screen in random order. The user has to put each group of sentences into a meaningful order. Published by Acornsoft/ESM.

Available from ESM, Duke St, Wisbech, Cambs PE13 2AE. Runs on the BBC micro.

Speedread: An authoring package designed for the creation of rapid-reading exercises. Teacher types in text, together with sets of multiple-choice questions to test comprehension. Student can vary the speed of presentation, from unlimited time to extremely fast. Published by Wida Software, 2 Nicholas Gardens, London W5 5HY. Runs on the BBC micro.

Storyboard: The original program from which *Copywrite* (q.v.) was derived. *Storyboard* and *Storyboard Plus*, a version which includes a set of texts by EFL specialist Andrew Harrison, are published by Wida Software, 2 Nicholas Gardens, London W5 5HY. Runs on the BBC micro, Apple.

Teacher's Toolkit: The original name of *Questionmaster* (q.v.)

Vocab: An authoring package which enables the teacher to create files of words, together with contexts/clues, which are then used as the basis for a variety of entertaining vocabulary games. Published by Wida Software, 2 Nicholas Gardens, London W5 5HY. Runs on the BBC micro.

Word Hunt: A program derived from the parlour game, in which participants attempt to create as many words as possible from the letters of a longer word. Published by Acornsoft/ESM. Available from ESM, Duke St, Wisbech, Cambs PE13 2AE. Runs on the BBC micro.

Word Sequencing: Presents groups of jumbled sequences of words on the computer screen, which have to be rearranged to form meaningful sentences. Published by Acornsoft/ESM. Available from ESM, Duke St, Wisbech, Cambs PE13 2AE. Runs on the BBC micro.

Yellow River Kingdom: Part of the BBC micro 'Welcome Package'. A game in which the user has to govern the imaginary Yellow River Kingdom, allowing for variations in the seasons and population. A useful simulation, making use of text and graphics. Published by British Broadcasting Corporation, 35 Marylebone High St, London W1M 4AA. Runs on the BBC micro.

Introduction to Chapter 3

In the first of two contributions to this volume, John Higgins has three objectives in mind. Firstly, to set CALL in a psycholinguistic context, exploring its relationship to three models of learning: what Kemmis has called Instructional, Revelatory and Conjectural paradigms. In elaborating on this triple perspective, Higgins not only reflects current applied linguistic interest in the links between acquisition and learning, but also suggests connections between patterns of teaching with CALL and teachers' views of the learning process. This issue allows him to focus on his second objective, the way in which grammar, in particular, can be taught and learned through CALL. What is interesting here is how a CALL perspective, informed by an analysis of modes of learning, can suggest even to non-CALL users, how they might more imaginatively go about working with grammar in the classroom. There is, as Higgins points out, more than one model for grammar teaching! Models, however, need practical illustration, and here the paper meets its third objective, that of providing the reader with an account of practical action in the classroom, making use of a variety of novel programs designed by the author and his colleagues. We are thus provided, not only with an example of emulatable practice, but one which is grounded in an awareness of varied learning and teaching strategy. Finally, the paper touches on a theme central to the book as a whole: how we can interlink computer-assisted research into natural language with the educational demands of the language-learning classroom.

3 The computer and grammar teaching

John Higgins

I wish I knew how to teach grammar. Of course I can carry out certain procedures which correspond to a conventional notion of teaching grammar. I can introduce well-contextualized examples of certain sentence patterns. I can demonstrate the similarities between these patterns and draw attention to the regular and predictable ways in which certain forms are selected in certain contexts. I can express these similarities and restrictions in the form of rules. I can make my students repeat patterned sentences or do drills which involve near repetition, so that they 'get their tongues round' the new forms. I can set them tasks based on transforming or completing sentences. When they make mistakes, I can review the rules and invite them to try again. I can point out ungrammatical features of their spontaneous speech and again draw attention to the rule which has been violated. But have I then taught them grammar?

Inconsistency

If I look for the answer in tests where the criterion is the ability to do what they have been doing in my class, the answer might be 'Yes'. If I look instead for an answer in the way they spontaneously manipulate and select forms in fluent speech, I am worried not so much by failure as by inconsistency. There is too much diversity of performance, a diversity which I cannot account for in the history of the way I have taught. There is no comfortable proportion kept between the time spent in my classes and the progress made. Mistakes persist, occurring frequently among some students, sporadically and unpredictably among others. The converse may occur. Some students seem able to cope with forms and relationships which I cannot remember having taught them; they seem to have deduced the rules for themselves.

Analysis

Obviously I am not the first person to feel worried about the way grammar is or is not learnt from conventional classroom presentation; this has been a major concern of the profession for at least half a century. In common with many others, I do not believe there is a clear solution to the problem. It follows that we may be unwise to try to 'computerize' conventional grammar teaching, since an essential prelude to computerizing any function is to analyse that function, to understand it fully, and grammar teaching is not well understood at all.

Models of the learner

It is, of course, easy enough to computerize most of the functions I described in the first paragraph, the things I do when I 'teach grammar'. Presenting examples, making statements in the form of rules, assigning mechanical tasks, and, to a lesser extent, error correction, are all well-understood. Accounting for errors, and thus giving the relevant explanation or correction, is probably something I do better than any computer, since I have more channels of communication open to my students and more knowledge of the students, whether as individuals or as archetypes. One way of describing this is to say that I have a better mental model of the student than I am capable of giving to the machine. I can distinguish, most of the time, between errors due to carelessness, those due to profound misunderstanding of a principle, and those errors which represent a kind of language exploration, an attempt to see if a principle applied in one context is also valid in another. (This kind of error can be called a language experiment, and is fairly common.) But I am not quite sure how I draw these distinctions, so I could not transfer my skill to a machine. Some researchers, however, are trying to do this under the banner of 'intelligent tutoring systems'.

Directed learning

Meanwhile no harm is done if computerized exposition and drill-and-practice material is made available to learners, since for some learners and on some occasions that is what is wanted. Such an approach has the merit of being familiar, and of removing oppressive responsibilities. If I wanted to learn, for instance, the game of bridge, I would certainly not relish having to deduce its rules from watching others play or indeed being required to join in a game. I would want a teacher or a book to explain the rules and give me advice on play using simplified example hands. I feel the same about tackling a new language. Both as a beginner and, too, at various intermediate stages I will want some other person to take the responsibility for directing my learning. If a good teacher is not available to me when I need one, I would accept a computer program as a partial substitute. The danger, though, comes in thinking of directed learning, learning in which the learner takes no initiatives, as being actually or potentially sufficient.

What is taught and what is learnt

Explicit teaching is demonstrably insufficient: the teacher will not have time to present in statement form all the facts which the learner needs to command. Frank Smith (1978, p. 69) has drawn attention to the enormous discrepancy between the vocabulary which learners come to command and the vocabulary which they have been explicitly taught. Very much the same point can be made about grammar. To describe a competent language user's grammar (native speaker or foreign learner) would require hundreds of thousands of separate statements, statements about when a particular tense is selected, when an article is required, which verbs are followed by *to* infinitives and which by *-ing* forms, why we say 'He is going to London tomorrow' and not (except with two tone groups) 'He is going tomorrow to London', and so on. In *The English Verb in Context* Jack Bruton plucked fifty paragraphs out of English fiction and journalism and invited comment on the verb forms which occurred in them (Bruton 1964). A glance at this book should convince any English speaker how much they know which has never been explicitly taught.

Learning and acquisition

Most language teachers would accept that there are conscious and unconscious processes at work when we learn languages. Stephen Krashen has characterized these as *learning* and *acquisition*, and makes strong claims that the two types of process operate independently and do not support each other. In particular he claims that what is consciously learnt cannot be used to initiate spontaneous language (e.g. Krashen 1982, p. 15). Not everybody will accept Krashen's conclusions, but most teachers would agree that the acquisition process is related to the effort to convey or interpret meanings and cannot flourish in activities which concentrate on forms. This has led several commentators on computer-assisted learning (notably van Campen 1980 and Odendaal 1982) to state that the computer should be used for formal grammar drilling which favours learning, thus releasing the teacher to run the freer forms of activity which will enhance acquisition. This seems at first sight very sensible. Teachers are good at conveying and interpreting meanings. Computers are good at processes which require patient repetition and attention to detail. Why not use each medium for the task it is best at?

Mediated and enacted learning

In the last paragraph I applied the word *medium* to teachers and machines, but it is only appropriate to use it when one is talking about learning rather than about acquisition. Olson and Bruner (1974) drew an interesting distinction between mediated learning, in which something is described, and enacted learning, in which something is experienced. In mediated learning the medium may be a book, a picture or a machine, or it may be the teacher. One is using the medium to learn *about*, rather than to learn *to*. Learning activities (using the word *learning* in Krashen's sense) require a medium. When, on the other hand, the class is engaged in activities which enhance acquisition, the process is, or should be, enactive; the teacher ceases to be a medium for experience but is part of the experience.

Linear versus random

Conscious learning, or mediated learning, is convenient in that it can readily be organized into a linear syllabus. Learners can be led through this syllabus, with periodic checks on their retention, and eventually given some attestation of what they have covered. Such a systematic approach not only appeals to teachers and boards of governors; it also has a powerful appeal to learners, who like the feeling that they are making systematic progress. Acquisition, on the other hand, depends entirely on the learner's readiness to absorb, and this is not under conscious control. Several writers have hypothesized an 'inner syllabus', claiming that new language features can only be acquired if the learner is ready for them. It is as if each learner is building up a mental jigsaw puzzle of the language, and a new piece will only be acquired if there is a place in the developing picture into which it fits. Thus an acquisition activity must be one in which language is 'thrown' at the learners, and perhaps only one 'piece' in a hundred will be acquired. One can 'tune' the language so that one

maximizes the amount which is at the learner's threshhold of understanding, what Krashen calls 'i+1' (standing for one step beyond
intelligibility), but the tuning can never be really fine, and with a
group must be quite rough if every member is to have a chance to
acquire something. Thus, inevitably, acquisition activities are
haphazard in the language they engender, and it is very difficult to
demonstrate that the teacher has covered any area of language
comprehensively, let alone that any learner has acquired comprehen-
sive grasp of an area of language. Acquisition is administratively
untidy.

Three models of grammar teaching

Thus grammar teaching can consist of
1. explicit statements and formal exercises, using a medium, systematically organized and consciously learnt;
2. activities in which meaningful language must be exchanged, in
   which formal accuracy is not the goal and will perhaps not be
   demanded, using direct experience, not following a systematic
   serial progression, and not demanding conscious attention to the
   language or any memorization;
3. other activities not covered by this dichotomy.

Rather than invent new names for 1, 2 and 3, I shall borrow terms
coined by Stephen Kemmis (Kemmis *et al.* 1977) and describe them
respectively as Instructional, Revelatory and Conjectural. (These
three terms were originally applied to what Kemmis called Learning
Paradigms, approaches to the teaching and learning task which were
implicit in materials which he was evaluating. He also identified a
fourth paradigm, Emancipatory, which is not immediately relevant to
this discussion.)

Instructional grammar

Of these three the Instructional model needs least explanation and
justification, since it has been in use for centuries. I have already
suggested that teachers are very good at applying an Instructional
approach where it is appropriate. Their lack of total success must be
attributed to the insufficiency of the approach itself. Computers, on
the other hand, are rather poor; compared with a human being they
are deaf, blind and stupid. Nevertheless, they have an interactiveness
which gives them occasional value as makeshift teacher substitutes.

Like books, they are simply displaced carriers of a human teacher's ideas, though for certain purposes they may be better than books.

Editing

Books, however, have been around for a long time and much care goes into their production. Computer programs are more of a novelty, and few producers of programs have yet learnt to apply to them the kind of editorial control which would be exercised by a book publisher. Many computer programs fail because they contain confusing explanations, ill-chosen examples, or simply statements which are untrue or irrelevant. In such cases there is no help for the student in the machine, though the machine's apparent responsiveness may lead to a greater sense of frustration than would be felt towards a badly-written book. It is easy to blame the medium for the failures of the human scriptwriter.

Metalanguage

During an Instructional session two types of language are in use, the language being studied and practised, and the language being used to talk about it. Paradoxically, it is only the second of these, the *metalanguage*, which is being used truly meaningfully, i.e. to convey messages. The metalanguage channel needs to be kept unobstructed at all times, so it is usually highly simplified and may be the learner's first language (in which case much potential exposure is lost). While conscious attention is being given to the language of the exercise, some acquisition may be occurring from the metalanguage of the instructions, comments and corrections. Therefore there can be some overlap between Instructional and Revelatory sessions. This, however, will not happen so readily with a computer, since the metalanguage of a computer exercise tends to be far more restricted and far less natural than that used by a human teacher. Computers do not 'chatter on', whereas good teachers often do.

Revelatory grammar

Although computers are mere makeshifts in the Instructional approach, they can take on a much more constructive role in Revelatory work, in activities designed to enhance acquisition. Here the division between language and metalanguage vanishes. Whatever language is present is meaningful, a part of the experience. Some of the language may originate with the computer in the form of displayed texts and instructions for a task. Far more of it will originate in the group round the computer who are tackling whatever task has been set. The machine becomes something to talk about rather than just to 'talk' to. The tasks can take the form of reading, discussion and decision-taking, as in branching stories, business simulations, or 'adventures'. The tasks can also be more abstract: puzzles or logic problems in which the computer has no role other than to provide a context for the use of language.

Advantages

Simulations and logic problems are perfectly familiar in uncomputerized forms, and it may be pertinent to ask what advantage the machine can bring to them. One advantage is that the machine can, with slavish accuracy, handle very complex procedures without the complexity being evident to the user. In a political simulation, for instance, it can calculate the likely effect of a particular decision on a candidate's popularity, using formulae derived from real-world political experience, and thus report the consequences of that decision at once. It can introduce random factors in ways which reflect the randomness encountered in real life. The complexity and diversity in such a program gives verisimilitude to what is a symbolic representation of one kind of reality. A second, and greater, advantage is that the machine's interactive facility allows it to act as the controller in a simulation, that neutral and austere role which is usually assigned by default to the teacher in paper-and-pencil simulations. The machine is both game-board and referee. The teacher is released to monitor the group or to join the group as a full participant.

Matching language to task

What, though, have such activities to do with grammar? The answer may seem to be 'rather little'. Many Revelatory activities or tasks can be slanted towards particular forms: a simulated police enquiry, for instance, will demand the use of past tenses, while a drawing program in which facial features have to be modified will provide a powerful context for comparative adjectives. But one cannot guarantee that a particular task will lead to the mastery or remediation of a certain form. Moreover, one cannot set out to cover a given syllabus by carrying out a fixed number of Revelatory tasks, each one slanted towards a target linguistic feature. Language and tasks cannot be matched up so neatly. One drawback of such activities is bound to be that little systematic progress can be perceived, and this may depress learners as much as teachers.

Dichotomies

Most of the professional debates in the language-teaching profession involve dichotomies, *structures* versus *notions*, *accuracy* versus *fluency*, or *learning* versus *acquisition*. Particular authorities may take up extreme positions, but the profession at large hears out the argument and adopts a compromise or blend. We are often not too happy at the blend, since we appreciate the inconsistencies in our position. The terms Instructional and Revelatory have some overlap with the pairs of terms I have just listed. However, they do not make a dichotomy but form part of a trichotomy (yes, the word exists), and when we add the third term, Conjectural, we may find it easier to find a position which suits us. After all, it is easier to sit on a stool with three legs than on one with two.

Conjectural grammar

Conjectural learning is what occurs when students sit down to work out rules from data, to form hypotheses and test them, or to rationalize their partial knowledge into a system which they can share with somebody else. It is an established part of good teaching and learning practice in the realm of vocabulary and extensive reading. Most teachers will discourage their students from running to the dictionary whenever they see an unknown word, encouraging them instead to use the context in order to guess the meaning and then refine their guesses as the word recurs. Not many teachers, however, will extend the principle to major features of grammar, since it seems that grammatical meaning is less easy to derive from common sense and knowledge of the world.

The question machine

I once took a class of post-elementary learners for an end-of-year two hour session on the kind of fine summer afternoon when nobody feels like a 'serious' lesson. I took in a sheet of cardboard, a pair of scissors, a roll of sticky tape, some pins, and a bag of Scrabble letters. Their task was, I told them, to build me a question machine, a box into which you pushed a statement and out of which the corresponding question would come. Of course one way of doing it would be simply to have some statements and questions ready-made on slides, so that the machine would look like this:

turning into:

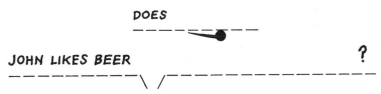

as the letters were pushed along. But such a machine would be ungeneralizable, and I explained that I wanted a machine which would be capable, in principle, of turning any correctly written statement into a question.

The first half hour was spent by the groups largely in drawing boxes, but one group led the way in observing that the elements JOHN LIKE and BEER did not change and could be assembled as units by taping letters together. (We were not using terms like Subject, Verb and Complement.) The problem was to extract that third person -S and insert DOES at the beginning. An early version of the machine looked like this:

DOES

JOHN LIKES BEER   ?

The gap in the bottom track would allow the S to fall through out of the way, and most of the rest of the time went into devising a switch which would allow the upper track to swivel and deposit the word DOES at the beginning of the sentence once the other words had gone past. There were still 'bugs'. An early run generated:

DOESJOHN LIKEBEER ?

until we sorted out the need for leading and trailing spaces in the slides.

The groups realized after a while that what they had could be used only for third person singular, and some of them started to think about what would be involved in creating a machine which would also handle plurals. We never built the Mark II machine, but the rough designs for it looked something like this:

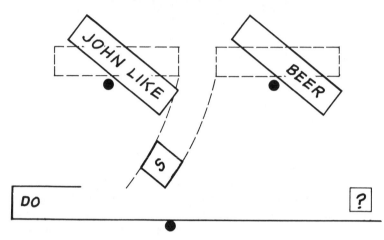

The problem here was that the S dropped off the verb and turned the word DO into DOS. It was no solution to have DOE waiting to collect the S, since then the plural form would emerge as DOE THEY LIKE BEER? We needed to have an E which would be collected by the S as it fell. A further problem would arise with a sentence like JOHN TEACHES ENGLISH. Now both the E and the S would fall, and the question form would come out as DOEES JOHN TEACH ENGLISH? unless something could be done about removing the intrusive E. We never achieved a mechanical solution, but at least the students became aware that there was a problem.

Two levels

This was a lesson which incorporated both Revelatory and Conjectural learning. At the Revelatory level, the learners were grappling with some very elementary engineering language (they were trainee engineers), words like *gap*, *switch*, *swivel* and *lever*, together with expressions like 'What's going to happen if we . . .'. At the Conjectural level they were concerned with some elementary grammar which in theory they knew well but which in practice was a plentiful source of error. I hardly saw any members of that class again, but I am fairly confident that they 'de-bugged' some of their ideas about the third person -*s* in English. This all happened in the seventies, and what none of us realized was that we were carrying out a form of computer programming without a computer.

Initiatives

What I hope is clear from this example is that the Conjectural approach combines analysis of what is passively or partially known with an external task to be performed. The task is often one which involves passing on the knowledge gained; creating the question machine was a kind of 'teaching'. One consequence of this is that most of the initiatives lie with the learner, who will decide in what order to tackle the different parts of the assignment. The responsibility for evaluation also lies to some extent with the learner, since he or she must judge when the task is 'finished'. A great deal of learning is by trial and error, and it may be objected that the learners cannot judge when a result is erroneous. This may be the case for very new and unfamiliar material, but in the case of familiar (but troublesome) grammatical concepts, as in this case, one can rely on the group collectively to spot almost all the errors generated by the process or the machine. The class supervisor can be a court of appeal, but rarely has to intervene.

Role reversal

The Conjectural approach, therefore, often involves students in a reversal of their conventional role; they will not spend their whole time as receivers of a ready-made language which belongs, initially at least, to others, but, instead, must marshal their limited knowledge and their access to outside resources and apply them to the task of teaching a communicative grammatical system to something less well equipped than they are. The computer makes an ideal recipient. There is a precedent for this. Studies of child language acquisition show that very young children spend at least a portion of their time not in learning language from their parents but in teaching their own form of language to them.

Dangers

It must also be pointed out, though, that conventional classroom approaches can stifle the habit of taking initiatives, and that students with no experience of autonomy in school learning may be baffled at first by a task which demands that they think for themselves. For this reason the first use of any Conjectural grammar activities may be very disappointing for the teacher. In my two hours with the question machine, the number of grammatical concepts dealt with was tiny, and, if I hadn't been expecting this, I might have thought the time wasted.

Building and testing

Conjectural activities are typically of two kinds: those in which one builds something up or those in which one tears something down. The first type is strongly associated with the work of Mike Sharples of Sussex University (e.g. Sharples 1983). His approach is to present learners with a rudimentary form of language generator, combining words more or less at random, and then to invite the students to refine the program so that the output becomes more grammatical and more meaningful. A similar activity has been used by Burkhart Leuschner in DIALOG-CRIT (see Higgins and Johns 1984, p. 60). In this case, however, the learner's task is not to modify the program but to edit manually the idiotic output that the machine generates. All such activities encourage the learner to think not only about the grammaticality of isolated sentences but also about the coherence of a piece of discourse. The same is true of a recent program, CHATTERBOX, which combines a form of the well-known ELIZA conversation simulator with an editor which allows the student to design new scenarios for future ELIZAs (Cook and Hamilton 1984).

Exploratory programs

The other type of Conjectural program is one in which the machine lays claim to a certain skill, and the learner's task is to find out what it can do and, if possible, to force it to make a mistake – a kind of testing to destruction. Such programs need not be elaborate, and some that Tim Johns has written for the Sinclair ZX81 occupy less than 1K of memory. The machine may, for instance, offer to carry out a regular morphological change, to add -S to a word (plural or third person), to put A or AN appropriately in front of a word or phrase, or to add -ING to a word. The learner, or more usually the group of learners, have to try it out with as many regular or exceptional forms as they can think of, in order to deduce the rules which have been programmed into the machine (Higgins and Johns 1984, p. 71).

Exploring stylistic choices

The same exploratory approach can be applied at a stylistic level. In LOAN the machine offers advice on how to ask for money. The user decides who the money is to be borrowed from (brother, uncle, best friend, bank manager, etc.) and the amount. The computer now displays a range of suitable request patterns. The learner's task is to explore the machine's use of language, observing when it uses *please* and *possibly*, indirect questions (*I wonder if. . .*), special words like *advance* and *overdraft*, and so on. Sometimes different groups, guided by worksheets, can study different parts of the range: one group can investigate close relationships and small sums of money, while another tries out large sums and formal relationships. I have worked on similar programs dealing with thanking for presents of different value, and apologizing for lateness, where the variables are the occasion and the number of minutes late (Higgins and Johns 1984, p. 73).

Grammarland

Another application of Conjectural grammar can be seen in a type of program which I have christened GRAMMARLAND. The model for this is Terry Winograd's classic research into natural language communication with machines, which yielded the program SHRDLU. (Winograd 1972). SHRDLU had 'knowledge' of a micro-world of coloured blocks, and was able to understand commands, answer questions and, within limits, to learn new facts about its world. Using the SHRDLU principle, one can create other micro-worlds which learners may experiment with. The learners' task is simply to communicate with the machine in an effort to secure responses and to manipulate the contents of the micro-world. For instance, the micro-world may consist merely of a drawing of rooms and people, and the learners' task depends on using the language of spatial manipulation: *here*, *there*, *bring*, *send*, *into*, and *out of*, for instance. Alternatively, the micro-world may be a shelf of goods in a shop, and the necessary language is now that of quantity and cost: *some*, *any*, *how much?* and so on. The machine is not offering to teach any of this language; it simply offers to communicate about the micro-world, as long as the learner can identify and stay within the limited competence that the machine possesses (Higgins and Johns 1984, p. 74).

Evaluating Conjectural grammar

Conjectural grammar is like Instructional grammar in that it has a clear linguistic focus: each Conjectural activity is 'about' a morphological change or a set of sentence patterns or a set of stylistic choices. But Conjectural grammar is unlike Instructional grammar in having no structure of its own. There are no clear starting and finishing points, and it would be virtually impossible to write an 'exit test' for a Conjectural activity to demonstrate what had been mastered in the session. For that reason, one cannot present evidence that it works. The learners are using trial and error, and have great freedom in deciding what trials to conduct; they are not usually following set procedures. The benefits may come in the form of sudden insights, and one cannot command or regulate learners to acquire insights at certain times. In practice learners vary greatly in the extent to which they enjoy Conjectural approaches and report gains from them, but there is anecdotal evidence that Conjectural activities may provide a kind of mental unblocking which the other approaches cannot. Papert, in a memorable example, quotes the case of a girl who, after working on a poetry generator, said excitedly, 'Now I know why we have nouns and verbs.' (Papert 1980, p. 48).

Conclusion

Each of the three approaches, Instructional, Revelatory and Conjectural, has a role in grammar learning. Elements of all three can be identified in the way infants learn their first language, and it is likely that no one approach in isolation is sufficient or efficient as a way of ensuring command of language. The computer has no necessary role in any of them, but it can greatly enrich the Revelatory and Conjectural approaches within the impoverished circumstances of mass teaching. Revelatory learning takes place when language is used for communication, and the computer can provide powerful contexts for communication. Conjectural learning takes place when language is played with and experimented with. The computer, within its limits, can behave like a patient mother or a slave, ready to play on demand. What may be even more important is that our experiments with computers are teaching us things about language and about the way it is learnt which we may be able to apply to other circumstances or feed back into the conventional classroom, so that the teacher who lacks the machines may still teach better because of them. Meanwhile, as far as the Instructional approach is concerned, a few well-constructed and attractively presented drill-and-practice programs on a library shelf or in a Christmas stocking may well help some learners to control some parts of the massively complex system we call grammar. If our life expectancy was a great deal longer, such programs might even do the whole job. But I doubt it.

Introduction to Chapter 4

As the Introduction to this book indicates, the origins of the papers collected here were in a course designed to explore relationships between CALL and computer-based language research. Given this practical and pedagogic source, it is appropriate, with this second of John Higgins's contributions, to include an account of a workshop session where participants were being introduced to ways of more rapidly communicating with programs. As in natural face-to-face communication, problems arise when extensive text needs to be processed, both in comprehension and in production. In this paper, Higgins outlines a number of standard ways in which the computer keyboard can be used to alleviate this processing problem for the learner: by integrating work with the screen and work with notes on paper; by using single keystrokes for inputting and accessing complex information; by using pointing devices and icons as ways of calling up particular routines. As a specific example, he adapts a routine first devised by Robert Ward for the entering of whole phrases by a small number of keystrokes, and illustrates it with an input routine for the Spectrum user.

4 Reading, writing and pointing: communicating with the computer

John Higgins

We are gradually becoming accustomed to the way in which computers communicate with us, namely by writing words on a display screen. If we still feel a residual discomfort, it is because we have a large investment in the conventions of our familiar paper and printing technologies. We like to see 800 words at a glance laid out across a double spread of pages, rather than the 130 or so which are displayed on a typical screen. As we turn a page, we enjoy the freedom to flick back and refresh our memories, a freedom usually denied by the computer. Letterpress printing with proportional spacing is more attractive than characters formed in an eight-by-eight matrix of dots.

A consequence of this is that the computer does not work well in tasks which demand rapid *extensive reading* from the screen of long texts. Books do the job better. The computer does, however, invigorate the task of *intensive reading*; computer activities which in-involve rebuilding or rearranging texts have proved their value. (This topic is covered fairly thoroughly in Higgins 1984a.)

Instructions

One is made specially aware of the problems of the computer as a reading medium when a program requires lengthy instructions. Full instructions, of course, combine some information required constantly and some needed only occasionally. The constant information is not really a problem. In a well-designed program there can be a reminder on the command line (e.g. 'N = NEW TEXT Q = QUIT'), and the user will quickly become familiar with the system. The problem arises with what is needed only occasionally, such as the procedure for correcting an error in input, or hints on play. When developing a program, most of us like to include all necessary instructions on screen, since it saves us from the labour of preparing and distributing paper documentation to those who will try out the activities. If the instructions require three or four screens of text, then one is soon made aware by users' complaints of the discomfort caused by lack of flexibility. One has to provide facilities to recall the instructions during the run of the program, since people are evidently not skilled at absorbing information in discrete screenfuls.

Mixing screen and paper

In one of my programs, a financial simulation, I made a virtue of necessity and prefaced the first screen with the words 'The instructions will be displayed once only. Make notes of the important points.' This perhaps points towards what we should do more often, that is integrate screen and paper presentations. David Clarke and Jeremy Fox are developing reading programs at Norwich in which the computer is the task-setter but in which the bulk of the actual reading is from paper (Clarke and Fox 1984). Complex instructions should really be in paper documentation rather than on screen. (If the program is commercially distributed and the documentation is properly printed, there is a further merit in that the honest person who has paid for the program has everything needed, while the person who has taken an illicit copy is usually deprived of the printed backup.) If we can assume that there is a printer connected to the computer, then we can provide an option to copy screenfuls of text to the printer for easy reference, but this is not a safe assumption nowadays, since printers are expensive and many institutions will not buy them for machines used by learners.

Time

Using a computer is normally a dialogue-like activity which involves turn-taking. Thus one component of the computer's communication is time: we have to consider not only what is displayed but also when it appears and where it is placed in relation to what was on the screen already. (This is another rather interesting difference between the computer medium and the traditional paper and print media: we do not normally watch a book being written in front of our eyes.) Programs written in the seventies often assumed teletype output. When adapted to screen presentation, they placed all new information on the bottom line and scrolled the screen up one line: the screen was treated as if it was a roll of paper. Modern programs are usually much more flexible, but one does still see, for instance, programs which involve filling in blanks but in which the word to be filled in is not written directly into the blank but at the bottom of the screen. The programmer saves some trouble this way, but the result is to heighten artificiality and risk confusion.

Keyboard frustration

When it is the user's turn to contribute to the dialogue, the normal medium is the keyboard, which in nearly every case is going to use the QWERTY layout. It is easy to blame the keyboard for our feelings of frustration. The layout looks haphazard, and, until we have learnt it, entering words or sentences is going to be by the aptly named 'hunt-and-peck process' and will be painfully slow. But learning to use the keyboard need not take long. A keyboard (and this applies to mechanical typewriters as well as computers) is an almost ideal learning environment, since it is totally responsive. You press a key and the corresponding letter appears. Most of us know our language and its alphabet well enough to provide the necessary evaluation. Was it the key we intended to press? If not, we have obtained the feedback necessary to modify our behaviour. In a few weeks nearly anybody can build up their rate of text entry to over twenty-five words per minute, and the editing capability of a word-processor, or even of BASIC's INPUT statement, allows us to be fairly tolerant of errors.

The speed gap

If frustration persists, it is due not so much to the keyboard as to the slowness of writing in general. A normal speaking speed is between 150 and 250 words per minute, but handwriting is limited to a range of 20 to 40 words per minute, depending on the neatness demanded. We are always going to find our thoughts and spoken words running ahead of our ability to write them down. The quasi-conversational style of interaction in many programs may well increase one's awareness of this speed gap, particularly since the machine's messages are normally printed out apparently instantaneously. We are made to feel lumbering by comparison.

Single key entry

In a great many programs the solution is to reduce the actions required of the user to single key-presses. If the available actions can be limited to half a dozen or so, and each can be identified by pressing a letter (chosen for its mnemonic value) or a number corresponding to a menu entry, then this speeds up the interaction to the point at which user and machine appear to be thinking at the same rate. Other conventions can be adopted in place of letters or numbers. One that is increasingly common nowadays is to display a menu of options with the first item highlighted in a contrasting colour. Pressing one key, usually the space bar as it is the largest and most prominent, will switch the highlighting to the next item, and one can step through the list in this fashion, reverting to the start after the last item. Pressing the ENTER key when the selected item is highlighted leads to that action being performed. The convention needs to be explained at first, but it is being adopted as the standard approach in the British Council's software project and by several publishers, so will soon be familiar to most regular users of software.

INPUT and GET

An advantage of single character entry is that it allows one to dispense with the INPUT statement. In a BASIC program, INPUT is used to halt operations while the user enters some text or a value. The end of the entry occurs when the user presses the ENTER key; if the user forgets to do this, the machine will wait indefinitely. Thus INPUT always requires at least two key-presses. The other method of allowing the user to communicate with the machine is by using the keyword GET or, on some machines INKEY$ (pronounced *inn-key string*). In this case the keyboard is scanned to see if any key is being pressed, but other processing can continue; for instance, moving graphics can be displayed while the machine waits for input, or a cursor can run along a list ready to be halted when it points to the item selected. In an earlier article (Higgins 1982) I suggested that the two keywords, INPUT and GET, provide an interesting metaphor for the conversational processes of *response* and *intervention*, and that dialogue which consists only of cue and response, as does much classroom dialogue and nearly all drill-and-practice CALL, is bound to be one-sided and unnatural.

Pointing

The use of GET or its equivalent does not limit one to the keyboard, since a similar continuous scanning process is used with devices such as joysticks, mice, and light pens. These can be used purely to point at something on the screen in order to identify a choice. In systems derived from Apple's Lisa machine, the mouse, a rolling ball whose movements are tracked by an arrow on the screen, is often used to point not at pieces of text but at 'icons', visual representations of office functions such as a typewriter for word-processing, a waste-paper basket for deleting unwanted files, or a calculator pad for financial calculations. Obviously one could create educational icons just as readily as office ones. Although all these devices are now rela-tively cheap, educational software tends not to make use of them, since they are not sufficiently universal.

Elaboration

Single key-presses or pointing will serve one's communication needs perfectly well as long as what one is communicating is decisions rather than messages or texts. In a multiple-choice quiz, for example, one selects an answer. In a simulation, it is usually enough to choose a direction or course of action. If the choices are elaborate and complex, they can be presented in the form of a succession of menus. Pointing or other forms of selection are not necessarily simplistic and limiting. They do, however, presuppose a fully worked out design and set of procedures. The program writer needs to have foreseen the range of paths that the user will follow in communicating a message to the computer.

Impoverishment

Such programs account for a part of what the learner of English will want to do with the computer, but to limit communication in this way would be to impoverish the medium. There are also many activities in which communication cannot be reduced to simple menu selection. In particular I am thinking of the exploratory programs and dialogue emulators, the descendants of Weizenbaum's ELIZA, which would of course lose their point entirely if one could not give them whole sentence inputs which the machine has to try and 'understand'. There is also good reason to design some problem-solving activities as dialogues in natural English, since the whole point of many such activities is to permit learners to cast around for solutions initially in a random way, so that they can evolve strategies for tackling the problem; menu selection can hardly avoid suggesting 'approved' strat-egies. It is precisely in these activities that frustration at the slowness of text entry can be most harmful.

Parsing

An approach used in some programs (including the British Council's FINDER program) is to parse the input letter by letter as it is entered, so that the machine immediately rejects any input that it is not equipped to understand. This can trap a faulty piece of text entry at an early stage and thus save the frustration of entering a long sentence and then having it rejected. There may, however, be just as much frustration due to the linguistic limitations of the parser. It is not too difficult to create a letter by letter parser with an augmented transition network (see Geoffrey Sampson, pp. 150 ff, this volume), but on a small machine it will only handle a limited range of sentence types and of vocabulary. In FINDER a display of all the language which is legal as input is available on help pages which can be called up at any point, even during the middle of text entry. This is probably necessary, and learners will need to be encouraged to use the help pages.

Whole phrase entry

A more relevant answer to keyboard frustration is that proposed by Robert Ward (1983) and his colleagues in the design for a group of logic and discovery programs for the BBC micro to be published by Acornsoft under the titles HIDDEN SHAPES AND SIZES and LANGUAGE AND THOUGHT. In these activities a masked out design has to be re-created by asking the computer a series of questions. The design consists of a four-by-four grid, in each cell of which there is a coloured shape. You begin by asking

> IS THERE A GREEN TRIANGLE?
> IS THERE AN ORANGE CIRCLE?

and so on. Having identified some elements, you can ask questions about their relative positions, such as:

> IS THE GREEN TRIANGLE TO THE LEFT OF THE ORANGE CIRCLE?

The most interesting feature of the program is the way in which the text entry is accelerated. Unshifted keys produce upper case letters, so all the text appears in capitals. Shifted keys produce complete phrases, but one must of course look up on a chart or memorize the phrase which belongs to each key. Thus shifted I might correspond to the phrase IS THERE A, while shifted R would produce TO THE RIGHT OF, and so on. It may seem unwise to be introducing additional complexity and a new learning burden, but the experience that Robert Ward reported when he presented the program in

Lancaster in 1983 was that the gains far outweighed the learning cost. It took only a few minutes (given the restricted language of the interaction) before students reached the point of being able to enter quite long and complex sentences with half a dozen keystrokes. They could go from thinking of what they wanted to ask to actually asking it in about the same time that they would need to utter the question in speech, and this enhanced their concentration and enjoyment.

The algorithm

The process does not require anything elaborate in the way of programming. A workshop session on the Lancaster course (see p. ix of the Preface) was intended to show this by creating on the spot an input routine of this kind for the Spectrum, which is reproduced below. I would recommend any language teacher with a Spec-

```
  10 REM Input routine for ZX Spectrum
  20 REM c. John Higgins 1985
  90 CLS : LET A$=""
  99 REM Input routine ********************************************
 100 LET I$=INKEY$: GO TO 100+(I$<>"")
 101 GO TO 101+(INKEY$="")
 105 IF CODE I$=12 THEN  LET I$="": LET A$=A$( TO (LEN A$-1)): CLS :
GO TO 150: REM Delete key pressed
 110 IF (CODE I$>96) AND (CODE I$<124) THEN  LET I$=CHR$ (CODE I$-32):
GO TO 150: REM Convert lower to upper case
 120 IF CODE I$<65 OR CODE I$>90 THEN  GO TO 150: REM Filter out non
alphabetic characters
 130 RESTORE 936+CODE I$: READ I$: REM Read new value for shifted
letter
 140 IF A$(LEN a$)=" " THEN  LET I$=I$(2 TO ): REM Delete duplicated
spaces
 150 LET A$=A$+I$: PRINT AT 12,0;A$: GO TO 100
1001 DATA " ARE THERE "
1002 DATA " BACK "
1003 DATA " CENTRE "
1004 DATA "D"
1005 DATA "E"
1006 DATA " FRONT "
1007 DATA "G"
1008 DATA " HOW MANY "
1009 DATA " IS THERE A "
1010 DATA "J"
1011 DATA "K"
1012 DATA " LEFT "
1013 DATA " MIDDLE "
1014 DATA " NEAR "
1015 DATA " OF "
1016 DATA "P"
1017 DATA "Q"
1018 DATA " RIGHT "
1019 DATA "S"
1020 DATA " TO THE "
1021 DATA "U"
1022 DATA "V"
1023 DATA "W"
1024 DATA "X"
1025 DATA "Y"
1026 DATA "Z"
```

Introduction to Chapter 5

The emphasis of earlier papers in this collection on the need to place the use of CALL in a learner and teacher-centred pedagogy is continued in this paper by Robert Lewis. More than merely suggesting, however, that the interactive characteristic of CALL matches a problem-solving view of the learning process, the paper touches on wider uses of the computer in language teaching and learning, which will be taken up by later papers in this book. For example, the use of databases to provide learners with extensive target language content, as well as with banks of information to facilitate the access to text, suggests ways in which learners can use the computer to go beyond the traditional limitations of data in textbooks, and can also be trained in researching answers to their own language difficulties. As a concrete example, Lewis offers a short program in German as a Foreign Language, designed to promote learner communication strategies, drawing not only on language knowledge but also on real-world experience.

5 Computers and language teaching

Robert Lewis

'What are you teaching your students and why?' Chris Harrison (1983a) begins a recent paper with this question and goes on to examine a number of computer simulations in English teaching.

This question provides a suitable starting point for an outline of computer-assisted learning (CAL) development over the last fifteen years. The rationale in science was to provide opportunities for student investigations in areas not otherwise accessible. Typically, students were given control over ecological systems or industrial processes and planned a series of experiments or trials in the process of gaining a clearer understanding of the scientific concepts involved. Evolving in parallel with this aim was that of a more detailed understanding of the processes of science through an examination of (largely mathematical) models (Lewis and Harris 1980). Examination of models was a natural activity for those concerned with the teaching of economics, and gaming was taken up by both economists and geographers (Watson 1984).

A characteristic of all this CAL development was the separation of the roles of teacher and computer. Both have their strengths and these were built upon. The teacher, with established skills in communication, analysis and diagnosis, was depended on to assist and, when necessary, assess the learner. On the other hand, the computer with limited communication was used to manipulate numbers and text. Other than checking the 'rules of the game', the computer was not used to assess students' knowledge or understanding. The development of CAL followed the strategy of the computer (plus software) providing feedback on students' ideas.

A similar philosophy was attached to later work in the use of databases. The characteristics of database use by computer are those of large quantities of data with a well-defined structure. This is found in large-scale scientific and sociological research but is not a characteristic of data used in schools and colleges. However, demographic data and some kinds of historical records, e.g. census data, are of this type and their use through computer databases is now gathering strength (Freeman and Tagg 1985).

But where does this lead in respect of language teaching? With experience of all the aspects of CAL development mentioned above, the Computers in the Curriculum (CIC) Project at Chelsea faced this question a few years ago:

> CIC units are often games or simulations. It was thus a considerable challenge to look at the potential for languages. The Project's philosophy has been to avoid cloze procedures and grammatical testing. Care has been taken to develop units that groups of students may use, rather than just single individuals. This enhances the amount of oral communication amongst the pupils both at and away from the keyboard during the sequence of a program. Many units may be used successfully as classroom demonstrations. [The Project] aims to capitalise on the experience gained in other subject areas to provide a motivating simulation or game during which English will be learnt and discussed. This, therefore, enhances the communicative approach that is the key to this languages feasibility study.[1]

As an example of foreign language material being prepared for fourteen- to fifteen-year-old pupils, STADTPLAN (see p. 58) provides experience in giving directions to reach a particular place in a town. Pupils may be required to express those directions in German, e.g. *immer geradeaus, erste Strasse rechts, zweite Strasse links, jetzt umdrehen*, or as single letter codes.

There is no single right answer to giving the directions but some microcomputers are able to time the journey. Not all the activities suggested in the materials use the computer; many other tasks involving reading and conversation are stimulated by the interaction which has taken place.

In a unit on exchange visits, pupils build up a profile of their own personal details and will see a number of 'bulletins personnels' on possible correspondents. The aims of the unit are:

1. to encourage contacts with young people abroad;
2. to reinforce purposeful reading and writing skills;
3. to encourage the pupil to assess his or her personal likes and dislikes, and to be able to express these concisely in French;
4. to introduce and rehearse personal vocabulary.

The non-computer activities include preparing a letter to the selected correspondent and conversations, in pairs, about their own correspondent's interests, etc.

This emphasis on providing additional opportunities for the exercising of language skills is a far cry from the drilling of irregular verbs, the earliest use of computers in the field. On the near horizon is the technical possibility of oral dialogue but, *beware*, this could lead us

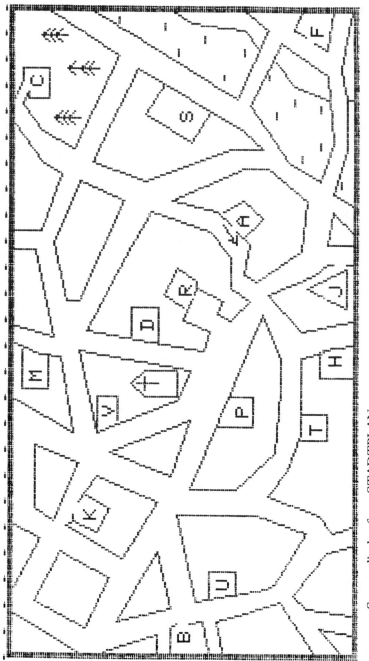

FIGURE 1 Screen display from STADTPLAN

back towards the assessment of learners by the machine. Enhancement of language games, with video-disk frames giving a stronger cultural element to the interaction, is also close at hand. The power of word-processing software also transforms students' attitudes to revising their initial thoughts, a desirable feature of all writing. An interesting series of papers on CAL in English Composition is to be found in the Spring 1983 issue of *Pipeline*.[2]

The pathway from science to language use of CAL techniques, outlined in this paper, could well turn full circle. The design of materials, for example, scientific adventure and other games stimulated by the work in languages, is a short-term accessible goal. This has already been achieved in the UK by the Association of Teachers of Mathematics in their game 'L'. The exchange of learning methodologies between disciplines has been promoted by educational analysis which underlies good CAL development. Teachers of most disciplines will be warmed by Chris Harrison's answer to his original questions:

> To return to the original questions: 'What are you teaching your students and why?', we may add 'How?' Taking the premise that our students learn English in order to build up their communicative abilities (although the cultural element also plays a large part), we may need to place more emphasis on fluency than accuracy activities, on interaction between students rather than on one-way teacher-student traffic. We need to allow the students to take risks without being threatened by penalties, to cooperate rather than compete, to introduce the unexpected and to take the initiative. By giving the 'information role' to a computer, and by the teacher taking on the 'analyst' and 'planner' roles, we can provide for all of these needs in a student-centred setting.

Notes

1. Extract from an information sheet of the Computers in the Curriculum Project, Chelsea College, 552 Kings Road, London SW10 0UA. Materials published by Macmillan.
2. *Pipeline* is the publication of CONDUIT, University of Iowa, 100 LCM, Iowa City, Iowa 52242

Introduction to Chapter 6

As is regularly the case with curricula, and especially with materials, more energy is expended on their conception and implementation than is devoted to their evaluation. This is certainly true of language-teaching materials, whether in CALL or elsewhere. Given the very rapid speed of CALL software development, it is more than ever necessary to provide a 'Which' guide to what is available for language teachers and learners. Although we hope that the programs referred to and exemplified in this book will in general contribute to this goal, the best way of developing such a guide is to offer practitioners a framework in which they themselves can evaluate what they propose to use in class. Annette Odell's contribution is to offer just such a way for teachers with limited experience of microcomputers to evaluate programs and thereby to make a contribution to our knowledge in general of CALL and in particular of software development. The paper addresses two main issues:

1. Teachers' uncertainty about the specific value of the microcomputer as a teaching aid;
2. Teachers' realization that there is at present a limited amount of software which reflects the best of current methodological practice.

In essence, to find out about CALL, CALL materials need to be more widely used, but to make any real contribution to software development, as Odell points out, we need a set of criteria by which to judge programs and their performance. Moreover, once obtained, we need an efficient method of storing this evaluative information.

6 Evaluating CALL software

Annette Odell

The body of this article looks at an experimental model for CALL software evaluation, using a database to store the resulting information.[1] The database store is divided into four sections:

1. *Section A: Specification*
   This section is intended primarily for administrative use (stock-taking, re-ordering, etc.) and could therefore be kept in a separate file. It contains such information as author, publisher, the number of copies, method of storage and supplier.

2. *Section B: Description and Classification*
   This section contains a description of the program content, student task and design objective as well as a simple classification system. It serves two purposes:
   a) It provides a framework for evaluation plus a record of individual applications.
   b) It provides teachers with a simple resource system (linked to section D) which can be used when searching for and selecting materials during lesson preparation.

3. *Section C: Evaluation*
   The evaluation section is divided into two major areas:
   a) *Program design evaluation* which concentrates on the more technical qualities of the program, such as 'bugs' and user-friendliness.
   b) *Pedagogic evaluation*: An evaluation both of the intrinsic quality of the program as language-teaching material and of specific applications.

4. *Section D: Ideas for use*
   This section contains information on *either* each application recorded in section B *or* those applications outlined in section B

which exploit the material in ways that may not seem initially obvious.

The focus of this article is on evaluation and, therefore, only the parts of the model which directly relate to evaluation will be discussed in detail.

The reasons for using a computer database to store the information are:

a) Unlike print, the database is a *fluid medium*. Information can be eliminated, changed or added quite easily. This is particularly necessary because the procedure for collecting the information is not linear and, therefore, is not collected in the same order as it is stored. In fact, the order will vary from program to program.

b) The computer database *can search for and extract information at a very high speed*. This means that we can compare and collate the results of evaluation in a variety of ways without tedious and time-consuming effort.

The model has been designed to suit as many teaching situations as possible. The following assumptions have therefore been made:

1. Most teachers work with a pre-designed syllabus. This implies that means (the material and activity selection) are restricted by prescribed ends (the need to reach shared goals in a set period of time). By extension, one of the central criteria by which materials are evaluated is their relevance to the syllabus objectives (a 'teaching' rather than 'learning' focus) which is reflected in the model.[2]

2. Time for such projects as CALL materials evaluation will be limited. Therefore the model should be flexible – able to be extended or restricted according to individual circumstance. Also, since time is precious, the long-term commitment of time and energy should have some short-term benefit of immediate practical value related to the central responsibility of planning and teaching. The resource classification system (see section B) is therefore an integral part of the evaluation model.

The procedure for collecting evaluative information is a two-stage procedure:

At *Stage 1 (pre-use)* we want to establish if the program is usable. The main reasons for rejecting a program at this stage is either that there are 'bugs' in the program which render it useless, or that the program content does not suit our students. The sections which must be completed at this stage are therefore 'specification' (section A) and a preliminary program design evaluation (section C). In addition, we want to establish at least the general area in which to experiment with use of programs which are not rejected, so as much of the classification section as possible is completed (section B).

At *Stage 2 (post-use)* fields which have already been completed are amended in the light of increased familiarity and experience, and previously incomplete fields are completed as the information is gained.

Sections of the model are now discussed in detail, with an example of a Stage 1 (pre-use) record at the end of each section. Fields within each record are shown here in bold type (on the computer screen they might appear in upper case letters). Since the examples are of a pre-use record some of the information is bound to prove to be irrelevant or inaccurate in the light of use, and therefore should not be taken as a reliable evaluation of the program in question.

Section B: Description and Classification

The general description of the program is divided into fields which provide a framework for the overall pedagogic evaluation in section C.

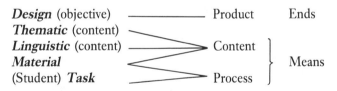

Design: Three types of program seem to exist:
a) Those designed to meet a specific objective.
b) Those which, because of inbuilt flexibility, can be used to meet a variety of objectives.
c) Those which, because of a vagueness or lack of objective in the design, have no immediately obvious area of use.
This field is therefore completed with the specific objective or general area, or possibly left blank.

Thematic (content): The topic(s) or subject matter. 'Adaptable' should also be entered where there is an authoring facility.

Linguistic (content): This is the general content (e.g. structure, discourse features, style, etc.), plus 'Adaptable' where there is an authoring facility.

Material: A description of the actual material.

Task: If there is a menu of options, each option should be briefly described.

Example:

Program:	Storyboard Plus Code: 001
Design:	Text reconstruction following deletion, using memory of content/prediction from title/redundancy/contextual clues, etc.
Thematic:	18 texts: varied.
Linguistic:	Informal written narrative style.
Material:	Text is completely deleted leaving a dash for each letter, and punctuation. Texts also on audio cassette.
Task:	Student selects one of 18 texts. Four options: see text for three varying lengths of time or not see text. Student deduces/guesses each consecutive word in text. Scores for correct completion and loses points for incorrect guess. Can use stock of points to a) 'buy' the first letter of the next word, b) 'buy' the word or c) see the text.

The programs are classified using fields which have been chosen to include the main criteria on which materials and activities are selected during lesson planning:

Type (material/activity)
Focus
Objective
Level
Interaction
Reference (to section D)
Supervision

These fields are presented in tabular form so that each individual application can be clearly recorded.

Type: Programs can be divided into two types:
a) Familiar, e.g. simulations, drills, mazes, clozed texts, quizzes, etc.
b) Innovatory, e.g. 'exploratory' programs.[3]
The classification of programs according to type is not only a useful part of the resource system but also a prerequisite to overall evaluation. A set of criteria already exists for familiar material/activity types, and therefore basic evaluation criteria are:
– Does the program satisfy the criteria for this particular material/activity type?
– What has been gained by the change of medium?
Since no established criteria are available for innovatory program types, it is necessary to ask a great many more questions which can only be answered after a considerable period of use.

Focus: There are two broad areas of focus in language training in current methodology which can be illustrated in polarized form as:

1	2
accuracy	fluency
enabling skills (functions, structures, etc.) in isolation	integrated skills in use
part	whole
content-based teaching	task-based learning

In practice, materials and activities exist on a cline between one pole and the other, according to intrinsic design and material type, but the method of exploitation can shift the focus. At the pre-use stage the program is classified according to its intrinsic focus, which establishes another set of criteria for overall pedagogic evaluation. Particular applications are categorized according to the focus in use. The classification bands used in the model are:
1. Narrow focus on one or two discrete items.
1/2. Wider pre-communicative focus on a number of integrated items.
2. Focus on communication practice using non-specified linguistic and non-linguistic skills.

Objective: The realities of working with a pre-designed syllabus have already been mentioned (see p. 62 above). One method of classification is to cross-reference the program to the syllabus, which has the advantage that entries are standardized and brief. However, the syllabus is a working document intended as a standardized base rather than as a statement of the sole objectives of teaching/learning for each individual student or group of students. Some additional form of classification is therefore necessary.

Since syllabi frequently consist of a set of discrete items, the main need may be for:

a) a classification system for programs which develop, or are used to develop, enabling skills not listed in the syllabus;

b) a classification system for programs which focus on, or are used to focus on, communication practice.

Since entries must be brief, the possible need for more information is overcome by providing detail in section D, possibly in print form, and a reference to the code under which the information is stored. Those programs with a communicative focus are classified according to broad skill area: S (Speaking: monologue), T (Talking: interactive), L (Listening), W (Writing), R (Reading). Combinations could show integrated skills work, e.g. R/W/T.

A classification for the program 'Mazes' could therefore be:

Type	*Focus*	*Objective*
Problem-solving	2	R

Level: This could relate to the specific levelling system used within a school or college.

Interaction: This field is intended to be of particular use when collating the results of evaluation in order to find out, for example, if students prefer a particular 'computer role', or to find out the type of interaction in successful applications compared to unsuccessful ones. It also attempts to distinguish the variety of methodological approaches possible in programs.

The coding system is quite complex initially, since it refers to possible 'computer roles' as well as the possible variety of interaction. The classification of interaction has been limited in the model to: S (individual student), Ss (pair or small group), G (group of between five and eight students), W (whole class).

1. Computer as 'teacher'   Code: T to (S, etc.)
The computer is in the traditional teaching or 'magister' role,[4] setting

the task, judging the student's performance, correcting, providing feedback, etc. Programs are therefore typically of the FOCUS 1, type (drill and practice, programmed learning, etc.).

2. Computer as resource for discovery   Code: (S, etc.) to D
This approach is used in 'exploratory' programs, where students manipulate the computer's 'knowledge' in order to make discoveries about language.

3. Computer as partner in the activity   Code: P to (S, etc.)
Many programs are based on the approach of a competitive or cooperative game between computer and student(s). The computer provides the context for practice, but does not usually evaluate the student's performance, though it may provide information for self-evaluation.

4. Computer as external resource   Code: (S, etc.) to (S, etc.)
Although the computer may provide the task, it does not take part in the interaction but provides a stimulus for the pair and group work going on around it. This computer role is often dependent on the method of exploitation, e.g. where an adventure game is used as a basis for oral interaction.

If we extend the example on p. 66, we can see how this field can clarify the contrasts between different applications:

Program: Mazes   Code 002

Type	*Focus*	*Objective*	*Level*	*Interaction*
1. Problem-solving	2	R		P to S
2.	2	T/R		S to S
3.	2	T/R		Ss to Ss etc.

Reference: This field, as mentioned above, gives a reference to any further information on particular applications of the program stored in section D.

Supervision: This field is completed 'Yes' if supervision is necessary and 'No' if it is suitable for unsupervised use, e.g. in an individual study unit.

The pre-use classification of the example program 'Storyboard Plus' could be:

Type: 'Extreme' cloze: text reconstruction.

	Focus	Objective	Level	Interaction	Reference	Supervision
1.	1/2	R	Int.	P to S	--	?
2.	2	T/R	Int.	P to Ss	--	?
3.	1	Awareness: Reading Strategies	Elem. up	P to W	001/1	Yes

Section C: Evaluation

Design evaluation

The first part of the evaluation focuses on the technical design of the program. Relevant information on 'plus' and 'minus' features of the program are established, using a checklist like the one below. The PLUS field includes a note of all the features of the program which seem particularly good and, therefore, should be included in similar programs. The MINUS field includes:
a) specific 'bugs' in the program;
b) features of doubtful value;
c) features which were missing, but should be included in future program design. The MINUS field is followed by RECOMMEN-DATIONS for use, or ways of compensating for faults in the design. The checklist used in the model is:

1. Loading and running the program
1.1 Time from loading to running selected program.
1.2 Ease of operation, e.g. Is it easy to
    a) manipulate the cursor? b) correct mistakes? c) get help?
    d) could you leave the program by mistake? etc.

2. Instructions
2.1 Quality of pre-program instructions, e.g. Are they
    a) brief? b) clear? c) at the appropriate language level?
2.2 Quality of documentation, e.g. Is it useful to students as well as teachers?
2.3 During-program instructions: as in (2.1) plus:
    d) is it easy to get help?

2.4 Post-program options and instructions, e.g. How easy to
   a) quit the program?   b) repeat the program?

3. Impression

3.1 Layout, e.g.
   a) attractiveness b) print size c) resolution d) amount on screen
3.2 Use of colour, e.g.
   a) constructive?   b) helpful?
3.3 Use of sound, e.g.
   a) constructive?   b) intrusive?   c) optional?
3.4 Computer 'personality', e.g.
   a) suitable?   b) intrusive or unnecessary comments?   c) over-
   friendly?

4. Flexibility

4.1 Options within program, e.g.
   a) sufficient?
   b) so many choices that student may become irritated or confused?
4.2 Authoring facility, e.g.
   a) clear instructions?   b) thorough?
4.3 Listing: Is it available, so that 'bugs' can be eliminated?

5. Specific 'bugs'

Pedagogic evaluation

The initial pedagogic evaluation is intended to provide clearer guidelines for use, primarily by evaluating the program's suitability in
relation to the projected uses recorded in section B. Information
gathered is stored in the same fields as the design evaluation: PLUS
(features of the program that merit inclusion in similar programs);
MINUS (limitations of the program which affect use and adaptations
which should be made in future design), and RECOMMEN-
DATIONS for use. This record is a summary of information gained
through a checklist of evaluative criteria which is based on the framework in section B.

The following is an example of the checklist used in the experimental model, completed at the pre-use stage for 'Storyboard Plus'.
Since the evaluation is conducted with reference to the specific
student body in each individual institution, those parts of the checklist which refer to the suitability of the program for the particular
students have, of necessity, been left blank, as are any parts where
the information has not yet been obtained.

	Yes	Adaptable	No	Comment
Objective (Design or specific application)				
Relevant to students needs/wants				
Relevant to syllabus objectives				Specify and enter in section B classification.
Sufficiently clear/limited		*		
Clear to students			*?	Not made explicit in pre-program information.
Perceived as relevant/useful by students				
Thematic content				
Suited to students' age, interests, etc.				
Intrinsically interesting			*	Topics not very interesting, sometimes odd.
Suited to objective	*			Any text suitable but authentic preferable.
Linguistic content				
Suited to objective			?	Structure and discourse organization often very
Suited to students' language level				simple but lexis difficult/unusual.

	Yes	Adaptable	No	Comment
Material				
Suited to objective (methodology)	*			
Suited to task	*			
Satisfies criteria for material type	*			
Suited to computer medium	*			
Task				
Suited to students (methodology)	*?			Competition/game element motivating?
Intrinsically motivating				
Suitable length				
Suited to objective (efficiency)			*?	Can only 'buy' next word, so encourages linear approach.
Suited to material	*			
Suited to computer medium	*			
Feedback				
Adequate/appropriate feedback during task	*?			Score may encourage students not to look back at text.
Adequate/appropriate feedback at end			*	More detailed feedback needed, e.g. words in context.

	Yes	Adaptable	No	Comment
Level				
Suitable for a variety of levels	*			18 texts are roughly graded in difficulty.
Interaction				
Suited to task	*			
Suited to objective		*		
Computer role				
Suited to students' preferences				
Suited to objective (methodology/approach)	*			
Suited to computer medium	*			
Support				
Support materials provided	*			Audio cassette of 18 texts.
Documentation provides useful pedagogic information.	*			*User Notes* include ideas for exploitation and a breakdown of text content, information on design.

Example pre-use record Section C: Evaluation

Program:	Storyboard Plus　　　Code: 001
Plus 1:	Use of layout and colour to distinguish instructions from student input, computer feedback and text.
Plus 2:	Thorough *User Notes*, including clear instructions and useful pedagogic information, especially ideas for exploitation.
Plus 3:	Language of instructions kept as clear and simple as possible.
Plus 4:	Provision of cassette support material increases flexibility of use.
Plus 5:	Suited to a range of language levels and objectives.
Plus 6:	'Game' element in task increases motivation.
Minus 1:	No authoring facility.
Minus 2:	Actual texts not the same quality as the basic material and task. Should be more varied and preferably drawn from life.
Minus 3:	Since the student can only 'buy' the next letter or word in the text, the program is not suitable for developing non-linear reading strategies. Preferable that student can 'buy' any word in the text.
Minus 4:	More feedback desirable at the end showing, for example, the words students did not guess in context, with an option to try to complete the text with only these words missing; the number of times the student looked back at the text.

Minus 5:	During the program a window with a summary of what to key in to 'buy' a letter or a word, to see the text, get help or 'quit'. These instructions should all be accepted in upper or lower case.
Minus 6:	An option on whether to have a score or not.
Minus 7:	Linguistic content may cause levelling problems; lexis is often unusual and difficult in relation to structure and discourse.
Recommendation 1:	If texts are unsuitable, use 'Storyboard' which has an authoring facility (N.B. No 'plus' of an audio cassette.)
Recommendation 2:	Provide students with a print summary of what to key in to 'buy', etc. as a reminder.
Recommendation 3:	Provide guidance on whether to ignore the score or not, according to the objective.
Recommendation 4:	If the objective is to train students to ignore words they do not understand which are not essential to working out the sense of a text, the program is not suitable, since they must work from beginning to end. In 'Storyboard' they can buy any word in the text and therefore choose any route to building up meaning.

Information gained from experimentation with individual applications will change and extend the database store. In addition, each individual application should be recorded and evaluated. The degree of formality with which this is done will obviously vary from institute to institute, depending on such factors as available time and degree of cooperation between staff. As a minimum, section B's classification could be divided into a record of successful applications and a separate record of ones that proved unsuccessful. Alternatively, records of individual applications could be recorded in section D.

Section D: Ideas for use

Section D is not part of the database store as records would prove too lengthy for the average database and, since they are 'one off' records, they can be efficiently stored in print form. This section includes only additional information on individual applications (as described on p. 73 or it could include a record of all applications, including the specific conditions of each pilot (the students involved and method of evaluation, for example) and results of evaluation.

The following is an example of a record of one projected application and shows the format used in the model: it is an extension of Application 3 recorded in the classification in section B. (See p. 68.)

Example

Reference: 001/1

Program: Storyboard Plus   Code: 001

Objective: Awareness-building: strategies for working out meaning when reading (guessing from context, predicting from topic or information in text, using redundancy, etc.)

Level: Elementary upwards.

Time: Computer activity: $\frac{1}{2}$ hour maximum

Text: Select text to suit students' level, interests, etc.

Preceding activity: Using a transcript of the text, delete words according to the specific focus of the activity (e.g. if concentrating on redundancy, gap out redundant words) or delete at random. Students work in pairs or small groups filling in gaps.

Preparation for computer activity: Key in the words up to the first gap on the computer. Explain to students that they can check their results against the computer. Get a volunteer to do the keying in.

Computer activity: Students suggest completions for gaps. Guide discussion on why a correct completion is correct and how students worked it out/why a suggestion is incorrect, or a viable alternative.

Elicit summary of strategies from students.

Feedback: None.

Follow-on: Students work in pairs or small groups around a terminal on the same activity using a different text. Tell them to aim for the highest score possible so that they do not look at the text too much but buy letters as clues when stuck.

Conditions of pilot 1:
Students involved (level, age, familiarity with computers, etc.):
Differences in procedure from above:
Text(s) used:
Time:
Interaction (size of groups and method of composition):

Method of evaluation:
Teacher (checklist, observation, impression):
Students (questionnaire, oral feedback, etc.):

Results of evaluation:

Specific evaluation objectives:
Did the procedure achieve the objectives?
Did students perceive it to be a useful exercise?
Was improvement in performance tested? If so, how? And with what results?
Was the computer activity (feedback on the preceding task) more efficient or motivating than using blackboard or OHP?
Did the change of 'knower' role from teacher to computer mean that the students did not feel 'judged' and participated in the discussion more freely?

The model is designed systematically to collect information about CALL's utility and also information which could form a basis for specific recommendations on future software design. The record reflects the particular conditions in the individual institution, and any conclusions drawn from evaluation or the results of experimentation cannot, therefore, be automatically used as a basis for recommendations to teachers working in dissimilar situations. The collective weight of experience, however, should answer some of the questions which surround CALL, for example, the optimum number for groups working round a terminal, the type of interaction that can take place, and the programs that seem to maximize learning.

Notes

1. The database used for the experimental model is not commercially available. However, any database that offered 50 plus fields in a file and 250 characters per record in each field should be suitable, although restricted. The major facility that would be missing would be the ability to access sections B and C independently, as if they were separate files.
2. It is further assumed that the syllabus implies a methodological viewpoint shared by the teachers within the institution and suited to the student population.
3. Examples of 'exploratory' programs are TWO STICKS and GRAMMARLAND. The background to this type of program is discussed in Higgins and Johns (1984).
4. The distinction between the computer in 'magister' (traditional teaching) and 'pedagogue' (slave) roles was made by John Higgins and is discussed in Higgins (1984b) and in Higgins (1983b).

Introduction to Chapter 7

Applied linguists concerned with language teaching and learning, as Scott Windeatt points out in this paper, are currently much involved in studying the processes of acquisition, both as a means of illuminating the development of interlanguage, and as a tool for evaluating the specific effects of instruction, with or without the aid of specially designed materials. Observing CALL in action, therefore, is not only timely: it offers a further mode of evaluating CALL materials to that proposed by Odell in the preceding paper. Specifically, experimental studies such as that described here permit a balanced assessment of some of the wilder claims made for CALL materials as facilitators of learning, promoters of interaction, resolvers of learner problems, and counsellors of their affective needs. It is equally, if not more important, that reading between the lines of this account we uncover (as with all interesting enquiry) further avenues of research. *Why* is there so little communicative interaction stimulated among learners or with the computer? *What* implications does this have for the design of software and the capability of hardware? *Why* does much software (cloze exercises are a specific example) offer little or no opportunity for recording learner-attempts in order thereby to facilitate the drawing of conclusions about the acquisition processes and the refinement of learners' self-diagnostic capacity? *How* can we design software so as to deliver data on, say intercultural and interlingual variability in user practices? *Where* can we locate CALL within the curriculum so as to maximize its effects on acquisition? The list could easily be taken further. What is important is that questions such as these, commonplace in the world of classroom research, achieve a central place in the framework of CALL development. Scott Windeatt's paper suggests what can be done, linking teaching and learning to action research.

7 Observing CALL in action

Scott Windeatt

Introduction

One thing which is missing from most discussions on computer-assisted language learning (CALL) is any evaluation of software based on observations of learners using CALL materials. Kemmis (1977) reports a wide-ranging study of different forms of computer-assisted learning (CAL), Strachan (1983) has provided a useful *Guide to evaluating methods* as part of the Microelectronics Education Programme, and Self (1985) has examined the pedagogical basis of current educational software. As far as language learning is concerned, however, Stevens (1984) is one of the few reported projects based on observations of learners using CALL software.

Such an omission may be a result of the relative novelty of the medium, but the development of observation techniques as part of a methodology for evaluating software is especially important at such an early stage in the introduction of computers into language learning, firstly in order to ensure that existing software can be used as effectively as possible, and secondly to provide guidelines for the production of improved materials. Such guidelines can be developed by investigating to what extent the software achieves its aims, and how the characteristics of the medium can best be exploited both by changes to the software, and by techniques for using it.

The subject of this paper is a project which makes use of such observation techniques, the stimulus for which was a series of informal observations of students tackling language-learning activities on the computer. (The students were mostly undergraduates or postgraduates at Lancaster who came to the Institute for English Language Education for extra language tuition.) From these observations I gained three main impressions.

The first impression was that the students appeared to like using the computer. Apart from the fact that they sometimes said they had enjoyed the activity, and clearly looked as if they were enjoying themselves, there were occasions on which they would insist on working on beyond the end of a lesson in order to finish a task on the computer – something which they rarely did with other activities.

The second impression, however, was that the students may have made a distinction between an interest in the medium, and the language-learning value of the activity. They occasionally qualified their claims that they had enjoyed doing the exercise with doubts about whether they would learn anything very useful from it.

Finally, although most of the activities were carried out in groups, there was much less discussion among the students during the exercises than had been expected. Since the solutions to the problems were often far from obvious, and in their computerized form they tended to encourage students to try out a number of guesses, it had been expected that there would be a considerable amount of discussion. However there was sometimes almost no discussion whatsoever, to the extent that in some cases the students would merely hand each other the keyboard if someone had a suggestion for an answer. In other words, the students appeared to be working as a number of individuals rather than as a group. And even when there was discussion, there tended to be a smaller range of types of exchange than might have been expected. For example, the students tended to limit themselves just to suggesting or rejecting answers without any explanation or discussion.

There may, in fact, be nothing particularly surprising about students using CALL materials in this way, since non-CALL materials are often used in a variety of unpredictable ways. How a particular task is carried out by a group of students is likely to depend not simply on the material itself, but on a number of other factors, including the instructions the students are given, the previous practice they have had, the way the classroom or equipment is organized, and the effect of individual personalities on group dynamics.

The question remains, however, as to what effects are due to the medium in which CALL materials are presented rather than to other factors, and what I am about to describe is a project aimed at examining under more controlled conditions the subjective impressions outlined above. The three main areas of investigation suggested by informal observations were:

1. the extent to which students were motivated by the medium in which CALL materials were presented;
2. the kind of communication which CALL materials encouraged among students;

3. the extent to which specific programs seemed to achieve the aims that had been set for them.

In addition, the project had the further aim of developing techniques for recording observations and descriptions of the way students use CALL materials.

Project description

Research design

In order to identify effects which were due to the medium in which the materials were presented, an activity was chosen which existed in both computerized and non-computerized form.

Next, the effect of differences among the subjects using the materials was minimized by matching students according to language level, according to their experience with computing, and, informally, according to personality.

Finally, in order to minimize differences due to the order in which the tasks were performed in the two different media, two tasks were selected. Group A did the first task in CALL form, with Group B doing the same task in non-CALL form. The situation was then reversed for the second task, with Group B doing it in CALL form, and Group A doing it in non-CALL form.

Subjects

The subjects selected for the experiment were 12 students on the Summer Study Skills course for overseas students conducted at Lancaster. The reason for selecting this particular group was that they were representative of many of the students in the Institute for English Language Education, though they were near the top end of the range as far as language level is concerned. They were all postgraduates, from a number of different countries, and from a variety of subject disciplines.

In order to ensure that the groups were as similar as possible in composition, students were allocated to a group on the basis of:
1. their results in a language test which had been given to them at the beginning of their Study Skills course;
2. their experience in using computers;
3. an informal assessment of personality characteristics (this was limited to an assessment of how talkative or quiet they were, and of how dominant they were likely to be in group work).

Materials

Current thinking in applied linguistics sees language teaching as being concerned not simply with helping learners to acquire specific linguistic products, but with providing opportunities for the practice of language-learning strategies and processes as well. Whilst the definition and identification of such processes is not unproblematic, a common interpretation would probably be that exercises which are concerned with reading strategies, negotiation between learners, and encouraging learners to form and try out their own ideas about how the language system operates are examples of 'process' tasks.

In order for the results of the project to have general relevance, the material to be used would therefore ideally exemplify such process-oriented tasks, and in particular, would, if possible, involve students in oral communication in groups, since the exchanges involved in such communication could be expected to provide clues to the nature of the processes which were taking place.

The material chosen was *Clozemaster:* a reading skills program which automatically provides cloze versions of texts, with a deletion rate which can be chosen by the user. Whilst it can be argued that this particular material does not represent the most imaginative type of language-learning task, or the most advanced use of the medium, it is typical of much of the kind of software which is available for CALL. In addition, the author suggests that the exercise has a number of advantages when presented in computerized form. For example, the program encourages users to try out a number of guesses in order to find the response that the computer will accept, so that, although 'Cloze is a well-established technique for testing reading skills. . . . Given feedback, and the chance to have another go after a wrong guess, the Cloze technique can become an equally effective learning device'. (Jones 1983, p. 4).

In addition, 'Cloze passages on paper are cumbersome and time-consuming to produce and, because the gap-frequency is chosen in advance by the teacher, the passage cannot be re-used by the same students. These constraints make Cloze particularly suitable for exploitation on the microcomputer . . .', because, once the user has selected a deletion rate, the program will automatically produce a gapped text with the appropriate words deleted.

There is, however, also 'a price to pay' for this 'flexibility'. In the cloze technique 'the student's task is to fill in the missing words by using the contextual clues offered by the remaining parts of the text. . . . and (by drawing) on all of his language resources as and when they are needed'. However, if by this process the learner finds a word which is an acceptable response to a particular gap, he may find his answer rejected, since ' ... this program only recognizes one right answer for each gap – that is, the word that the computer originally deleted from the text'. Nevertheless, Jones claims that, 'used as a learning device ... this limitation is less important; the student is playing a game – the game of trying to identify the deleted word – and in a game it is acceptable, even motivating, that luck should be involved'.

Finally, Jones also provides some advice on how the students can be helped to use the program most effectively. 'Students should ... be encouraged to use the 'help' facility and to 'cheat' where necessary.' (Students can ask the computer for help, in which case they will be given the first letter of the deleted word, together with a dash for each of the other missing letters, or they can 'cheat', in which case the computer will tell them the right answer.) 'They will get more out of each text, too, if they work not alone but in pairs or groups, and discuss the various possibilities before typing in an answer.'

The program allows the user to type in his own texts, and for this project two texts were selected which had been used in previous experiments with students from the Institute. One was of a general 'literary' nature, on the subject of Cervantes' *Don Quixote* (see Appendix A), but hopefully accessible to students from across a range of disciplines. The other was of a more specialized nature, on economics.

Hypotheses

The hypotheses that were selected for investigation were the following:
1. that students would be equally motivated by the task whether presented in computerized or non-computerized form;
2. that the two forms of presentation would lead to the same kind of interaction among students in the group;
3. that the reading strategies practised by the activities in both com-, puterized and non-computerized form would be the same.

Observation techniques

The observation techniques used had therefore to allow the identification, recording and analysis of:

a) affective reactions;
b) interaction among members of the group;
c) the processes and strategies involved in tackling the task;
as well as the stimulus from the materials which accompanied or was responsible for these.

The procedure adopted was to record the groups on videotape while they worked on the task. For the CALL task, a split-screen technique was used; the students were recorded on the bottom half of the screen, whilst the computer monitor which they were referring to was recorded on the top half of the screen. In this way a record could be kept of the part of the text which they were reading or discussing at any particular moment, and of the answers which they keyed in.

The students were also asked to complete a short questionnaire (see Appendix B) before each session and a longer one after it, and a brief discussion was held with them.

Analysis of the data

Hypothesis 1: Students would be equally motivated by the task whether presented in computerized or non-computerized form.

Evidence from the questionnaires

The term 'motivation' can be interpreted in a number of different ways, and the degree to which a particular task is motivating can similarly be measured by reference to a number of different criteria, including 'enjoyment' (question 1), an appreciation of 'usefulness' (question 2), a perception of 'learning' (question 3), a willingness to repeat a similar exercise (question 4), and persistence in working to solve a problem or complete a task.

The students' answers to question 1 suggest that the exercise on the computer was slightly more enjoyable than the non-CALL exercise, though the answers also suggest that they liked both the CALL and non-CALL exercises. A comparison of their answers to this question and to the pre-task questionnaire suggests that the experience of doing the exercise confirmed rather than altered their expectations of how enjoyable the experience would be.

The answers to question 2 suggest, however, that the students found the non-CALL exercise slightly more 'useful' than the CALL exercise, although the answers to question 3, on the other hand, suggest that the students felt they learnt slightly more from the CALL exercise.

The answers to question 4 suggest that there is little difference in the students' expressed willingness to repeat a similar exercise. The second part of question 4 on the questionnaire given to students after the CALL exercise was intended to investigate the possibility that students might be willing to work on the computer again, but preferably on a different kind of exercise (possibly suggesting more interest in the medium than in the exercise itself). The responses do not, however, support this interpretation.

These data suggest at least three conclusions:

1. this type of exercise is equally motivating, whichever medium it is presented in;
2. the students themselves were highly motivated, and would be motivated by, and make the most of, whatever learning opportunity was presented to them;
3. there may have been differences in motivation which the questions did not identify.

Evidence from other sources

Three other sources of information about motivation are available to us. Firstly, taking 'motivation' to mean 'enjoyment', a subjective impression suggested that the students working with the computer were enjoying themselves, for much of the time at least, whilst those working on the non-CALL exercise appeared more sober and serious during most of the task. The observation that students using computers actually look so happy, except when the exercise becomes particularly difficult, may be a major source of the claim which is frequently made that CALL is particularly motivating, though this study has not provided convincing evidence from other sources to back up these subjective impressions.

Secondly, in a brief discussion at the end of the task the notions of 'usefulness' and 'learning' were pursued. Since there was no obvious way of measuring what the students had learnt as a result of the exercise, they were simply asked what they thought they had learnt. They mentioned only one or two items of vocabulary – particularly *humdrum* in the text on *Don Quixote* – although there is some additional evidence in the transcripts of individuals asking for clarification of particular items of vocabulary (*tore*, for example and *embodiment*) which may well have been new to others in the groups as well, and may therefore have been learnt by more than the particular individual asking the question. It seems, however, that what they felt was 'useful' or was 'learnt' from the task may well have related to the process of carrying out the task – for example the opportunity to discuss or to try out different answers – rather than to specific linguistic products. The discussion did not identify any obvious differences between the CALL and non-CALL tasks in this respect.

Finally, interpreting 'motivation' as meaning 'persistence in trying to solve a problem or complete a task', the students tended to spend considerably longer (perhaps two or three times as long) on the CALL than on the non-CALL exercise. Whilst this may be due to the time which was needed to key in the answers, it may also be an indication that they felt the enjoyment of the task, or benefit they were deriving from it, justified spending considerably longer on it.

Conclusion

The evidence from these results is not conclusive, but tends to suggest that, in this case at least, the students were not more motivated by having the activity presented in one medium rather than the other. Nevertheless, observation of the students using the CALL materials suggests that there may be an interest aroused by the medium which was not identified by the questionnaire, but which might be identified by an improved questionnaire, or by other means, such as follow-up interviews, or long-term studies of students working with different media. In addition, the students who took part in the project were likely to be relatively highly motivated, and so representative of only a particular category of student; it would therefore be useful to investigate the effect of CALL materials on other, and especially less highly motivated, students.

Hypothesis 2: The two forms of presentation would lead to the same kind of interaction among students in the group.

This hypothesis was investigated by analysing the videotapes and transcripts of the tapes. Three particular areas were investigated:
1. the number of turns taken by each participant, and the direction of contributions within the groups;
2. the competition for turns;
3. the content of the turns.

The number of turns taken

Although individual participants in the activities took different numbers of turns, they all contributed to the discussion, and the different number of turns taken by each student was not necessarily dependent on the medium in which the materials were presented. For one of the groups there is little evidence of any significant difference between the CALL and non-CALL exercises in terms of the number of turns of each participant, and the direction of contributions within the group. This may be a result of group dynamics, since one member of the group tended to take charge of the discussion in the non-CALL exercise, and in the CALL session the same student operated the computer keyboard, with the result that the discussion had to be channelled through him.

There is some evidence, however, that the direction of the contributions – who talked to whom in the group – may have been at least partially determined by the medium for the other group. Although one student did tend to dominate the discussion during the non-CALL session, that student did not take over the keyboard in the CALL exercise, and so discussion was channelled through someone else. The evidence is not clear-cut, however, since discussion in the non-CALL session was occasionally diffuse, with the group talking to each in pairs or threes.

The competition for turns

One of the characteristics that one would presumably want to find in a 'communicative' exercise is that of competitive turn-taking. As van Lier (1982) says: 'If turn-taking is rigidly (predictably) controlled, and our aim is to enable the learners to communicate in the target language outside the classroom as well as inside it, then there is something wrong, because outside the classroom competition for turns is standard procedure.' In this respect, interaction during all of the sessions, whether the groups were using CALL or not, can be said to have been 'natural', and so 'communicative'. It is interesting that both the CALL and non-CALL procedures were far more satisfactory in this respect than the procedure followed at the end of a non-CALL exercise whereby the teacher checks the answers with the students; in this case turn-taking is fairly rigidly controlled by the teacher.

A comparison of the CALL and non-CALL procedures with the procedure in which the teacher checked the answers does, however, suggest one interesting difference. There are a number of examples in the data of students suggesting answers which are correct, but which are consistently ignored by the other members of the group. In the non-CALL exercise, whether or not a student is taken notice of appears to depend on his or her strength of personality, or persistence in trying to make the others take notice. In the CALL exercise, on the other hand, most or all of the students get a chance to try out their ideas, unless someone comes up with the correct answer reasonably quickly. A similar phenomenon is found in the procedure during which the teacher checks answers, as the teacher tends to allow all of the students a chance to try out their ideas. To that extent it could be said that the CALL exercise is distorting 'natural' conversation, since the computer is acting to some extent as a teacher, though the distortion in this case would presumably be considered beneficial.

The content of the turns

It was anticipated that the discussions would consist predominantly of suggestions and counter-suggestions; explanations for suggested answers, and reasons for rejecting them; and general expressions of agreement or disagreement. It was also expected that the CALL sessions would contain a certain amount of discussion related to the working of the computer and the program – for example, explaining to the person at the keyboard that they had pressed the wrong button, or how to scroll the text.

The variety of types of content appears, however, to have been rather more limited than expected. Mostly the students made suggestions for answers to the gaps, or rejected answers and offered counter-suggestions, with few examples of explanations for those suggestions or rejections. There was little difference in this respect between the CALL and non-CALL activities. The CALL activity also contained relatively little discussion related to the working of the program or the computer; this may have been because the instructions for the program were straightforward (although one group did manage to exit from the program by mistake) as well as because the students had had an introductory session on the computer. In addition, if there was a problem over which button to press, students would tend to lean over and press the correct button, rather than try to explain to the person at the keyboard.

The evidence therefore tends to confirm the second hypothesis.

Hypothesis 3: The reading strategies practised by the activities in both computerized and non-computerized form would be the same.

Taking the author's suggestions for the aims of cloze texts (see p. 82 above), what we would want to try to identify in the task is the following:

1. evidence of attempts to find and agree on the correct, or an acceptable, word to complete the gap;
2. evidence of students 'drawing on all their language resources as and when they are needed' in order to complete the gaps;
3. evidence of students using the contextual clues offered by the remaining parts of the text to fill in the missing words.

Evidence of attempts to find an acceptable word to complete the gap

There is ample evidence of students attempting to find and agree on an acceptable word to fill the gap, in both the CALL and non-CALL situations. There are, however, two striking differences that the data reveal between the CALL and non-CALL exercises. The first is that the students using the computer tend to try a larger number of guesses, and the second is that students doing the CALL exercise tend to get stuck on particular gaps. They seem reluctant to use the 'help', or 'cheat' facility, and as a consequence they spend a great deal of time and effort in trying to find the single correct answer. The non-CALL group, on the other hand, with some exceptions, tend to agree on an acceptable answer and move on to the next gap rather more quickly.

Evidence of students 'drawing on all their language resources'

There is some evidence, though perhaps surprisingly little, of students 'drawing on all their language resources as and when they are needed' in order to find suitable words to fill the gaps. Clearly, it is difficult if not often impossible to infer with any confidence what thought processes a student is using, simply from external observations, but it had been expected that, if they were working in groups, there would have been a good deal of discussion indicating why a particular solution to a gap was being suggested. Indeed, there is some such discussion, on the lines of 'it must be a verb here', or 'it must begin with a vowel because the article is *an*'. However, given the number of gaps where several guesses were considered before the correct one was found or an acceptable one agreed upon, the amount of explanation of why a guess was suggested or rejected was surprisingly small.

Evidence for the use of contextual clues

It is equally difficult, of course, to infer whether students are using the contextual clues offered by the remaining parts of the text to fill in the missing words, since there may be few external clues to the students' reading strategies and their thought processes. It was expected, however, that there might be three kinds of clues to whether this was happening.

Firstly, and most importantly, it was expected that students would discuss their suggestions by reference to other parts of the text; these references would give some indication of how far ahead the students had read, and of how far back they would refer in order to find, justify, or reject an answer.

Secondly, it was expected that there might be some reading aloud of the text, as they were working in groups rather than individually.

Thirdly, it was expected that the way in which the CALL students scrolled the text on the screen would give some indication of how far backwards or forwards they were reading.

There is surprisingly little evidence in the data of students referring to other parts of the text in considering the suggestions for answers. There is a considerable amount of reading out loud of parts of the text by both the CALL and the non-CALL students, which gives an indication of the extent to which at least some of the students read back or ahead. Clearly, however, it is not possible to claim that evidence that any particular student is doing this is necessarily evidence that other students are doing the same. Nevertheless, it is interesting that when the students used the computer they rarely, if ever, scrolled the text other than when they had completed all the gaps in one screenful of text and wanted to reveal the next gap. In other words, they treated the text a screenful at a time at the most, even though each passage contained three screenfuls of text.

In this context it may be useful to point out that there was some apparent difference in the way the two groups tackled the tasks. One group, for example, appeared to tackle the CALL and the non-CALL tasks in a similar way, that is, by considering each gap in turn, rather than reading the whole of the text first. The other group, however, when they tackled the non-CALL task, chose to spend a considerable amount of time reading the whole of the text through first individually, before discussing suggestions for the missing words. When that group tackled the CALL task, there is some evidence from the reading aloud that they read the whole of the first screenful of text before beginning to consider suggestions for the gaps. They did, however, stop at the last word on the first screen, and not scroll any further ahead. One possible interpretation is that they were trying to apply the same reading strategy that they had applied to the non-CALL text, but were discouraged from doing so – perhaps by the form of the presentation, i.e. one screenful at a time rather than all on one page; perhaps because they were reading one text as a group; or perhaps because of unfamiliarity with the program or computers (though when they were asked afterwards if they had not scrolled the text because they weren't sure how to, they denied this).

The evidence, therefore, tends to reject the third hypothesis.

Conclusions

Comparing CALL and non-CALL activities

The decision to compare similar exercises in CALL and non-CALL form would appear to be justified in that it has provided evidence to suggest which of the effects observed are due to the medium in which the task is presented, and which are inherent in the task itself. The evidence, however, raises certain questions not only about the difference between computerized and non-computerized cloze texts, but about the cloze technique in general, and in particular about the extent to which the cloze technique may be used to foster efficient reading strategies. These questions arise for the following reasons.

Firstly, if an efficient reading strategy is one which relates the way we read a text to our purpose in reading that text, then it is difficult to see how the exercises used in this project can be fostering or practising efficient reading strategies, since there is no particular purpose that the students have for reading the text, other than as a language exercise.

Secondly, whilst guessing the meanings of unknown words is one of the reading strategies we use, the exercises presented here appear to imply that all unknown words in a text are of equal significance; presumably part of the process of reading efficiently consists of making decisions about which unknown words are and are not of importance for a reader's own understanding of the text.

Thirdly, one of the strategies which the cloze technique purports to be practising is that of using contextual clues from elsewhere in the text to find the meaning of an unknown word. A random cloze technique, however, may not be particularly effective in encouraging such as strategy, since there may well be words deleted for which there are no clues elsewhere in the text. The evidence from the data suggests, in fact, that the students may be using clues only from immediately before and after the missing words.

These comments apply to both the CALL and non-CALL activities, but the evidence suggests that the CALL program may be exaggerating two of the characteristics described above. Firstly, there is some evidence that students using the computer were less likely to read very far ahead or back in the text. Secondly, in achieving its aim of encouraging students to make a number of guesses the CALL program also appeared to be encouraging the idea that all unknown words are of equal significance in a text, since the learners persisted in looking for a single correct answer rather than settling for an acceptable guess. Part of the reason for this was that the program seemed to be particularly successful in encouraging the game element which was one of its stated aims. The students appeared to be engaged in the game of 'beating the computer' as much as in the process of decoding the text, and were therefore reluctant to use the 'help' or 'cheat' facilities in the program, to the extent that they sometimes reached the point of trying suggestions which they must have known were clearly unacceptable rather than 'give in' to the computer. To some extent, then, in computerizing the exercise in this way, the nature of the activity itself seems to have been altered.

Implications

Software and methodology

A single study of this kind cannot come to any significant conclusions about the advantages or drawbacks of computer-assisted language learning. Nevertheless, it seems clear that, as with activities in other media, the techniques used for instructing and training the students in how to make the most effective use of an exercise may have an important effect on the value of the activity. Encouraging students to scroll the text and read it through before beginning the exercise, pointing out examples of words which could be guessed from clues elsewhere in the text, suggesting that they note down examples of words which were rejected by the computer but which they nevertheless think were acceptable – techniques such as these might make the material more effective as a 'reading skills program', whilst retaining some of the advantages of the game element, and the automatic production of exercises.

To exploit the full potential of the computer, however, changes to the software would be necessary, and the facility for automatically producing exercises might have to be sacrificed. (Should we really expect the computer to produce good exercises on its own?). The program discussed in this paper is neat and well-constructed, but may be restricted by the limitations of the hardware on which it is run. The potential of the medium, however, suggests a number of exciting possibilities which it would be difficult or impossible to implement in other media, especially in the provision of clues and help facilities. A variety of clues could be provided as part of the help facility, at different levels of explicitness. For example, parts of the text which provide clues for a particular gap could be highlighted. In addition, while leaving students free to decide how to complete the task, prompts could be provided suggesting, for example, that if they are stuck on one gap they should move onto another gap, or ask for help. The program could also be written to allow acceptable alternatives for gaps, as well as to allow modified cloze, i.e. the selection by the teacher of the words to be deleted. None of these suggestions seems particularly difficult to implement, though there are other more exciting possibilities such as linking programs to dictionaries and databases which hold promise for the future.

Observation techniques

It is essential to develop observation techniques in two directions. First, we need to gather information from the students themselves in more detail. To some extent this can be done by questionnaire, but more useful would be interviews with the students, reporting sessions during which the students talk about what they are doing while they are working on an exercise, as well as talkback sessions during which they watch part of a videotape of themselves doing the exercise, in order to clarify or explain some of the details observed during that exercise.

In addition to techniques for gathering information in more detail, it is necessary to develop techniques for gathering information in quantity. These would include simplified observation schedules allowing useful information to be gathered by less sophisticated means than split-screen filming, and which could be more quickly analysed. One way, for example, of determining how much of a text students read in order to find the answer to a gap is simply to ask students at regular intervals to tell you which part of a text they are reading, and which gap they are working on.

Appendix A: Sample cloze exercise

Name: _____

Quixote

For more than three centuries readers in all countries
--1-- been delighted by the adventures of an
absurd gentleman --2-- Don Quixote and his
squire Sancho Panza. The masterpiece --3--
Miguel de Cervantes, a Spanish contemporary of
Shakespeare, 'Don --4--' tells of a poor gentleman who tries to relive --5-- heroic days of old
by seeking adventure in the --6-- of the knight-
errant of medieval romance. Don Quixote's
--7-- is not caused merely by his being delight-
fully ridiculous, --8-- comical nuisance, an
absurd figure apt to get into --9-- wherever he
goes. Beneath his humorous surface Don Quixote
--10-- the embodiment, even though he is also
the exaggeration, --11-- a great idea – that life
holds more than the --12-- routine of everyday
affairs, that true greatness is to --13-- found
only in the spirit of service to an --14--.

That for Don Quixote the ideal is an illusion
--15-- not detract from its fascination, though it
does make --16-- a pathetic figure. To attempt
the impossible for the --17-- of honor, to add to
the store of human --18-- by risking everything
without the hope of material gain. --19-- en-
dure danger and hardship because endurance itself
is noble – --20-- is the quixotic ideal; this is the
secret of --21-- Quixote's universal appeal. We
must laugh at his absurdity, --22-- we are
moved by it as well; if there --23-- any chivalry
or generosity in us, we cannot help --24-- on
his side, however innocent his victims. We know
--25-- cannot win, but his misguided valor ex-
cites our pity --26-- our laughter.

1. _____
2. _____
3. _____

4. _____
5. _____
6. _____

7. _____
8. _____
9. _____

10. _____
11. _____
12. _____
13. _____
14. _____

15. _____
16. _____
17. _____
18. _____
19. _____

20. _____
21. _____
22. _____
23. _____
24. _____

25. _____
26. _____

Appendix B: Questionnaires

(The questionnaires for the CALL and non-CALL tasks were identical except where indicated.)

Pre-task questionnaire (CALL task)

Please answer these questions:

Name: _____

1. Have you used a computer before? _____
   If the answer is 'yes', please give brief details:

2. Do you think you will enjoy doing an exercise on the computer?
   Very much _____ A little _____ Not very much _____ Not at all _____

Pre-task questionnaire (non-CALL task)

Please answer these questions:

Name: _____

1. Do you think you will enjoy doing the exercise?
   Very much _____ A little _____ Not very much _____ Not at all _____

Post-task questionnaire (CALL task)

Please answer these questions:

Name: _____

1. Did you enjoy doing the exercise on the computer?
   Very much _____ A little _____ Not very much _____ Not at all _____

   If you want to explain your answer, please write your comments here:

2. Did you find the exercise useful?
   Not at all _____ Not very _____ Fairly _____ Very _____
   If you want to explain your answer, please write your comments here:

3. How much do you think you learnt from the exercise?
   A lot _____ A little _____ Not very much _____ Nothing ___
   If you want to explain your answer, please write your comments
   here:

4. Would you like to do an exercise on the computer again? Would
   you like to do:
   a) the same kind of exercise?
      Very much _____ A little _____ Not very much _____ Not
      at all _____
   b) a different kind of exercise?
      Very much _____ A little _____ Not very much _____ Not
      at all _____
      If you would like to explain your answer, please write your
      comments here:

5. If you would like to make any other comments, please write them
   here:

Post-task questionnaire (non-CALL group)

(The non-CALL post-task questionnaire was identical except for
questions 1 and 4)

1. Did you enjoy doing the exercise?
   Very much _____ A little _____ Not very much _____ Not at
   all _____
   If you want to explain your answer, please write your comments
   here:

4. Would you like to do the same kind of exercise again?
   Very much _____ A little _____ Not very much _____ Not at
   all _____
   If you want to explain your answer, please write your comments
   here:

Introduction to Chapter 8

Language testing, at first sight, is an obvious area for the application of computers and their associated software. Charles Alderson's paper discusses the implications for language testing of recent developments, focusing especially on current practice and research into CBELT (computer-based English language testing). It begins by examining pitfalls arising out of the apparent ease with which tests can be constructed, using existing programs. In particular, the paper identifies the frequent lack of any validation of test items constructed with the aid of such commercially available programs, and their consequent limitation as a valid measure of student performance. Ease of complex calculation using statistical packages, for example, has in Alderson's view a consequent devaluing of the need to preserve face, content and construct validity. All is not necessarily rosy in the world of CBELT. As is argued in Thomas's paper which follows, however, there are considerable and innovative advances which can be made. Specifically, the paper focuses on an increasingly sensitive diagnostic testing of learners, with an accompanying possibility of adapting test levels of difficulty and range of coverage to the perceived performance range of the testee. Results from such adaptive testing would, of course, not only be useful to the learner; they would provide a continually updatable record of individual and group performance over a given period of instruction. Learners would then be assessed against group norms, rather than against criteria often unrelated to the actual programme of study in question. Once again we can make use of computers as a force for greater learner-centredness, and what is more, in a field of applied linguistics which has often come under attack for its normative and impersonal stance. Finally, the paper offers a provocative argument for CALL benefiting in its exercise and task design from the rigour required by CBELT techniques. Indeed, as the paper makes clear, the much proclaimed distinction between teaching and testing, at least as far as learner activity and task are concerned, may prove to be no longer reasonable.

8 Computers in language testing

J. Charles Alderson

Computers in language testing: some problems

According to Davies (1983): 'Language testing is an obvious computer application.' Indeed testing is frequently associated with computation and computerization. In a recent discussion of computers in language education, Higgins and Johns (1984), deal with well-established uses of computers in testing, namely statistical operations and computer test marking, and such uses are probably typical of a tester's use of computers. In my own research I have used mainframe computers for two main purposes – test marking and statistical calculations. My research has involved 12 cloze tests of 50 items each, taken by 60 subjects, i.e. 720 subjects in all. Marking the tests and analysing the results by hand would have taken a very long time and the marking might have been inconsistent. This problem was solved by getting the computer to score all the responses to all test items, using keys developed with a text editor. It was thus possible to apply any scoring criterion required, and indeed I used six:

1. the exact word;
2. any acceptable word;
3. any word from the same form class;
4. any word from an acceptable form class fulfilling the same grammatical function;
5. any grammatically correct word;
6. a score that gave non-native speakers credit for responses also given by native speakers.

In addition to the marking, the validation of so many tests potentially involved huge calculations in order to correlate and factor analyse results and so the use of a computer-based statistical package was very important.

Mainframe computers have long been used to calculate the statistical properties of tests. Programs for the analysis of test items – in terms of facility and discrimination, at least – have been available for some considerable time, and so have statistical packages which enable one to analyse test performance through calculation of zero order, multiple, and partial correlations, regression analyses, factor analysis, analysis of variance, and the like. The development of psychometry was closely associated with developments in hardware and software that enabled necessary calculations to be performed routinely and with minimal effort. Most budding testers and language test researchers are familiar with statistical packages like SPSS, which have been in use, especially in the USA, for well over fifteen years. Indeed almost every MA and PhD thesis in testing I read seems to rely on the use of such packages. Latterly, packages for use on microcomputers have become available and the disadvantages of main-frames and batch-processing with punch cards have been overcome through interactive terminal use. Software like INTROSTAT for the Apple or UNISTAT for the Spectrum or BBC B can handle quite large data sets and perform a useful range of calculations. Because these packages are interactive, they can also be used for hands-on experience in teaching statistics, often necessary on testing courses.

The ready availability of such packages has, however, some severe disadvantages and these are likely to increase with the advent of cheap micros and associated packages. The disadvantages include an increased emphasis on the statistical properties of tests, and a concentration on calculations of various sorts, where less attention is being paid to the design of the instrument, to its face, content and construct validity. Any number of statistics cannot improve a bad test. Indeed, they may not even show the need for improvement of a test since the evidence for such a need may not be readily quantifiable. Thus, computers may be directly connected with an overemphasis on statistics, often to the detriment and neglect of equally or more important aspects of test development. In addition, the ease with which calculations can now be performed has simply outstripped the ability of many researchers and test developers to understand and interpret the results, so that often one is faced with a mass of partially digested data which the progenitor or the reader has no means of properly interpreting. This is particularly common when the researcher enlists the assistance of a statistician to prepare the data and run the package. Thus, the use of computers in testing to provide statistics can be problematic.

The other use I exemplified above – that of test marking – also presents problems. Although it is possible to use computers to mark verbal responses to test items, this can be difficult if one's procedure is not *a posteriori* (as mine was through a text editor) but is instead *a priori* – having a key established in advance. This problem was typically solved in large-scale testing, where there was and is a need to mark large numbers of scripts rapidly, by using multiple-choice tests rather than limited response or open-ended items. In addition, the input of responses to the computer can be tedious. In the case of my own research, each response by each subject to each item (36,000 responses in total) had to be keyed to disc by data preparation personnel, and then verified for accuracy, before listing programs could be run to allow me to edit scoring keys. The problem of data input is greatly reduced by multiple-choice tests, and the use of machine-readable answer sheets, usually with optical scanners. For a long time now, test-takers have been required to provide answers to multiple-choice tests on such answer sheets. In other words, responses can be directly fed into the computer for marking and analysis. Such uses are convenient for the tester, in that they allow large numbers of examination scripts to be processed and results to be made available extremely rapidly, but such uses are unremarkable in terms of their effect on test development. Moreover, the instructions required to ensure that testees complete the machine-readable forms properly are often much more complex than the test tasks. This, understandably, can also have a negative effect on student performance by raising anxiety levels and creating greater opportunities for unreliability through transfer errors from test booklet to answer sheet. Indeed, the use of peripherals like optical scanners linked to computers has not to my knowledge led to new and desirable developments in test techniques but rather to the reverse. The increasing use of optical scanners and the associated convenience and ease with which such tests can be marked has led to the continued survival of so-called objective tests, especially multiple-choice tests, when developments in thinking in applied linguistics and language teaching have emphasized the disadvantages of such techniques. Thus, paradoxically, the computer has been a force for conservatism and lack of innovation in testing techniques: technological innovation has discouraged innovations in content validity.

The development of devices capable of reading testees' handwriting is, to my knowledge, a long way off. But even when testees can produce responses in readable form, i.e. through the keyboard of a terminal, other problems remain. As these are common to other aspects of CALL, I do not wish to dwell on them, but will simply mention that they include both response *recognition* (tolerance of spelling errors, misuse of space bars and non-letter keys, program break keys, etc.) (Last 1984, pp. 37–77 and 87–9, contains a useful discussion of this) and response *judging*. Where marking/judging schemes are laid down *a priori*, as they probably have to be in inter-active use, how can the scheme cope with unpredicted or indeed unpredictable responses that might be correct? This problem is obviously particularly important for tests, which by definition involve judgements of acceptability of response.

To summarize the discussion thus far: computers have been used for a considerable time to mark test responses, and to perform stat-istical calculations. Computers are therefore not new in testing. I have pointed out some dangers, however, inherent in their use that have come from experience. The ease of performing statistical calculations has led to a proliferation of statistical analyses, an overemphasis on their statistical properties and a neglect of non-quantifiable test issues (e.g. backwash effect). In addition, since multiple-choice or fixed response tests are much more convenient to mark by computer, there may be a reluctance to develop different test instruments which could be less convenient to score, especially by computer.

I see, however, two further problems arising out of the recent avail-ability of microcomputers and associated software and these are the production of a 'test' by computer without proper validation and trial, and the use of suspect testing techniques because they are easily programmed and produced. The two are related, as I hope to show by means of the example of the cloze test.

It is normal, indeed, mandatory practice in test development to *trial* the test one drafts in order to refine and improve the instrument. This includes detecting unsuspected ambiguities and possible alternative responses, and ensuring that those students who *have* the ability being tested can perform adequately on the test. In other words, all tests need validation during trialling. There is no such thing as an automatically valid test technique. Yet we now have packages like *Clozemaster* and *Questionmaster* which allow us to create tests on the computer *without* trialling. This is especially true of *Clozemaster*, where the machine selects items to be deleted, and supplies the response key. From an input text, the computer 'automatically' produces a supposed test. The superficial ease of construction of cloze tests – simply select a number and then mechanically delete every nth word – has always been one of its seductive and dangerous attractions. Now that cloze tests can be produced by machine they are even more attractive, but no less dangerous. What I wrote about cloze in 1979 remains true:

> The procedure is in fact merely a technique for producing tests, like any other technique, for example the multiple-choice technique, and is not an automatically valid procedure. Each test needs validation . . .

> (Alderson 1979)

A procedure cannot be valid – it is the resultant test that is or is not valid. Moreover, tests need trialling to ensure their validity. The warnings I issued five years ago about *assumptions* of validity instead of *proof* of validity are even more likely to be ignored when all one apparently has to do is input texts and let the machine do the rest. Indeed, we apparently do not even have to construct tests. That was and remains a nonsense; tests have to be constructed, probably by human agency based on principles deriving from learning and linguistic theory, and they have to be validated. In short, computers cannot produce automatically valid tests.

The other problem mentioned above is the use of easily programmed and produced test techniques. Considerable research, including my own, has already shown that the cloze procedure may not do all that is claimed for it. In particular, given the apparent insensitivity of many cloze items to long-range constraints on meaning, it has been suggested that perhaps the tests produced by the procedure tend to measure lower-order skills relating to short chunks of context – four or five words preceding a gap – rather than to extended discourse. Two further considerations are important here:

1. It is well known that students' reactions to cloze tests are negative, much more than to other tests, even including multiple-choice.

2. Reading clozed texts may encourage students to read in inefficient or counter-productive ways. In particular, students seem to pay little attention to text *beyond* a gap, and seem not to bear in mind – or indeed even to read – the overall or developing meaning of a text when clozing gaps. This was reasonably well attested some time ago, and Scott Windeatt's research (pp. 79–98, this volume) provides further confirmation of this.

Yet cloze tests are a particularly common form of CBELT, presumably because they are easy to produce. Such ease is, unfortunately, deceptive. It is important to consider the relative lack of acceptability of the cloze procedure for testees. It is also important to consider the possible undesirability of the behaviours it encourages. Whatever the ease of production of a cloze test, we must always pay attention to what it is that cloze tests might be capable of measuring.

So far, I have presented a fairly gloomy picture of the dangers and disadvantages of CBELT as I see them. What Davies (1983) sees as the main advantages of the computer – speed and memory – may seem to present possible disadvantages: undesirable educational testing practices, as well as teaching and learning practices, are in danger of being encouraged by the use of computers. Of course, any tool can be misused and its advantages can obviously become dangers – that is as true of axes and knives as it is of computers. There are, however, interesting positive possibilities for developments within language testing, given the increasing availability of cheap microcomputers.

Computer-based English language testing (CBELT)

Davies (1983) has claimed that CALL and CBELT can now provide 'a large enough item bank memory and a swift enough access . . . [to produce] reliable and valid diagnostic instruments'. In principle, diagnostic testing of grammar, vocabulary, and pronunciation has always seemed a good idea – as Davies says, 'something highly desired but somehow unattainable'. It may be that CBELT through micros will allow us to *explore* the possibilities.

Indeed, this is one exciting challenge to testing and applied linguistics which comes out of CBELT and CALL: *Can* we diagnose learners' errors and language problems? Language diagnosis has been called a pseudo-procedure, perhaps because of the lack of memory and computational capacity to carry it out. We now apparently have this capacity, through advances in technology, to allow us to test the claim. Thus CBELT, through diagnostic testing, can not only feed from but also contribute to our understanding of learners' language. CBELT diagnostic testing could proceed by predicting likely errors – possibly based on previous research into learner interlanguages, or based on its own database of previous performances of similar individuals on CBELT tests. Learners could then be presented with choices. Responses thus elicited could be evaluated by the computer, and a score assigned, or the learner could be given clues based on the nature of his response, to help him on a second try. Such preprogrammed feedback could clearly also serve a pedagogic purpose.

Results on a set of items would lead to a profile of performance which would minimally be in the form of a set of scores which could then be used for *placement* purposes, or, pedagogically more interesting, could be presented in the form of a compilation of the preprogrammed feedback which would in effect *describe* weaknesses, or idiosyncratic rule systems. It is interesting to note that the challenge consists less in writing the software than in identifying suitable areas of language proficiency that are amenable to such description, diagnosis and rule-based feedback.

A further possibility that the computer offers is adaptability. It is said that diagnostic tests, to be reliable, require large samples of performance. However, tests could be constructed to be administered in such a way that if an individual passes, or indeed fails, a given number of items, the computer either stops presenting him with parallel items, or presents him with further items in order to probe and explore the particular weakness or strength in depth. I return later to this aspect of CBELT, which is becoming known as 'adaptive testing'.

I noted above the possibility of the computer using stored records of previous performances on a test, either by the same student or similar students (on whatever criterion: same school, age, sex, language background, etc.). Any particular test-taker could be presented with only those items which have proved relevant (because easy, difficult, discriminating or whatever) for a relevant peer group. Tailor-made tests thus become a real possibility. In addition, an ongoing record of the performance (of items or individuals or groups) raises the interesting possibility of the computer calculating a constantly updated item analysis of those tests on file, which could lead to the automatic deletion or modification of items, in the machine, based upon accumulating evidence of performances. Thus the computer offers very real possibilities of continuous test updating. If responses are classified by test group, however defined, it also offers the possibility of differential item analyses for different target groups. This could lead to a determination of items which were suitable for some groups but not others — tailor-made tests.

If a record of group performance were maintained by computer, a student/testee could receive credit for his response, relative to the frequency (difficulty, etc.) weighting of responses given by criterion groups. This would obviate the need for test constructors to specify in advance what the correct answers *should* be, but rather allow the computer to grade according to what proved to be popular answers for criterion groups.

Indeed, such a procedure has already been developed for use with cloze tests, and is known as the clozentropy scoring procedure. Cousin (1983) has developed a clozentropy program using interactive terminals and a mainframe computer (IBM 4331), for use on self-assessment programmes within self-directed learning programmes. Overseas students taking the cloze tests are scored according to the frequency of responses given by peer non-native groups, at present. The aim, however, is eventually to produce entropy scores based on appropriate native-speaker criterion groups. So far the project has only been piloted on small groups, but indications are that there is considerable interest on the part of testees in getting feedback on their performance, by comparing their responses with those of native speakers.

Although the investigation uses cloze tests as the testing instrument, the procedure need not be confined to cloze tests. Simple entropy scores can be calculated from the performance of whatever reference group one wishes to select, based upon any testing instrument.

Although cloze tests, i.e. pseudo-randomly produced tests, might be unsuitable for use in CBELT tests, gap-filling tests might be much more interesting. Unlike the cloze test, deletions in gap-filling tests are made in accordance with the tester's purpose, and in terms of what he wishes to test. Such tests are constructed according to psycholinguistic or linguistic criteria. Thus one might ask testees to restore cohesive items, or words carrying main ideas, or structurally redundant items, or key vocabulary items whose meaning is deducible from context. *Unlike* cloze tests, however, such tests cannot yet be constructed by computers. How could one program a machine to identify items restorable from an understanding of the context? Such gap-filling tests would have to be constructed by humans, with one possible exception. It may be that deletion pattern programs could be interfaced with computer language corpora, of the LOB (Lancaster-Oslo-Bergen) variety, in which case there is a possibility that, say, words of a particular form class could be systematically deleted by computer. Although this may hold some promise for the future, until the computer is able to process 'meaning' it is unlikely to be an interesting possibility, and humans are likely to remain the best constructors of such theory-related gap-filling tests.

A major development, however, that is already taking place relates more to test administration than to test construction, and that is adaptive testing, alluded to above. To quote Canale (1984):

> In contrast to a traditional test in which each testee is essentially required to respond to the same set of questions regardless of his or her individual ability to do so, an adaptive test is one that can be tailored during its administration to the level of performance of each testee.

Based on feedback from performance on initial tasks, the test administrator (in CBELT, the computer) selects subsequent test items to correspond to that performance. Thus if performance on items 1–5 is poor, easier questions might be selected. Typically this is what happens in oral interaction tests, typified by the FSI (ILR) tests (Foreign Services Institute (Interagency Round Table) of the United States), where the interviewer adjusts his questioning to the success of the testee on previous items. It is increasingly commonplace in the CBELT literature to make the analogy of a hurdle race. Suppose we are interested in knowing about hurdling ability and we have hurdles in series that increase in height by 10 cm, starting at 10 cm and going up to 100 cm. If a runner knocks down the first five hurdles there would seem to be little point in asking him to go ahead and knock down the remaining five. Similarly, if most runners clear the first five hurdles effortlessly, their clearing the 30 cm hurdle gives us sufficient information about their ability to clear 10 cm and 20 cm without our having to subject them to those hurdles. In general, we can learn little by asking questions that are too difficult – we just frustrate testees. Thus tests that can be adapted to the level of the testee would not only be more efficient and less time-consuming, they might also be more acceptable to testees, and by being concentrated at the ability level of the testee, they would provide a more accurate account of ability with the same number of items. Such tests are likely to be less wasteful, and more accurate. There are, however, considerable problems in adaptive test development to be overcome. These include the large database required, which means almost certainly that present micros could not handle more than a trivially small area of language. The item would need to be calibrated and to be independent of person (sample) bias. This probably requires a testee sample size of 1000 (Tung 1984).

High discrimination is required for such items – .65 rather than .2 – and so there is likely to be a high wastage rate in trials. In addition, there are the problems of entry and exit levels: when, at what point, should a student begin a test; which items should he or she be presented with? And when does one decide that one has gained sufficient information to allow the testee to stop the test? In spite of these practical problems, organizations like Educational Testing Services are investing in developments of Computerized Adaptive Testing. According to Wainer (1983), the advantages of computerized adaptive testing are:

1. improved test security;
2. the individual can work at his or her own pace, and the speed of response can be used as additional information for assessment;
3. each testee stays busy productively: all are challenged, none discouraged;
4. physical problems of answer sheets are removed (interactive terminals are used);
5. immediate feedback;
6. new items can be easily and unobtrusively pretested;
7. faulty items can be immediately removed.

A further advantage of CBELT – not just adaptive testing – is that it also allows continuous testing to be a practical possibility. CBELT is unlikely to be feasible when large numbers of students have to be tested. However, when testees appear in small numbers yet continuously, as they often do for placement purposes, then CBELT tests are highly efficient. They need not be innovative, since individualized administration is itself a sufficient advantage. For such uses authoring software like QUESTIONMASTER can be extremely useful. These programs are designed to allow users to input existing tests to a computer without any knowledge of programming. Thus tests whose properties are known (I emphasize the importance of this since there is no substitute for validity and validation) can be simply administered at otherwise inconvenient times. Feedback of results can be immediate, to the institution or indeed to the individual, either after each item, or after a subtest, or after the whole test. CBELT might thus remove the inconvenience of test administration to small numbers of subjects.

Importantly, the use of CBELT is breaking down the supposed differences between a test and an exercise. It is frequently claimed that there is a big difference between the two. Although the two clearly differ in *use* and the consequences of a particular level of performance, I believe that there is very little difference in *design*. A test is essentially a device for eliciting relevant behaviour (which then becomes describable) and some procedure for judging that behaviour (which implies a set of criteria for adequacy and acceptability). Thus language or language use is elicited and then judged. Exercises do essentially the same, by eliciting behaviour and then, however inexplicitly, allowing the possibility of its evaluation (which is what we often call teaching). Perhaps there are only three important differences between a test and an exercise in this regard:

1. Exercises do not typically explicitly provide criteria for the evaluation of the elicited performance (although perhaps they should do so);
2. When doing exercises learners typically receive support and guidance from peers and teachers. They are not expected to work alone, without help. But in a test, a learner is typically alone without support and guidance.
3. In most fields we normally receive feedback on a performance once it has been completed. Whereas in tests, feedback may be considerably delayed – perhaps indefinitely – partly for fear of contaminating future behaviour, and thereby invalidating one's non-interventionist validity. The Navaho child quoted in Canale (1984) illustrates this well. After doing his first test item, and

before going onto the next, he turned to the tester and asked: 'Did I get it right?'

With the possibility of immediate feedback on performance from the computer, however, even this distinction between testing and teaching activities becomes blurred. What may distinguish them is how the results are used, rather than what the elicitation procedures – the exercise types or test techniques – look like. Thus testers will do well to look at recent and future developments in CALL methodology – exercise types – in order to incorporate them into tests. It seems to me that a good CALL activity must also make a potentially good CBELT technique, always with the proviso that testers have to be more rigorous than exercise developers (unfortunately for CALL). There is an onus on testers to show that the tests resulting from their techniques are valid and reliable. Would that the same could be said about exercise and materials writers! I hope that CBELT will benefit in the near future from CALL developments, and equally that CALL will benefit from developments in CBELT types and techniques.

To conclude, the advent of CBELT does hold out interesting possibilities. I have warned of the danger of unsound educational practices, or the use of poor pedagogic techniques in CBELT, but this applies equally to CALL. Those developments that play to the computer's strengths of speed and memory and accuracy without losing sight of their *inherent* applied linguistic justification are to be encouraged as the most likely to succeed. There can be no doubt that the computer can be misused and can be a restraint on development, for example, of non-multiple-choice items. An awareness of this is essential but it does not mean that computers cannot or should not be used to advantage in language testing.

What makes recent developments in hardware more interesting is the possibility of increased *interaction* between the testee's performance and:

a) possible evaluations of the performance;
b) test/item content.

Input to computers can be readily stored and this may lead, interactively, to:

1. research data on processing and learning;
2. modification of test items;
3. administration of a different Next Item.

The possibility of interactive provision of immediate feedback leads to:

1. the breakdown of the distinction between test and exercise;

2. the possibility of fine-tuned diagnosis;
3. pedagogic intervention via clues and guidance after a test (or item);
4. a consideration of the value (or lack of it) of one-shot (irrevocable) performance, and the possibility of allowing learners to review their responses before they are 'finally' stored in memory. (The learner could review all his responses before committing himself, and it may be possible to elicit and take account of the learner's degree of certainty about the 'correct' answer, and thus make allowances for such uncertainty in one's calculation of test scores).

A test is not only an elicitation procedure but also a judgement. In CBELT this judgement can be *a priori*, made by humans, and thus fed into a marking key which can be referred to by a computer scoring system. This has the disadvantage that one cannot predict all possible or plausible outcomes. Or the judgement can be *a posteriori*, made by humans (although this then reduces the advantage of the speed of the computer). The judgement could also be made by machine, comparing responses with a database, which could be either other responses (clozentropy, for example), or computer-based corpora, either directly or by rule application, on the lines of the parsing system under development at Lancaster for detecting typing errors (see Atwell 1983).

What is clear is that CBELT offers a unique opportunity to experiment, to try out ideas, and test theories. By recording responses and learners' routes through data or tests, one might begin to discover what effective feedback might be. One might, through CBELT, develop one's theories of what diagnostic testing should or can be, and perhaps thereby gain greater understanding of the nature of language learning.

Introduction to Chapter 9

Jenny Thomas's contribution falls into two distinct but related parts. It provides a short critique of current CALL, identifying in particular the pedagogic limitations of many programs and their heavy production costs in relation to their range of applicability. One drawback she identifies is the limitations imposed by the restricted processing power of most home computers and the inappropriateness of BASIC for anything other than relatively simple language tasks. As a contrast to this salutary criticism, however, (in which she echoes at least one of the discussion sessions of the course from which the papers in this book are drawn) she offers in the second part of her paper an exciting innovation for CALL: one which does not replicate what many teachers have been doing in their non-computerized classrooms, but which makes accessible to learners analysed corpora of language data on which they can draw. Using a powerful database program (dBase II), she provides extensive illustration of work in conversational pragmatics, specifically the selection of sociolinguistically appropriate realizations of chosen speech acts. What this example shows is the potential for such linguistic databases in classroom language learning. Not only can learners access very large and varied input data, they can also, in principle, draw on the results of linguistic analysis as an aid to their own problem-solving. Used in this way, CALL has a liberating effect on the learner, and suggests considerable changes in the relationship between teachers and learners. Indeed, it may well be in Jenny Thomas's application that we will see the greatest area of cooperation between CALL and current theories of language learning and classroom pedagogy.

9 Adapting dBase II:[1] the use of database management systems in English language teaching and research

Jenny Thomas

1 Introduction

This paper is divided into two distinct parts. The first part is a very brief overview of the criticisms most frequently levelled at CALL in its present state and with which, on the whole, I concur. The briefness of the account means that I may unfairly include in my condemnation some very worthwhile work and for this I apologize in advance. My concern is to show in general terms that the current approach to CALL is misguided, not to suggest that all the work in the area is irredeemably unsound! I shall argue that we should be aiming at the 'top end' of the market, at very advanced learners, perhaps those undertaking pre-university courses, where the need to individualize tuition is greatest and where powerful microcomputers are available. I shall further argue that instead of 're-inventing the wheel' by producing every program from scratch (and, of necessity, doing it rather badly), language teachers should be looking to see how 'off-the-peg' software can be adapted for their purposes.

In the second part of the paper, I shall describe how a very powerful commercially-produced database management system – Ashton-Tate's dBase II – can be adapted for use in English language teaching and research. I shall show how an analysed corpus of English can be easily accessed by language learners or teachers and describe how dBase II can also serve as the basis for an intelligent knowledge-based system. I shall argue that, unlike most current work in CALL, the approaches I am outlining have a sound pedagogical basis and use the computer to accomplish tasks which no teacher can.

2 Criticisms of current approaches to CALL

CALL is under fire at the moment, by no means all of it is coming from benighted computer-illiterates, fighting a rearguard action against a technological revolution they fear will leave them dispossessed! Classroom language teachers and applied linguists alike are expressing serious doubts about the pedagogical value of CALL programs. Those who believe that introducing the computer into the language classroom is a worthwhile enterprise ignore such criticism at their peril. In the section which follows, I summarize briefly the most obvious criticisms of CALL, focusing particularly on those criticisms I think can be answered by the approach I am suggesting. For a far more detailed and authoritative criticism of educational software in general, see Self (1985).

2.1 Pedagogical criticisms

The main thrust of teachers' criticisms of CALL programs is that at best they do no more than an averagely talented teacher could accomplish using simple visual aids, or than a good textbook does already – at far less cost. At worst, they are based on teaching methods which run counter to desirable teaching practices and which bear little relation to what we know about second language acquisition.

As an example of software in the first category one could take a program called COPROB being developed at the Computers in the Curriculum Unit at Chelsea College and which, in spite of the very limited graphics employed on the pre-publication version I saw demonstrated, is enjoyable enough to use. The student receives hints as to where a robbery is taking place and then tries to get the police to the scene of the crime before the criminals escape. If it is used properly,[2] one could expect that at the end of the game the player might have practised using or learnt the names of some twelve places in a French town (*poste, station service*, etc.), the appropriate preposition to put in front of them (*au, à la, à l'*, etc.) and perhaps how to give directions. All of which is fair enough, except that, even relying on a great deal of development-time freely given by teachers, the program cost many thousands of pounds to develop and achieves little more than could have been done for pence using an overhead projector or a games-board.

Into my 'at worst' category comes one depressingly typical example of CALL teaching materials based on an impoverished understanding of the process of second language acquisition, as described in an article by Roberts (1981, p. 126):

> Basically, two methods can be used to 'teach grammar'. For the ablest pupils the learning of rules is used which, when learnt and internalised, allow the production of new unheard utterances. This is ultimately the most efficient method. This is where the computer can help.

He then goes on to describe a 'slot and filler' approach to teaching *ce/cet/cette/ces*, before conceding (p. 127) that 'most pupils cannot apply rules even if they can learn them. For perhaps the majority of pupils the only method is repetitive drills'.

Clearly, a behaviourist approach to language teaching is not restricted to CALL and many designers of CALL software obviously have given a great deal of thought to appropriate methodologies (e.g. Higgins and Johns 1983; Higgins 1984), even if they have been unable in practice to implement them in their programs. That so many CALL programs do nevertheless adopt a pedagogically unsound approach is not difficult to explain. In the first place, to develop truly innovative educational software is not simply beyond the average classroom teacher, but beyond most professional programmers too (see Self 1985). In the second place, people appear to become so engrossed in or overwhelmed by the task of actually programming that they lose sight of the original pedagogical goals. Avner (1979, cited in Self 1985, p. 109), reports that teachers 'became so involved . . . that the production of impressive sequences of animation or simulation became almost an end in itself . . .'. This certainly appears to be the case with Kenning and Kenning (1983) who devote an entire article to the virtues of the 'drill facility' of EXTOL (East Anglia and Essex Teaching-Oriented Language), without ever appearing to question whether or not the drill is an effective and appropriate language-teaching technique.

2.2 Technical criticisms

As John Self pointed out at the Conference from which this collection of papers originated[3] and reiterates in his book (1985, p. 98), it is simply not reasonable to expect enthusiastic hobbyists, working on very modest home computers, such as the Sinclair Spectrum or the BBC micro, and using an inelegant programming language like BASIC, to accomplish much of worth. 'Basic was not intended for writing even modest-sized programs for practical use – it was designed for beginners to write small programs.'

What he did not say, but what those same enthusiasts (myself included) felt on hearing his criticisms, was that such proficiency as they had achieved had been painfully acquired over many years and that the simplistic programs he criticized so forcefully had been painstakingly produced over many months! No one wants to gestate like an elephant only to be told they have given birth to a gnat, but the sad truth is that one can dedicate a disproportionately large amount of time and energy to developing CALL materials and still have nothing worthwhile to show for it at the end. The shortcomings of the materials are certainly not due to any lack of dedication on the part of their creators, but to the inappropriate nature of the technology they are able to afford, to the inherent limitations of the programming language they use and also, perhaps, to their view of language and learners and of the place of CALL in the curriculum.

2.3 'Ideological' criticisms

This is not a criticism I have heard made explicitly, but one I sense lies beneath the accusations of 'elitism' which are often directed at any language teacher able to tell her ASCII from her elbow. In Britain, teachers have struggled for many years to liberate themselves from having their curriculum and teaching materials imposed from above and have no wish to lose their hard-won freedom to innovate and to adapt materials to suit their own needs, just because they lack the necessary computing skills to create their own programs or to modify other people's. Quite reasonably, they are not prepared to devote excessive time to acquiring such programming skills, but yet have no wish to exchange one tyranny for another.

2.4 Practical considerations

2.4.1 *The use of CALL with young beginners*
Perhaps for the technical reasons I have outlined above, most CALL software is aimed at young students in the early stages of learning a second language. Yet it seems to me that for a number of practical reasons these are precisely the groups least likely to benefit from the essentially individual learning resource provided by the computer. In the first place, they need the stimulus of group activity and immediate, intelligent response – not the type of interaction which even the most 'user-friendly' computer can as yet be programmed to provide. Secondly, the emphasis in the early stages of language learning is on

the spoken word – for which the computer is not an appropriate medium. Thirdly, it is rather easy in the early stages of language learning to predict the needs of the whole group – such individualized tuition as computer programs can currently offer is unlikely to be productive at this age or stage. Finally, few language teachers in secondary schools have more than one computer at their disposal and even then it can normally only be used under close supervision, so that even if individualized learning were seen as desirable, it would rarely be possible.

Some CALL advocates, apparently making a virtue of necessity, argue that a single computer, used by the teacher or a couple of pupils in front of the class is ideal. This has not been my experience. VDUs are not designed to be viewed by more than one person and students accustomed to operating their own computers at home are irritated by being passive observers at school. Indeed, on those occasions during the Lancaster course when CALL software was being demonstrated during a lecture, the people more than one row back, who could not see and who were not among the lucky two or three chosen to press the keys were murmuring rebelliously and discontentedly after a few minutes. And these were highly motivated and reasonably well-behaved adults!

2.4.2 Financial considerations

I do not wish to labour this point, which must be clear from the foregoing criticisms: CALL is extremely costly – either in money for commercial software or in time for home-produced materials. We need to be very sure it is worth it.

There is, however, another related issue, which I find deeply disquieting – the reluctance, not just on the part of individuals, but also on the part of publicly-funded bodies, to submit their products for normal evaluation by others professionally involved in language education. This can be explained in part by the fear of programs being pirated, but is, it seems to me, also motivated by a fear of having the programs exposed to informed criticism before they can be marketed and some of the enormous development costs recovered. The present government's desire to see practical applications without being prepared to pay for the necessary preliminary research, may prove costly in the long run, not just for the educational establishments which purchase software of dubious quality, but also in terms of academic integrity.

3 In defence of CALL

Unable to respond satisfactorily to mounting criticism, particularly of the sort I have outlined in Section 2.1 above, proponents of CALL have been forced back on to two defensive positions. The first has been around in various guises for many years, the second is relatively new.

3.1 The computer as motivator

In the ten years that I have been involved in language teaching, the 'ed. tech.' industry has proposed a variety of panaceas for re-motivating the disaffected language learner – film-strips, comic-style textbooks, television, video and now:

> ... the microcomputer holds an *innate attraction* ... (especially for teenage boys, when interest in French is waning!) and can have a great self-motivating effect.
>
> (Roberts 1981, p. 121)

Leaving aside the quaint sexism and questionable logic of the quotation, there is no evidence whatever in the extensive research literature on the affective and motivational aspects of second language acquisition (see e.g. Gardner 1979; Heckhausen and Weiner 1972), to suggest that the computer – or any other extrinsic motivator – will have more than a very short-term effect in enthusing the jaded language learner.

As for the motivating force of the CALL software currently available, no student who has played ELITE is likely to be won over to language learning by BOMB THE WORD. And the more glamorous the software to which the student is exposed at home or in other classes, the duller and more de-motivating the CALL material will seem by comparison. In my experience, it is much more likely to be the semi-(computer)-illiterate teachers who are enthralled by CALL software than the average blasé teenager!

3.2 Never mind the quality, feel the interaction!

A more recent tack adopted by CALL enthusiasts, forced to accept that the majority of software currently available is pedagogically weak, is to assert that: 'It is not the quality of the software which is important, but the quality of the interaction it engenders.' It is, of course, quite true that all sorts of improbable things can generate real communication. The most lively (for want of a better word!) language

class I ever conducted in the Soviet Union followed an encounter
on the stairway with the dead body of a Dean. Now, few teachers
(even in these dismal times, when promotion prospects are so bleak!)
would encourage the wholesale slaughter of senior academics just to
pep their classes up a bit, any more than I would countenance
spending time or money on meretricious CALL programs which may
or may not do the same. If 'quality of interaction' is what you are after
and if – which has yet to be established – playing computer games
really does generate 'authentic communication', there are plenty of
trashy space invader games available extremely cheaply from any
corner shop, together with many excellent 'adventure games' such as
DUNGEONS AND DRAGONS, THE HOBBIT or MACBETH.

I would certainly concede that the activity of using a computer may
in itself, at least in the short-term, get students talking, but using a
computer for this purpose can scarcely be considered to come under
the heading of CALL. The use of the computer in these circumstances would be purely incidental and no one, as far as I am aware,
has suggested that the language generated by showing someone else
how to operate a computer is any richer than that generated by
explaining how to construct an object from Lego bricks or by playing
any of de Bono's 'lateral thinking' games.

4 Summary

This all sounds very depressing and may seem ungenerous to those
enthusiasts who have devoted a great deal of time and thought to the
production of CALL programs. Obviously, it is not always possible
to foresee what, if anything, will come of new ideas and approaches
until one has tried them and the attempt was, in my view, worth
making even if the results have not been encouraging. There have
been positive spin-offs from the efforts of individual CALL enthusiasts. In the first place, that teachers become computer-literate is in
itself a very good thing; it will not be until large numbers of language
teachers and linguists have a good grasp of the problems, possibilities
and limitations of computing that real progress will be made.
Secondly, the enthusiasm of the teacher for the software he or she
has produced will transmit itself to the students, almost regardless of
any intrinsic value the materials may have.

Developments in computer hardware have been very dramatic in
recent years in terms of memory size, speed of processing, etc. In fact,
improvements in hardware are outstripping even expert computer

programmers' ability to keep up and manufacturers are now deliberately holding back innovations in hardware. At the same time, prices
are dropping almost monthly. There has been no parallel revolution
in software production. Indeed, as far as language teaching is
concerned, the introduction of the computer has often meant the
unthinking re-adoption of techniques long since discredited. At the
same time, there are many pressures on teachers and institutions to
be seen to be using the new technology and the temptation to get on
the computer bandwagon/gravy train is strong. This has been
accompanied by a marked reluctance to subject CALL materials to
any rigorous evaluation or to question the theory of learning implicit
in such materials. Pedagogically unsound material, particularly if it is
over-promoted (and there is every sign that it will be) will rapidly
bring the whole CALL enterprise into disrepute. The language
laboratory fiasco of the fifties and sixties is still in many people's
minds and uncomfortable parallels are already being drawn (Underwood 1984, p. 35ff).

The time has come for a radical rethink, for examining the questions we should be asking about CALL and the criteria used to assess
CALL software.

5 Re-thinking CALL

In my view, the only justification for the wholesale introduction of
computers into the language-teaching classroom is if they can be
shown to do something which research into second language acquisition suggests is pedagogically well-motivated and that they can do
something which either is not being done at present, or can do it more
cheaply or efficiently than it is being done at present. As Self (1985,
p. 12) remarks, computers should 'supplement not replicate the
teacher'. In the second part of this paper, I shall discuss one program
which will do just this.

Most CALL materials have been developed on an ad hoc basis,
by individual hobbyists. The few institutions taking an interest are
under-financed and under pressure to produce quick results. All
have failed to ask the right questions and their common point of
departure seems to have been: 'What can we use the computer for
in the language class?' What they should have been asking is: 'What
would I like to be able to accomplish that cannot be done (or done
efficiently) without a computer?'

In the following sections, I shall begin by describing how I answered this question in relation to my own research and then show how precisely the same methods and principles can be used to provide a worthwhile resource for the language teacher.

6 The computer in linguistic research

The data I needed to analyse related to the Cross Cultural Speech Act Realization Project (CCSARP). Briefly, the aim of the project is to establish a database of speech-act realizations across (initially) ten different languages or language varieties and to analyse them in terms of surface grammatical structures and underlying pragmatic features. Our aim is to discover and describe the most probable speech-act realization in a given language in given circumstances and to pinpoint likely areas of cross-cultural pragmatic failure. For each language, the data consists of eight apologies and eight requests, elicited from two hundred native-speaking informants by means of a 'discourse completion' task (see Appendix A) in which the parameters of social status and size of imposition are manipulated. A full account of the CCSAR Project is given in Blum-Kulka and Olshtain 1984.

6.1 Hardware

Although my colleagues on the CCSAR Project had processed their data on mainframe computers using SPSS, I deliberately chose to restrict myself to a microcomputer because I was already considering the implications of our research for language teaching and wanted the data to be readily available for people to use at institutions which did not have access to mainframe facilities.

The machine I use is an ACT Sirius I, which is a particularly good 'business' microcomputer, but any personal computer with a minimum of 256K RAM would do (e.g. ACT Apricot, IBM PC, DEC Rainbow). Such machines are not cheap, but they are now available from £1,600 and should soon come within the price range of most educational establishments.

6.2 Software

Finding suitable software was much more difficult, as all the 'user-friendly', 'menu-driven' database management systems (e.g. FRIDAY!, CARDBOX) were far too inflexible: the maximum field size was often as little as 32 bytes (hopelessly inadequate for entering natural language data) and the processing possibilities were largely pre-determined and extremely limited. The only package I found which answered my requirements was dBase II from Ashton Tate.[4]

dBase II is a relational database management system and is designed for both the first-time user and the experienced programmer. It operates on two levels. The first level provides commands which can be entered interactively, allowing an absolute novice to create a database, enter data, sort according to user-defined criteria, etc. It took me less than a week to master level 1 completely. The second level is a powerful high-level programming language, which enables the user to perform an infinite variety of data management tasks using procedures or sub-routines. It is this programming facility which is so important for language-teaching purposes, since it allows complete beginners to access the data by means of menus (see section 7.2.2 below).

6.2.1 Designing the database structure
dBase II allows three field types to be used: 'character fields' (any keyboard character may be entered), 'numeric fields' (only numeric data may be entered) and 'logical fields' (accepts only yes/no, true/false statements). Logical fields are very useful for fast sorting. The maximum field size is 254 characters (1,000 in dBase III) and the maximum number of fields is 32 (128 in dBase III).

Figure 1 (p. 122) shows the database as I originally designed it. The field names may appear rather arcane. This is because they cannot exceed 10 characters. However, a more elaborate screen-format can be designed to make it easier for other people to enter data (see Figure 2). In fact, the 'front-end' can be made as user-friendly as is necessary, and Figure 3 shows a version which a complete novice could use.

The structure was designed so that fields 1–12 contain personal details of the informant, 13–23 give information about the speech act of requesting and 24–32 are for tagging apologies. Much of the personal information can be entered automatically using a simple 'global replace' command, but each speech act has to be tagged individually according to a coding scheme developed by all the project participants and designed to capture the most significant generaliz-ations in the different languages. Ninety-nine basic tags were used for coding requests and fifty-eight for apologies, but it is perfectly possible to add tags to capture language-specific usages or to refine the analysis. Figures 4 and 5 are examples of the way in which a request and an apology are tagged.

FIGURE 1 **Normal database structure**

FIGURE 2 **'User-friendly' screen format**

PRIMARY USE DATABASE

FLD	NAME	TYPE	WIDTH	
001	SURFACE	C	254	SURFACE STRUCTURE
002	INF:NUMBER	N	004	INFORMANT NUMBER
003	FEMALE:Y	L	001	IS INFORMANT FEMALE? ANSWER Y/N
004	SIT:NUMBER	C	002	SITUATION NUMBER
005	LANG:QUEST	C	002	LANGUAGE OF QUESTIONNAIRE
006	SAMELANG:Y	L	001	IS THIS INFORMANT'S MOTHER TONGUE? Y/N
007	M:TONGUE	C	002	IF NOT, STATE MOTHER TONGUE
008	SAMEPOB:Y	L	001	WAS INFORMANT BROUGHT UP HERE? Y/N
009	LENGTHSTAY	C	002	IF NOT, HOW LONG HAS S/HE LIVED HERE?
010	DATE:QUEST	C	004	YEAR QUESTIONNAIRE ADMINISTERED
011	POP:TYPE	C	002	TYPE OF INFORMANT (E.G. PRE-UNIVERSITY)
012	AGE:INFORM	C	002	AGE OF INFORMANT
013	REQUEST:Y	L	001	IS SPEECH-ACT A REQUEST? ANSWER Y/N
014	ADD:TERM	C	002	FORM OF ADDRESS USED
015	REQ:PERSP	C	002	REQUEST PERSPECTIVE
016	REQ:STRAT	C	002	REQUEST STRATEGY/DEGREE OF DIRECTNESS USED
017	DOWNGR:SYN	C	002	SYNTACTIC DOWNGRADER
018	DOWNGR:OTH	C	002	OTHER DOWNGRADER
019	UPGRADER	C	002	FORM OF UPGRADER
020	SUPPORTIVE	C	002	TYPE OF SUPPORTIVE MOVE
021	MODE	C	002	MODE (NEUTRAL, SARCASTIC, ETC)
022	MODAL:TYPE	C	002	TYPE OF MODAL
023	MARKED:SYN	C	002	MARKED SYNTACTIC FORM
024	TERM:ADDR	C	002	TERM OF ADDRESS IN APOLOGIZING
025	IFID	C	002	ILLOCUTIONARY FORCE INDICATING DEVICE
026	INTENSIF	C	002	INTENSIFIER
027	RESPONSIB	C	002	RESPONSIBILITY
028	EXPLANAT	C	002	EXPLANATION
029	REPAIR	C	002	OFFER OF REPAIR
030	FOREBEAR	C	002	PROMISE OF FOREBEARANCE
031	MINIMIZE	C	002	ATTEMPT MADE TO MINIMIZE OFFENCE?
032	CONCERN:Y	L	001	IS CONCERN EXPRESSED FOR HEARER? Y/N

FIGURE 3 **'Idiot-proof' version of screen format**

1. Enter the surface structure in precise form in which it appears on the questionnaire.

2. Enter the informant number from section 1 of the questionnaire.

3. Is the informant female? Enter Y for yes, N for no.

4. What is the situation number? Enter number from 1 - 16.

5. What is the language of the questionnaire? Enter 1 for Australian English, 2 for British English, 3 for Hebrew, 4 for Danish, 5 for American English, 6 for German, etc.

FIGURE 4 A request (a brief explanation of the coding is given in
brackets)

```
001   SURFACE        Please could you tidy up the kitchen soon?
002   INF:NUMBER     0001
003   FEMALE:Y       Y
004   SIT:NUMBER     01
005   LANG:QUEST     02 (British English)
006   SAMELANG:Y     Y (Informant is a native speaker of British English)
007   M:TONGUE
008   SAMEPOB:Y      Y
009   LENGTHSTAY
010   DATE:QUEST     1981
011   POP:TYPE       01 (University student)
012   AGE:INFORM     19
013   REQUEST:Y      Y
014   ADD:TERM       00 (None)
015   REQ:PERSP      01 (Hearer-oriented - "could you", c.f.
                     speaker-hearer oriented "shall we")
016   REQ:STRAT      (Preparatory Condition)
017   DOWNGR:SYN     (Interrogative)
018   DOWNGR:OTH     (Politeness marker - "please")
019   UPGRADER       (Time intensifier - "soon")
020   SUPPORTIVE     (Grounder - S enquires about H's
                     ability to perform request)
021   MODE           (Neutral - c.f. 82 Sarcastic)
022   MODAL:TYPE     (Specify form of modal used - "could")
023   MARKED:SYN     (None - conditional, passive,
                     negated proposition, etc. are classified)
```

FIGURE 5 An apology

```
FLD   NAME

001   SURFACE        Oh, I am so very sorry, but I
                     forgot it, Sir.  I'll bring it tomorrow.
002   INF:NUMBER     0601
003   FEMALE:Y       N (Informant is male)
004   SIT:NUMBER     04
005   LANG:QUEST     02 (British English)
006   SAMELANG:Y     N (British English is not informant's mother tongue)
007   M:TONGUE       06 (Informant's mother tongue is German)
008   SAMEPOB:Y      Y (Informant was born and brought up in West Germany)
009   LENGTHSTAY     1 (Informant has been in Britain for up to one year)
010   DATE:QUEST     1981
011   POP:TYPE       01 (Informant is a university student)
012   AGE:INFORM     20
013   REQUEST:Y      N
024   TERM:ADDR      09 (Honorific - Sir)
025   IFID           01 (Sorry)
026   INTENSIF       01 (Adverbial intensifiers)
027   RESPONSIB      06 (Implicit responsibility)
028   EXPLANAT       01 (Explicit account of reason for offence)
029   REPAIR         01 (Explicit offer of repair - I'll bring it tomorrow)
030   FOREBEAR       00 (No undertaking that the
                     offence won't be committed again)
031   MINIMIZE       00 (No attempt to minimize the offence)
032   CONCERN:Y      00 (No concern expressed -
                     e.g. I hope you didn't need it urgently)
```

6.2.2 Processing the data

Once the data has been coded, the possibilities for processing the data are virtually limitless. For example, address terms (field 15) are coded in the following way:

00 NONE
01 TITLE/ROLE (Dr., Prof.)
02 SURNAME
03 FIRST NAME
04 NICKNAME
05 ENDEARMENT TERM
06 OFFENSIVE TERM
07 PRONOUN
08 ATTENTION GETTER (e.g. excuse me)
09 MARKED ADDRESS TERM OR HONORIFIC
10 TITLE + SURNAME
11 LANGUAGE SPECIFIC FORM

Looking only at address terms (which is far from being the most interesting feature, but is very easy to explain!) one might compare the two speech acts and ask whether in a 'costly to hearer' speech act like requesting (see Leech 1983, p. 107) the address form is different from that used in a 'costly to speaker' speech act like apologizing? We could compare mother-tongue usage and ask whether there is a significant difference in the use of address forms in German and in British English. And is the difference carried over to any significant degree when Germans speak English? Is there any difference in male and female usage and if so is the difference parallelled cross-culturally? (The answer to all these questions is 'yes'.)

Any number of conditions can be set on commands in order to access all and only the information required. If the fieldtype is 'logical' (true/false) it is sufficient to enter the true condition (in the examples which follow, the upper case words represent commands in dBase II):

Example 1
COUNT FOR FEMALE: Y would give the total number of female informants.

For a 'character' or 'numeric' field, the equal to (=) or not equal to (<>) symbols must be used:

Example 2
COUNT FOR AGE: INFORM = '19' (Count the number of informants aged 19)

Any number of Boolean operators (and, or, not) can be strung together. Supposing, for example, I wanted to look only at the form of apology used by male speakers, I could do this interactively with one command:

Example 3

LIST SURFACE FOR .NOT. FEM:Y .AND. (.NOT. REQUEST:Y)

[i.e. list the contents of the field called SURFACE (surface structure) for all records where the truth condition of the field called FEMALE:Y (is the informant female?) is false and where the truth condition of the field REQUEST:Y (is the speech act a request?) is also false.]

If you wanted to find out what a nineteen-year-old female university student who is a native speaker of British English would use as an abusive form of address to a man who was pestering her,[5] you *could* enter the following command interactively:

Example 4

LIST SURFACE FOR FEMALE:Y .AND. SIT:NUMBER = '3' .AND. LANG:QUEST = '2' .AND. SAMELANG:Y .AND. POP:TYPE = '2' .AND. ADD:TERM = '6'

However, beyond a certain point (particularly if you will want to access this information frequently) it is simpler to put exactly the same commands into a subroutine (known as a 'command file') called, say 'FEM:ADDS' (Address forms used by females) which could then be executed simply by typing DO FEM:ADDS. It is very simple to modify or extend these command files (it can even be done using a word-processor), or to present a novice with a menu-driven version, as I shall show in section 7.2.2 below.

7 Feeding into language teaching

The value of a powerful commercial database management system in linguistic research should be obvious from the example I have given above, but how can it be justified in language teaching?

7.1 Practical justification

The type of programmable database I have described seems to me to offer a useful middle path between leaving everything to the professional programmer (with all that that implies for teachers in terms of relinquishing autonomy) and what I consider to be the educationally deficient programs produced by hobbyists. Authoring systems may eventually offer a similar middle path, but at present they are restricted (as far as language teaching is concerned) to generating one type of activity only, such as multiple-choice tests, cloze tests or rather limited simulations. Self (1985, p. 111) comments that:

> Apart from technical limitations, there are two main problems with authoring systems. The first derives from a conflict inherent in the design of any high-level programming system, that is, in the balance between easing the programmer's (or author's) task and in limiting what he can, in fact, do. Most authoring systems are best suited to the development of text-based, 'tutorial' lessons which follow a pre-specified pattern. It is often difficult to specify, for example, the model needed for a simulation ... More generally, authoring systems, with their rigid frameworks, may stunt any teacher creativity.

A program such as dBase II is expensive but, unlike an authoring system, can be used for any number of purposes: I have shown how I use it for research in pragmatics, but it could equally well be used in grammar, sociolinguistics, for any subject where it is useful to manipulate data (history, geography, English) as well as for bibliographical and administrative purposes (after all, huge organizations like UNESCO use it for their administration!). It allows the computer to do what it is best at and turns it into a powerful and flexible teaching resource.

7.2 Pedagogical justification: the computer as resource

There are three properties of a powerful microcomputer which are potentially invaluable for the language teacher: it can store, access and analyse data. Textbooks can do this too – although, of course, the computer can store more data than most books can and it can be processed incomparably faster. The really important difference is that on computer the database itself, the systems of accessing and analysing can all be modified to suit the needs of the user. This is true in theory, at least. In practice, the degree to which they can be modified is a function of the software or the programming skills of the operator. I shall shown how in dBase II this can be done without an inordinate degree of programming knowledge.

7.2.1 Modifying the database
The storage capacity of modern microcomputers is vast – the ACT Apricot, for example, could store over 2,000 of the records shown in Figure 1 on just one floppy disk. The implications of this in language teaching are enormous. We no longer need to regard the database as 'given' once and for all. It can be updated, replicated or modified at will.

The data we used for the CCSARP were elicited, but it would be very simple for a student to add to the database naturally-occurring data, data from different languages or socio-economic groups, to include different speech acts, data obtained in 1985, etc. I have shown in Figure 3 how the system of data entry can be made simple enough for anyone to enter extra data to an already existing data file. To teach someone to create his or her own data file from scratch would not take more than half an hour.

We collected the data in order to compare speech-act strategies across languages, but making available a huge database means that it is unnecessary to restrict or predict the purpose to which other people might put it. You could, if you felt so inclined, use it to find out how many university students know how to use apostrophes correctly! To give a concrete illustration, one overseas student at Lancaster wanted to know the difference in usage between *standpoint, point of view* and *viewpoint*. None of us knew exactly (or cared!) and no grammar book or dictionary dealt with the question adequately, but within a few minutes we were able to get a printout from the LOB corpus of every occurrence of these words and he could answer the question for himself. This may seem a trivial example, but it made this student independent of his teachers and gave him the information he wanted when he wanted it. A further instance of a corpus fulfilling a need which had never been predicted by its designers, is that of a linguist who wanted all the instances of 'scare' quotes from newspaper extracts in the LOB corpus.

7.2.2 Accessing the data

The most valuable function of a well-programmed computer is that it can give rapid access to a vast body of information. A system such as dBase II allows the information to be given in a variety of different ways, presenting all and only the information the user wants at a given moment. I have sketched out in 6.2.2 how this can be done interactively, or how subroutines can be written to do it more efficiently. The command files can be modified using a word-processor if the user is not confident enough to use the screen-editor, so that a student could ask, say, for female informants in example 3 (p. 125 above), simply by erasing '.NOT.'.

Alternatively, a menu-driven system could be created which the student could operate using one or two keystrokes:

Example 5

Do you want to specify sex of speaker? Enter Y for Yes, N for No.

If so, do you want to restrict yourself to male speakers or female speakers? Enter M for Male, F for Female.
Is the sex of addressee a relevant consideration? Enter Y for Yes, N for No.
Is the status of the addressee a relevant consideration? Enter Y for Yes, N for No.
etc.

I should say at this stage that what I am proposing is emphatically *not* an expert system, which will give the 'right' answer to questions such as: 'How would a native speaker make a request of someone of higher status where the size of imposition is great?' Expert systems might be justified in grammar, but are inappropriate in pragmatics. What I have in mind is a non-expert option-generator, a program in which the basis for decision-making is made explicit by asking questions such as: 'Is the status of the addressee an important consideration?' Such an approach involves drawing the user's attention to potentially relevant factors, rather than the replication of expertise.

To create a menu-driven program of this order requires some degree of expertise in the dBase II programming language. I was able to write such a program after about two months of teaching myself,[6] but there are programming aids available to speed up the process of programming and creating 'user-friendly' screen-formats.[7]

In my experience, language learners are keen to exploit the resources of large corpora such as LOB, CCSARP and the Corpus of Spoken English – the problem has always been a practical one of accessing the data. In my opinion, the main advantage of the computer is the enfranchisement of learners: allowing students to approach the task of information-retrieval with their own questions, such as 'Why do Russians sound impolite when they speak English?' or 'What is the most useful request form to teach?' However, there is no reason why the learners' minds should not be focused on certain tasks if that is considered desirable. This could be done in a variety of ways. For example, a student could be asked to use the CCSARP corpus to find the most likely area of mismatch between a native and non-native speaker, or to investigate what is the most likely factor to affect the degree of indirectness used in a given language or culture.

7.2.3 *Modifying the system of analysis*
Many systems of analysis – both in grammar and in pragmatics – have hidden ideologies. To take a simple example, coding a double negative as 'ungrammatical' involves a particular view of the status of standard English. My own inclination would be to code 'endearments'

used as terms of address to unknown women as 'offensive', but non-feminists might not subscribe to this point of view. By typing the command DISPLAY STRUCTURE, the student can see displayed the coding system and the basis on which decisions have been made. If he or she then wishes to modify the coding system, or extend it to capture different features, this can be done very simply using the command MODIFY STRUCTURE.

8 Conclusion

I have no wish to make exaggerated claims for the approach I am taking – bombast is one of the few commodities not in short supply in CALL. What I do claim, is that it is possible to accomplish something intrinsically worthwhile for language learners and teachers, which cannot be done without the computer; that it can be done at a reasonable cost, with software which is readily available (and which can justify its purchase price by being used for other things in an educational institution), which requires minimal skill to operate and does not require inordinate expertise to adapt extensively and which still leaves room for contributions from both teachers and students. Finally, it can be done now, and not in that 'very near future' which has, for decades, been just around the corner!

Appendix A Part of CCSARP questionnaire

CCSA Research Project

Please fill in the following information
1. Date: _____ 2. University of Lancaster
3. Name: _____
4. Age: _____ 5. Sex: M/F (Please circle)
6. Mother tongue (if it is not English)_____
8. If English is not your mother tongue how long have you studied
it? _____

In each of the following 16 situations, one sentence is missing in the dialogue. You are asked to fill in the missing sentence, so that it fits into the ENTIRE TEXT. Please read each situation TO THE END before writing your answer.

Example
A woman is talking to her twelve-year old son.
PETER: Do you know where my shoes are?
MOTHER: They're in your cupboard and they're filthy. _____
_____
PETER: I don't want to do it now; I want to watch Dallas.

Possible answers you might give:
               Go and clean them right away.
               You'd better go and clean them.

N.B. No solutions are suggested. Simply complete each dialogue in the way which seems most appropriate, bearing in mind THE CIRCUMSTANCES in which the interaction is taking place and the RELATIONSHIP between the participants.

1. In a student flat

Larry, John's flatmate, had a party the night before and left the kitchen in a mess.
JOHN: Larry, Ellen and Tom are coming to dinner tonight and I'll
               have to get on with the cooking soon. _____
_____
LARRY: OK. I'll get on with it now.

4. In a professor's room

The student has borrowed a book from her professor, which she promised to return today. However, she realizes she has forgotten to bring it along.

PROFESSOR: Mary, did you remember to bring the book?

MARY: _____

PROFESSOR: OK, but please try to remember it next time.

Notes

1. dBase II is the trademark of Ashton-Tate.
2. I wrote 'properly used' advisedly, since children rapidly develop techniques for 'getting the right answer' without going through the reasoning process the program-designer had in mind. I myself achieved consistently high scores on a 'problem-solving' simulation whilst stabbing at the keyboard with my eyes shut! The same, of course, is true of many other forms of teaching material (see Hosenfeld 1976).
3. Course on 'Computers in English Language Education and Research', University of Lancaster, 16–28 September, 1984.
4. A more powerful version of dBase II, dBase III, became available after I started my research.
5. For those who are burning to know: in 1981–83 the most likely offensive address term to be used in these circumstances was 'you creep' (80%). Interestingly, only 12% of replies from women were abusive or obscene, compared with 24% of replies from men. Asked why this should be, women students replied that offering direct abuse in these circumstances was liable to provoke violence.
6. dBase II is often used to introduce novices to programming (see Freedman 1984) and a large number of introductory books on dBase II and dBase III are available (see bibliography).
7. For example QUICKCODE and dUTIL from Fox and Geller.

Introduction to Chapter 10

Together with the two previous papers by Alderson and Thomas, Gerry Knowles's contribution moves away from CALL in the narrow sense towards broader educational applications of computers, and moves closer to the final papers in the collection which highlight computer-based linguistic research. In a partly documentary vein, Knowles surveys the uses made of computers in the teaching of undergraduate and graduate courses in English phonetics at Lancaster over the last few years.[1] He identifies general arguments in favour of computer use, for example, in their speed in handling transcription and their ability to be programmed with interesting learning tasks for students. But the strength of the paper lies in its clear documentation for would-be computer users of the range of phonetic operations that can be successfully undertaken. Firstly, the capacity to handle a variety of transcription systems, using the capacity of many micros to have new characters defined by their specialist users; secondly, the capacity alluded to above to program the computer to undertake automatic transcription from orthographic texts of various kinds, lists, written originals, and (with an accompanying tape-recording) spoken samples. One of the more challenging aspects of the paper is the suggestion it makes for using the computer to test theoretical ideas about phonology, using a corpus of stored text. This, linked to a brief discussion of further research possibilities into speech synthesis, concludes the paper, illustrating how phonetics teaching and the computer is nicely poised between the pedagogy of CALL and the explorations of fundamental research.

10 The role of the computer in the teaching of phonetics

Gerry Knowles

Why use the computer?

There are many reasons for using the computer in phonetics teaching. One is that innovation and increased efficiency are essential if phonetics is to maintain its position in linguistics and language teaching. A more positive reason is that the subject can be taught more effectively with a computer than without. A third reason is that it is actually jolly good fun, and makes teaching more enjoyable and more interesting than it was before.

The traditional method of teaching is highly labour-intensive. Phonetics is not the sort of subject the student can go away and read up in the library. It is not possible, for example, to learn to associate phonetic symbols with their conventional values just by reading about them. If basic phonetics is to be taught effectively, it takes up a large amount of contact time. In a large department with several phoneticians and just a few students, there may be sufficient time available. However, the growth in the coverage of linguistics over the last twenty years or so has meant that less and less time can be devoted specifically to phonetics: so a more common situation is that a small number of staff have to teach a large number of students. In practice, we have to choose between teaching the subject inadequately, and finding new and more efficient ways of using teaching time.

If the computer is to be used effectively, there are two important principles to be observed. First, it should do something that a human teacher cannot do, or at least cannot do as efficiently. The computer can write on the screen much faster than a human teacher can write on the blackboard, and can do lots of totally predictable and repetitive tasks which for humans are time-consuming and rather dull. This gains useful time for the teacher to do things that humans do better than computers.

The second principle is that the computer should leave the user with interesting tasks to carry out. There is no point in making the computer do all the work, as that reduces the user to a passive onlooker. Nor is much to be gained by giving most of the boring work to the computer, if the task itself remains boring. This will very quickly associate the computer with boring jobs. The challenge of the new technology is that it gives us a chance to transform the tasks themselves, so that they actually become interesting.

In phonetics, the beginner has to learn to cope with exotic symbols and an unfamiliar terminology, and to write speech down in a way which clashes with the familiar writing system. This learning has to be done before basic skills and knowledge can be applied. Beyond this point, phonetics becomes an increasingly interesting subject; but it must be said that the majority of learners never arrive. For many, the subject remains a matter of upsidedown e's, voiceless labiodental fricatives, and remembering not to use capital letters. Our challenge is to rethink the approach to the subject, and give the learner a stronger motive. The computer can help with the acquisition of basic knowledge, and also with motivation.

Phonetic symbols

Defining IPA characters

A preliminary problem for computer work in phonetics – as in mathematics and other subjects which use special symbols – is to get nonstandard characters displayed on the screen, and printed on paper. This is a factor to take into account when buying a computer or a printer.

Fortunately, many micros allow the user to define a number of characters. On the BBC model B, for instance, it is easy to create up to 32 characters with ASCII values in the range 224–255.[2] It is actually possible to create more than 32, but this requires some understanding of the innards of the machine. Some IPA characters can be formed by overprinting, e.g. /θ/ can be made by printing '-' over '0'.

To print the characters on paper, we can use a *daisy wheel* printer, which has a set of ready-formed characters like a typewriter, or a *dot matrix* printer, which creates each character as a pattern of dots. In view of the better quality of print which it produces, a daisy wheel printer might seem preferable. However, even assuming a phonetic daisy wheel could be found, it would be necessary for someone to stand over the machine changing the daisy wheels to switch from printing IPA characters to conventional ASCII characters, and back again. In practice, one would need a printer with two daisy wheels.

A more realistic choice is a versatile quality dot matrix printer with the facility to create special characters. The Canon PW-1080A has two qualities of print; a fast low quality, suitable for rough drafts or listing programs, and a slower 'near letter' quality (NLQ), suitable for final drafts. New characters can be created for both qualities, in such a way that the printer can switch back and forth from the standard ASCII set to the user defined set.

Using phonetic symbols

Having defined the necessary characters, the next problem is to use them. If, say, shwa is created as character number 240, the command PRINT CHR$(240) will result in shwa being printed on the screen or on the printer. Although this works well from within a BASIC program, another method needs to be devised for the program user.

Some micros have special keys which can be programmed to print phonetic symbols directly. In practice there are likely to be rather more symbols than available keys. To print the remainder, it is necessary to choose keys which are not normally used in the same text as phonetic symbols, e.g. £ $ % & ~, and to use these as substitutes. By testing every key-press, it is possible to intercept the substitutes, and replace them on the screen with the phonetic symbols.

The easiest way of intercepting key-presses is to use GET. In BBC BASIC

    LET K$ = GET$

will GET the first key pressed and assign it as a value to K$.

Suppose we have created /ʃ/ as character 250, and selected the dollar sign as its substitute. Given the instruction

    IF K$ = "$" THEN PRINT CHR$(250);

the computer will print /ʃ/ on the screen whenever the user presses the dollar sign.

If key-presses are being intercepted anyway, it is worthwhile adding another check to ensure that only lower case letters are sent to the screen irrespective of whether the user types in capitals or lower case. The simplest method is by means of the instruction

    PRINT CHR$(ASC(K$) OR 32);

This adds 32 to the ASCII values of the capital letters (65 to 90) converting them to lower case (97 to 122), while leaving the lower case letters unchanged.

Using the ordinary keyboard to input phonetic symbols does have its limitations. It is fine for users who are already familiar with the QWERTY layout and with phonetic symbols. For the majority who are not, it proves rather cumbersome. An improvement which we hope to introduce shortly will involve using a CONCEPT keyboard.[3] On this keyboard the consonant symbols can be laid out on the conventional grid, and vowels on the conventional quadrilateral, and the user simply finds and presses the desired character.

Transcription systems

Since phoneticians use a rather peculiar set of symbols, it is only reasonable that they should have to create their own characters, and devise a method of printing them from a keyboard. A more serious problem for the beginner results from the lack of a standard set of symbols for transcribing British RP. Contrary to the widespread belief, there is no such thing as an 'IPA' transcription for RP. Scholars are free to choose their own symbols from the International Phonetic Alphabet: and different scholars make different choices. Problems arise when students mistakenly believe that they have learnt the 'IPA' transcription, and then come across different symbols in other textbooks, and on other courses.

Fortunately, although different sets of symbols are used, they actually label the same set of RP phonemes. This means that they are exactly equivalent. While it may be confusing for the human learner, it is possible for the computer to translate from one set of symbols to another.

The task is made easier by the fact that contemporary transcription systems derive from the kind of 'broad' transcriptions used at the turn of the century. Transcriptions in the computer use ASCII characters which are either acceptable as IPA characters, or else substitute for them. These correspond directly to the symbols of a 'broad' transcription. By recapitulating the development of transcription systems in the present century, we can convert a transcription from this 'ASCII' system into any of the more familiar ones.

At present five systems are catered for in programs in use at Lancaster:

1. the ASCII system for which ASCII characters are substituted as necessary for IPA characters;
2. Daniel Jones's 'broad' transcription, the first system given in *The Principles of the IPA*;[4]

3. the later 'EPD' transcription used by Daniel Jones in the *English Pronouncing Dictionary*;[5]
4. Gimson's system used in his *Introduction to the Pronunciation of English*;[6]
5. the system used by Wells and Colson in their *Practical Phonetics*.[7]

To illustrate the differences between these systems, here is a test sentence[8] transcribed in each. The sentence is:

> This good warm weather we're enjoying today is truly a pure pleasure but I daresay tomorrow could easily show something of just how far the British climate can turn treacherous.

1. /&is gud wo:m we&8 wi8r ind3oii9 t8dei iz tru:li 8 pju8 ple38 b8t
ai de8sei t8mor8u k8d i:zili $8u sʌm0i9 8v d3ʌst hau fa: &8
briti$ klaim8t kan t8:n tret$8r8s/

2. /ðis gud wo:m weðə wiər indʒoiiŋ tədei iz tru:li ə pjuə pleʒə bət
ai deəsei təmorəu kəd i:zili ʃəu sʌmθiŋ əv dʒʌst hau fa: ðə britiʃ
klaimət kan tɔ:n tretʃərəs/

3. /ðis gud wɔ:m weðə wiər indʒɔiiŋ tədei iz tru:li ə pjuə pleʒə bət
ai dɛəsei təmɔrəu kəd i:zili ʃəu sʌmθiŋ əv dʒʌst hau fɑ: ðə britiʃ
klaimət kæn tɔ:n tretʃərəs/

4. /ðɪs gʊd wɔ:m weðə wɪər ɪndʒɔɪŋ tədeɪ ɪz tru:lɪ ə pjʊə
pleʒə bət aɪ dɛəseɪ təmɔrəu kəd i:zɪlɪ ʃəu sʌmθɪŋ əv dʒʌst haʊ
fɑ: ðə britɪʃ klaɪmət kæn tɜ:n tretʃərəs/

5. ðɪs gʊd wɔm wɛðə wɪər ɪndʒɒɪŋ tədeɪ ɪz trulɪ ə pjʊə pleʒə bət
aɪ dɛəseɪ təmɒrəu kəd izɪlɪ ʃəu sʌmθɪŋ əv dʒʌst haʊ fɑ ðə brɪtɪʃ
klaɪmət kæn tɜn tretʃərəs/

The ASCII transcription uses ordinary Roman lower case letters, plus a few non-alphabetic characters for phonemes which have no single letter spelling, e.g. [$&90] for [ʃðŋθ]. To convert this into Jones's 'broad', it is necessary only to change the non-alphabetic substitutes into conventional IPA characters. The EPD transcription uses exotic symbols for some of the vowels, and these can be derived from Jones's 'broad' by context-sensitive rules, for example:

a remains   /a/   before i, u
   becomes   /ɑ/   before :
   becomes   /æ/   elsewhere

Gimson introduces more exotic vowel symbols, and these can be derived by additional rules. The last system is like Gimson's, but omits colons for long vowels. There are also minor differences, such as the use of Greek 'ɛ' instead of Roman 'e' for the vowel of *bed*: this too is handled by a context-sensitive rule.

This ability to switch from one transcription system to another gives considerable flexibility, and is a considerable advantage over conventional printed phonetic texts, for which one is forced to choose one system or another.

However, having obtained this flexibility, we must ask what it is for. Why on earth are phoneticians using so many systems in the first place? To defend the exotic symbols, appeal is made to alleged principles of transcription, and to the system of Cardinal Vowels. But these principles are notoriously contradictory, largely irrelevant, and inconsistently applied: there is no set of principles to defend (say) the use of the Cardinal 14 symbol /ʌ/ for the vowel of *cut* and the Anglo-Saxon letter 'æ' for the vowel of *cat*. A rather odd consequence of these 'principles' is that the letter 'o' is outlawed altogether: surely this cannot be taken seriously? Here the computer helps to separate out the real theoretical issues from matters of fashion and scholastic debate.

Parallel orthographic and phonetic texts

The computer is used in two different ways for transcription. In the one, an ordinary written text is input, and a program – or, more precisely, a suite of programs – produces a phonetic transcription automatically. In the other, texts are stored in parallel orthographic and transcribed versions, and the program produces the transcription simply by reading a stored transcribed version. Both approaches are under development at the University of Lancaster. The former is primarily a research project,[9] but it is already having an important effect on the way phonetics is taught. The latter is concerned purely with basic phonetics teaching, and I shall deal with this first.

The texts used are written in WORDWISE and read from a BASIC program. The only minor complication here is that in order to read a WORDWISE file, one has to load it one character at a time by BGETting the ASCII value of each character. Each text is divided into 'chunks' using '*' as the delimiter. Each chunk consists of a group of words of the right size for processing together. The reading procedure builds up BASIC strings character by character until '*' is read.

Types of text

The texts are of three kinds. The first is a beginners' word list. This contains a hundred English words which do not vary much from one variety of English to another. They range in difficulty from *cat* to *characteristic.* When this is selected, the whole text is read into an array, and items chosen by random number. The words are transcribed in their citation form, without considering the influence of context.

The second kind of text is a written original, ranging from an extract from a seed catalogue to St Luke's account of the Nativity. The transcription is predictive in nature, suggesting how the text would be spoken. (Ironically, the catalogue extract is the one most commonly chosen by students even though it is very unlikely to be read aloud in normal circumstances.)

Texts in the third group are spoken originals. This part of the program is not yet fully implemented, but is potentially the most interesting. As well as sending a written version phrase by phrase from the disc to the screen, the program also uses a Tandberg computer-controlled cassette recorder (TCCR).[10] which plays the original spoken phrase. This can be repeated as many times as required.

A feature of the TCCR is that it can find and start playing at any position on the cassette measured in minutes and seconds from the beginning. It was initially used for the beginners' word list. However, although the winding speed is extremely rapid, it still takes a little too long if the hundredth word is chosen and followed by the first word.

Choice of transcription system

The user selects the transcription system to be used. The computer then reads the transcription from the disc, and converts it into the chosen system.

Although beginners are expected to learn to transcribe texts, it is not easy to find samples of actual transcriptions for them to study. The kinds of example used by linguists and phoneticians tend to be very short, and designed to illustrate a particular point, and not to demonstrate how to transcribe. Texts for the beginner – such as Abercrombie's phonetic texts,[11] are only really suitable if they happen to be printed in the system wanted. This is a problem with which the computer can cope easily, by doing something which cannot really be done in any other way.

Choice of activity

Users can choose what they do with the chosen text in the chosen transcription system. The beginner who has never done phonetics before can see a fair copy of the text on the screen. For someone who has already learnt to use some other system, it is easy enough to display for comparison parallel transcriptions in two different systems. (The main effect of this is to show just how trivial the differences are.) Since Gimson's system is the most widely used for RP, that is the one recommended to most students. Nevertheless, in any year there are several students, particularly at the postgraduate level, who have already learnt one of the other systems, and there seems little point in forcing them to change. Here again the computer can instantaneously do something which could in theory be done with blackboard and chalk, but which would in practice take far too long.

The third option is for the user to do the transcription, which is displayed on the screen. When <RETURN> is pressed, a fair copy is displayed below the user's version. The user is left to compare the two versions.

Ideally, the program should evaluate the user's version. The simplest way to do this would be to GET the user's version character by character – instead of INPUTting it as a whole string – and reject any character which mismatched the stored version, perhaps sounding the bell as a warning. A more sophisticated procedure could identify errors arising from the confusion of different systems or of transcription with conventional orthography.

Although beginners certainly do make obvious errors, and lots of them, they also make intelligent 'errors'. Some of these are due to shortcomings in transcriptions systems, e.g. the use of the same symbol for the two vowels of *city* /sɪtɪ/. Nor is it obvious whether words ending *-ation* should be transcribed with shwa or not: both /eɪʃ ən/ and /eɪʃn/ would be acceptable. Some words, e.g. *February*, have several pronunciations, and students are often misled by differences between the RP described in the textbook and their own variety of English. The diagnosis of errors is not something to be handled by a simple mechanical procedure. To do it properly would require the program to be radically re-designed. To begin with, in order to handle errors caused by the user's variety of English, the stored phonetic text would have to be not in RP, but in an abstract pandialectal representation from which the RP version could be generated, along with non-RP versions. This is an area in which further work needs to be done.

Automatic transcription

A more challenging approach to phonetic transcription is to make the whole process automatic, getting the computer to imitate what a human phonetician does when making a transcription of a written text.

Superficially, phonetic transcription might seem to be an intellectually uninteresting, almost mindless activity, simply translating one sequence of symbols into another. Getting the computer to do it reveals just how much it really involves. An automatic program has to contain much of the content of an elementary phonetics course, including vowel and consonant theory, syllables, accent or 'stress', and the relationship between sounds and spellings.

A program of this kind is perhaps not as directly applicable to basic teaching as is transcription with parallel texts. However, by enforcing us to re-examine some basic assumptions, and the relationships among the parts of phonetic theory, it will lead to a more integrated and internally consistent description of English. Areas of English phonetics and phonology which are conventionally taught as matters of faith take on a greater degree of credibility when the ideas on which they are based can actually be shown to work. This is bound to have indirect but positive consequences for teaching.

Interpreting English spelling

To make an automatic transcription, we have to interpret English spelling conventions. There is a – rather superficial – school of thought according to which English spelling is so erratic, irregular and inconsistent that it cannot be said to have rules at all. (On this see the work of opponents to the 'phonics' approach to reading, e.g. Smith (1973).[12]) In fact there certainly are rules of spelling, and they are familiar to anybody who is literate in English. It is our knowledge of these rules that gives us a good idea how to pronounce words the first time we see them. For instance, you are unlikely to have heard the words *sesquipedalian* or *agathokakological* actually spoken, but having seen them in print, a native speaker of English will probably know how to pronounce them.

Although we are intuitively aware of the rules, it is far from easy to formulate them consciously and precisely in a computer program. If we try out tentative rules and find that they do not work, that does not mean the rules do not exist: it just means we have failed to formulate them properly.

In some cases it is easy enough to identify individual rules, but the difficulty is in showing how groups of rules work together. Take the case of these four rules:

1. the 'magic <e> rule' that <e> lengthens the preceding vowel but is itself silent;

2. the 'soft <c> rule' that <c> represents /s/ before <e, i, y> but /k/ elsewhere;
3. the rule whereby <s> is sometimes voiced to /z/;
4. the rule that <ph> represents /f/.

How do these rules cooperate in words like *fake, face, phase?* Let us assume that they apply in the order given above:

	fake	*face*	*phase*
1. magic <e>	/feɪk/	feɪc	pheɪs
2. soft <c>		/feɪk/	
3. <s> = /z/			pheɪz
4. <ph> = /f/			/feɪz/

This is clearly wrong, as *face* comes out identical in pronunciation to *fake*. The optimal order is in fact the reverse order:

	fake	*face*	*phase*
1. <ph> = /f/			fase
2. <s> = /z/			faze
3. soft <c>		fase	
4. magic <e>	/feɪk/	/feɪs/	/feɪz/

If we formulate the rules correctly, and get them in the right order, the number of irregular spellings in English reduces dramatically. There remains a hard rump of genuine irregularities which simply have to be listed. No spelling rules, for instance, can predict that *Cholmondeley* is pronounced /tʃʊmlɪ/ or /tʃʌmlɪ/!

Structure of the program

The spelling rules group naturally into blocks, and as a result there are four (unequal) stages in the transcription of words:
1. morphological analysis;
2. graphemic analysis;
3. syllable division;
4. accentuation.

Morphological analysis
In the first, morphological stage, we have to identify suffixes. In some cases this is because suffixes have special rules governing their pronunciation, e.g. the suffix *-s* of *was* or *goes* is pronounced differently than the final *-s* of *gas* or *Lewes*. Secondly, some suffixes can affect the accentuation of the word, and consequently the nature of vowels in the word.

Morphological analysis is part of a more general grammatical analysis. In some cases, it is necessary to identify the word's part of speech, e.g. *that* is pronounced /ðæt/ as a demonstrative, but usually /ðət/ as a conjunction. Grammatical analysis is unfortunately beyond the scope of a program that will fit into the 32K of a BBC micro. Texts have to be pre-edited manually to mark the part of speech where necessary, or the job could be done on the mainframe,[13] and the edited text transferred to the micro.

Graphemic analysis
In the second stage, some graphemes can be interpreted directly as phonemes or phoneme sequences. For instance the combination <sh> can be re-written /ʃ/ as in *fish* or *ship*, and <ch> usually as /tʃ/, e.g. *chip*, except before /r, l/ where it is /k/, e.g. *chrome, chlorine*.

Syllable division
The main idea behind the concept of the syllable was explained long ago by de Saussure,[14] and is concerned with the opening and closing of the vocal tract in producing sequences of sounds. Briefly, the syllabic (normally a vowel) is the most open sound, and the segment at the boundary between two syllables (normally a consonant) is the closest segment. This idea is implemented in the program.

Accentuation
A theory of accent has to account not only for the position of accents in a word, but also for consequent vowel lengthening and reduction. In the program, changes in vowel quality are handled by procedures which are called from within the accentuation procedure.

Spellings and the development of pronunciation

If we consider English spelling in its historical context, it is found to represent not modern pronunciation, but that of the late Middle Ages, of the time when our spelling conventions were established. In a commercial text-to-speech system, this historical dimension might be regarded as irrelevant, and a purely synchronic approach might be thought more appropriate. Indeed, most accounts of English spelling are strictly synchronic.[15] But if our program is to be linguistically realistic, history must be taken into account. Since the English spelling system has developed over several centuries, it would make sense to recapitulate the development of pronunciation in the program.

In practice a knowledge of history is directly beneficial in formulating rules. In a purely synchronic account, some rules are entirely arbitrary, e.g. that <oa> represents /əʊ/ in *boat* /bəʊt/, but /ɔː/ in *boar* /bɔː/. Historically, long vowels have developed differently before /r/ than elsewhere, and the easiest way to deal with this is for vowels before /r/ to branch off the main set of vowel rules.

Since it is a matter of historical fact that spelling represents medieval pronunciation, there is no way we can actually avoid history anyway. To explain why the letter <i> of *five* is pronounced /aɪ/, we can either talk about the magic <e> in the primary school manner, or about apocope and the Great Vowel Shift in a historically explicit manner. We have to account for the history of the system in one way or another.

Spelling and varieties of English

Since the same spellings are used for all varieties of English, and are not exclusive to RP, words are represented in certain stages of the program in just the kind of pan-dialectal manner referred to on page 140 above. An intriguing consequence is that if a program can be written for RP, it can equally well be written for other varieties of English: a well-designed program could output a choice of varieties of English.

Most of the variables in modern English pronunciation have developed over the last 500 years or so. (I am referring here to the kind of urban English spoken by the mass of the population in Great Britain, the USA and Australia, and not to the traditional rural dialects spoken by retired farmhands in isolated hamlets in Northern England or Southern Scotland.) By an accident of history, our spelling conventions conveniently pre-date variations in pronunciation, e.g. *card, for, year* are spelt with an <r> which has long since disappeared in speech in most parts of England, but which survives in Scotland, Ireland and the USA. This means that if we adopt the historical approach to the interpretation of spelling, we can generate different varieties of English as a by-product.

Automatic transcription and phonological theory

In the long term, the computer will contribute not only by the interesting things individual programs do, but by its effect on the way we approach linguistic problems. A computer program of the kind sketched above can contribute by improving procedures for testing individual hypotheses, and also the compatibility of different parts of the overall phonological theory.

In the conventional approach, the phonologist selects a certain amount and kind of data, and sets up a hypothesis to account for it. For instance, one might choose the list of words *convict, transport, indent, produce*, and set up the hypothesis that in this type of word, nouns are stressed on the prefix and the corresponding verbs on the root. Of course, the data is handpicked and so does not really test the hypothesis, but merely flatters it. What about *detail, debate, research, comment*, etc., in British and American English? With the computer, it is possible to establish a corpus of texts which can be used to test theoretical ideas. Since there is no guarantee that only desirable data will be used – indeed real texts can almost be guaranteed to contain awkward data – inadequate hypotheses are very quickly disposed of.

Secondly, the program sketched above necessarily incorporates a phonological theory which has to be internally consistent. For instance, if one part of the program assigns 'word stress' and another 'sentence stress', it is essential that these two kinds of 'stress' are compatible. There is a notorious credibility gap in this area in traditional accounts of 'stress'. Human beings may be content to deal with one aspect of a complex problem at a time, and to make intuitive leaps of faith over the gaps. But before writing a computer program, one has to make all the logical connections explicit.

Future developments: speech synthesis in phonetics teaching

A phonetic transcription is a kind of code in which the symbols represent speech sounds. To end a program with a transcription is to give up in the middle of the job: the logical next step is to speak the transcription aloud. For the student, this provides the point of the whole exercise, and explains why anybody would want to transcribe phonetically in the first place.

Some cheap synthesizers costing just a few pounds contain a small set of speech-like sounds – erroneously called 'allophones' – and words are synthesized by stringing appropriate sounds together. A simple procedure identifies the sounds corresponding to the symbols of a phonemic transcription, and with sufficient faith and imagination it may be possible to recognize the spoken output. Some of these synthesizers are claimed to speak any language you like: perhaps one should add '. . . as long as it sounds like American English'. They are good value at the price, and fun to play with, but not suitable for serious work in phonetics.

Using a more versatile synthesizer, such as the LSI formant synthesizer,[16] we first have to get from the phonemic level to a more detailed phonetic level. By applying distribution rules for allophones, and making arbitrary choices for the occurrence of free variants, we can predict a detailed phonetic specification from a string of phonemes. At this point the job of programming is handed over to the electronics engineer to convert symbols into sounds.

An expected spin-off is that this program will demonstrate the distinction between 'phonemic' transcription and true 'phonetic' transcription. By conventional methods, it is difficult to give more than a few cursory examples of this, e.g. the distribution of 'clear' and 'dark' /l/, or the aspiration of /p,t,k/, and the point of making the distinction probably eludes most beginners. As part of a speech synthesis program, beginners can see as many examples as they want. The reality of the distinction should quickly become clear: a word synthesized with the wrong allophone is likely to sound odd or unintelligible.

Conclusion

In this paper I have discussed the role of the computer in the specific area of phonetics teaching. Some general points could probably be made equally well for other areas of language teaching, and indeed for other subjects.

Before using the computer as a tool, one has to think out exactly what one is trying to do, and how the job can be done. Instead of solving problems by an intuitive leap of intelligence, we have to break problems down into their components, and tackle them step by step. The immediate result of this is that the computer can take over highly predictable tasks, including some that might not previously have been thought predictable. This allows teaching time to be spent more profitably: instead of spending time on phonetic transcription, for example, one can describe the patterns of the spoken language which phonetic transcription represents.

In the longer term, the computer is likely to change the nature of the subject itself. The discipline of writing a program brings with it new insights and understanding: English spelling, for instance, works in mysterious ways, but it is useful to know for certain that at least there are rules to be discovered. The procedure for converting from one transcription system to another indicates quite clearly that the changes are matters of fashion – or at best of packaging – and do not represent any serious theoretical development. Weaknesses in the subject are revealed as vague metaphors and woolly thinking, since they prove impossible to program, and have to be replaced by precise algorithms. In short, the computer will enable us to build up a coherent and integrated body of knowledge which is demonstrably correct, and immune to the vicissitudes of fashion and personal taste, or to the rise and fall of schools of linguistics.

Notes

1. The computer used is a BBC model B with a disc drive and a WORDWISE word-processor. Texts are prepared on the word-processor, and read and processed from BASIC programs.
2. Details of how to create non-standard characters are given in the BBC *User Guide*. A clear and detailed account – intended for children, but equally useful for adults – is given in J Smith (1984) *Micro Knowledge* (Ladybird). Other micros use different methods.
3. The CONCEPT keyboard is available from Star Microterminals, 22 Hyde Street, Winchester SO23 7DR.
4. *The Principles of the IPA*, obtainable from the secretary of the IPA, Department of Linguistics and Phonetics, University College, London.
5. This was used by D Jones (1918) *An Outline of English Phonetics*. Heffer, Cambridge. It is better known for its use in Jones's *Everyman's English Pronouncing Dictionary*. Dent (13th edition 1967, revised by A C Gimson). Note that for the vowel of *go* Jones used the symbol /ou/, and that this was changed to /əu/ in the later editions of the EPD to reflect a change in pronunciation. I have used the latter symbol.
6. Gimson, A C (1962, 3rd edition 1980) *An Introduction to the Pronunciation of English*. Edward Arnold.
7. Wells, J C and Colson, G (1974) *Practical Phonetics*. Pitman, London.
8. This sentence contains all 44 RP phonemes, and was contributed by J Windsor Lewis (1979) 'British English in strict IPA transcription', *Journal of the IPA* 9(2): 72–3.
9. This work is supported in part by IBM (UK) Ltd.
10. The TCCR530 is available from Tandberg Ltd., Revie Road, Elland Road, Leeds LS11 8JG.
11. Abercrombie, D (1964) *English Phonetic Texts*. Faber, London.
12. Smith, F 'The efficiency of phonics' in Smith, F (ed.) (1973) *Psycholinguistics and Reading*, Holt, Rinehart and Winston, New

York. (I am not defending phonics here, I am merely attacking superficial and ill-informed criticism.)

13. Grammatical tagging programs have been developed on the mainframe at the University of Lancaster by the Unit for Computer Research on the English Language.

14. de Saussure, F (1918) *Cours de linguistique générale.*

15. For example Venezky, R L (1970) *The Structure of English Orthography* Mouton, The Hague, or Albrow, K H (1972) *The English Writing System: notes towards a description* (Schools Council Programme in Linguistics and English Teaching. Papers, series 2, vol 2) Longman.

16. Made by Loughborough Sound Images Ltd., The Technology Centre, Epinal Way, Loughborough LE11 0QE, and obtainable from Millgrant Wells Ltd., P.O. Box 3, 7 Stanley Road, Rugby CV21 3UF.

Introduction to Chapter 11

Critics of the use of microcomputers in education frequently identify as a drawback the narrow limitations which small machines and restricted programming languages impose on machine capacity. As Thomas discusses in this volume, this has the effect of constraining the range of user input, and, correspondingly, the range of machine response. Of course, as Geoffrey Sampson points out, the mechanistic nature of the computer precludes open-ended choice, but in his imaginative use of augmented transition networks (ATNs) he drives the typical micro to its limit in offering a responsive and active partnership with the learner. His proposals, fully exemplified in the paper, greatly increase the speed of machine response to learner input. They do so, essentially, by means of recognizing the potential of the input before that has been completely keyed in. Analysis thus takes place during the keying-in process, much as a human being analyses a text in the process of reading. One useful by-product, as Sampson points out, for the second language learner or immature writer, is the capacity of ATNs to tolerate imperfect input while nonetheless keeping an account of the errors in question for later remediation, and for immediately signalling to the user that errors exist.

11 Transition networks for computer-assisted language learning

Geoffrey Sampson

Introduction

My article concerns a programming technique which, I believe, has a great deal to offer to people producing CAL software in the area of language skills. The concept of 'transition networks', and specifically the concept of 'augmented transition networks' (or 'ATNs' as they are usually known), have up to now been current only within the rarefied domains of artificial intelligence and cognitive psychology. But the concepts are inherently simple; and they can be used to solve very practical problems that face someone such as a teacher with a hobby-type interest in writing educational software.

One of the offputting things about the computer as a potential partner in the teaching process is that by its nature it tends to force the learner into a passive role. The most obvious way to use computers in teaching anything is almost always to set up a program in which the computer provides information or response-eliciting stimuli that may be complex, subtle, perhaps even beautiful or fascinating, but in which the range of acceptable responses from the learner is miserably restricted. A screen of material is presented by the machine, followed by a direct question: 'Answer y or n'. Or a multiple choice of answers is proffered, and the learner presses A, B, or C. The objections to this state of affairs need little emphasis.

Not every use of the computer as a teaching tool falls foul of this problem. Readers of Seymour Papert's marvellous book *Mindstorms* (1980) will appreciate that the point of the Logo language which Papert invented is precisely to get away from this situation, and to hand over the initiative to children in their interactions with computers. A child using a computer running Logo is learning by playing with the machine; sometimes the machine does things which surprise the user, but it does nothing except in response to the user's initiatives and the user acts creatively in deciding what to make the computer do.

Logo is excellent at encouraging intellectual creativity and experiment, and I have little doubt that it succeeds very well in leading children to learn the sorts of knowledge it teaches. Having said that, one must go on to say that the virtues of Logo do not appear to be capable of generalization to other areas of knowledge. Logo teaches concepts of number and geometry, and it teaches them in a marvellous way that could not be matched, I believe, by non-computer teaching techniques. There is no obvious way, though, that language teaching (or the teaching of many other non-mathematical subjects) could use Papert's approach. Fundamental mathematical knowledge lends itself to Papert's technique partly because it is almost purely conceptual – grasping the ideas is what matters. With language learning, on the other hand, there is a great deal of non-conceptual, factual material to be mastered. You really do have to learn what the past participle of *savoir* is, or the order in which to place perfective and progressive auxiliaries in an English clause containing both. So, here, the idea of CAL techniques in which the learner has *all* the initiative does not arise. If the computer can help the language teacher at all, it will be as a device that helps inculcate fairly concrete pieces of knowledge and skills in the learner. The trouble is, even the teaching of concrete facts and skills can be done in ways which involve active participation by the learner or in ways that leave him passive, and introducing the computer as teacher seems to imply a new and heavy pressure towards the passive-learning end of the spectrum.

Let me say immediately that I see no complete solution to this problem, and certainly ATNs do not amount to one. The problem is real, and I sympathize with sceptics who doubt the usefulness of computers as teaching tools other than in a few very special situations. As someone who has been interested in and involved with computers since the mid-1960s, I have been baffled by the way in which, for almost all of that twenty years, the general educated public has been content to remain entirely ignorant of these fascinating machines, while during the last two or three years they have abruptly come to be perceived as holding the answers to all life's problems. In the introduction to their survey of the CALL field, *Computers, Language, and Language Learning* (1982), Graham Davies and John Higgins begin by condemning as a 'myth' the belief by many language teachers that computers are tools for scientists and businessmen rather than for themselves; yet at the same time they concede that 'high quality courseware ... especially the sort the language teacher might wish to use' is 'hard to find'. For Davies and Higgins this very lack makes it 'vital that language teachers overcome their natural scepticism' in order to demand better CALL programs, but I feel dubious; why should one take it for granted that computers are the coming thing in the language class, if their current contribution is admittedly quite poor? The steam engine in its day was an excellent invention that made great contributions in a number of domains, but did people in the early nineteenth century see it as manifestly destined to replace paper and pens as a writing technology?

Nevertheless, I certainly agree with Davies and Higgins that if we are going to use the computer in language teaching at all we should use it as well as it can be used, rather than tolerating indefinitely the unimaginative, mechanical language-drill software which is the easiest kind to write. Transition networks are attractive because they offer the possibility of language-learning software that can cope with a much wider range of linguistic inputs by the user than the kind of program which asks for a response and checks it simply as matching or failing to match a target. Transition networks open up the possibility of linguistic interaction with the computer that is less totally mechanistic and rigid than more obvious techniques allow. But let me stress that this is only a matter of degree. ATNs, at least of the limited complexity that can be produced by semi-amateurs and held in the memory of a micro, are far from offering the possibility of open-ended conversation with the machine.

The problem of response speed

Before explaining what ATNs are, let me discuss a specific problem to which I applied them. I helped to produce a suite of Basic programs, *Telling the Time*, intended to help children learn to read clocks. The package involved a progression of tasks of different degrees of complexity: the child saw a clockface drawn on the screen, and could use the keyboard to manipulate the hands so as to set the clock to given hours, later to half-hours, quarter-hours, and so on, and he would be shown clockfaces with hands set in different orientations and invited to input the corresponding time at the keyboard. At most stages of the progression, times were written in numeral form; but I wanted to include a final stage at which the user named the time in words. (There is room for argument about what age it is appropriate to teach children the skill of spelling out time-names, and whether this task ought to be linked to the much simpler task of learning to read a clock; but for present purposes I shall bypass this issue, since it is not relevant here.)

The difficulty in writing a program to accept and recognize time-names written out in words is that there are many alternatives. My program dealt only with times that were multiples of five minutes, so that on a twelve-hour clock there were just 144 namable times; but each of these can be named in more than one way. For instance, the time which is written numerically as '8.35' can be called *eight thirty-five* (with or without a hyphen or a space between *thirty* and *five*), or it can be called *twenty-five to nine*, or *twenty-five minutes to nine*, or (as I normally call it) *five-and-twenty to nine*. '12.00' can be *twelve*, or *twelve o'clock*, or *noon*, or *midday* – or *midnight*. And so on. The total range of possibilities is not open-ended, but it is quite large.

In the first version of my program (before I thought of using a transition network), the user was asked to spell out the time, and his attempt was accepted as a string via an INPUT statement. The program then simply worked out which English time-name (if any) the string represented, by applying what I might call brute-force analytic techniques. For instance, the string was searched for an occurrence of the substrings *past* or *to*; if one of these occurs, the string must be an example of the 'traditional' rather than 'modern' style of time-name (e.g. *quarter past three* rather than *three fifteen*), and the program went on to look for a number representing hours in the following rather than in the preceding substring.

Since there is only a closed class of valid time-names, this brute-force approach does ultimately yield the correct analysis. One problem, though, is that it takes a very long time to do it. A child would get interested in the task, type in his attempt to name the time he was reading on the clock, press the RETURN key, and then he would have to sit twiddling his fingers for quite an appreciable period while the program wrestled with the analysis of what he had written. Pedagogically this was disastrous. If the child's input had been mistaken, by the time the machine noticed what was wrong and responded, e.g. with 'look at the big hand again' the child might have forgotten what he had written and would need to re-read it off the screen to make sense of the machine's comment. If the child was correct, the congratulatory message came after the psychological moment had passed.

There are various ways one might think of dealing with this difficulty. If I were able to program in machine-code, the same algorithm would execute so much faster that the delay might cease to be noticeable. But there is little possibility that creators of educational software in general can become machine-code programmers. Writing machine-code programs is a highly demanding, expensive skill which is worth investing only in lucrative commercial software, particularly software that can be left unchanged once perfected because it fulfils an unchanging need (e.g. word-processing, spreadsheets). The field of educational software is not like this. Financial returns will presumably always be modest; producing the material will resemble textbook-writing in being a sideline rather than a full-time career for almost everyone involved; and it is highly desirable for software to be flexible, easily added to or adapted by different teachers rather than rigidly fixed. All these factors imply that educational software must be written in high-level languages (and, while manufacturers persist in installing BASIC as the standard resident language on their machines, most of it must inevitably be written in BASIC); which means that it will run relatively slowly.

In the case of my problem about time-names, the ATN proved to offer a complete solution to the difficulty about response speed (as well as yielding other advantages which I shall discuss later). After I hit on the idea of using an ATN, I was able to re-program my time-telling package so that the machine's response is effectively instantaneous. My program is written wholly in BBC BASIC; a touch-typist can key in a complex time-name at full speed, pressing RETURN immediately the name is finished, and only occasionally will he or she be able to perceive a split-second hesitation by the machine. For a learner, whose inputs are naturally slower, response time is much faster than needed – it could even be desirable to slow it artificially.

How ATNs work

Speed is not the only or even a particularly crucial virtue of ATNs. But, before going on to discuss their other virtues, let me now explain what they are.

I will begin with an extremely simple artificial example. Suppose we are interested in sentences like 'I know, you know, he knows, I know that you know, he knows that I know that you know that he knows, you know that I know that I know that he knows that you know', and so on (letting the sentences get as long as you like). This range of sentences can be represented by the network in Figure 1 opposite.

In this diagram, the circles are 'states' of the network; arrows linking states are 'transitions'. There is a single entry point to the network, represented by the arrow arriving from the left. After this arrow is taken, any particular sentence in the class of sentences we are inter-

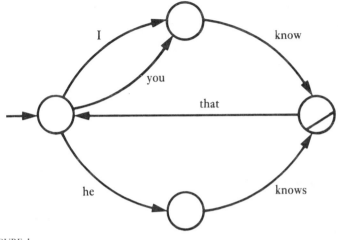

FIGURE 1

ested in corresponds to some path following the transitions through
the network and finishing at a 'terminal state': in this network there
is just one terminal state, indicated by the diagonal line across the
circle. (A terminal state is a state where one *may* stop; it is not a state
in which one *must* stop, and in our simple example all the sentences
except the shortest involve passing through the terminal state
repeatedly.)

One way of thinking of the network is as a representation of a
speaker, with the labels for each transition representing words the
system utters. For present purposes, though, it is more relevant to
think of it as representing a hearer who checks whether what he is
hearing is English or not: in this case, the labels are inputs to the
system which drive it from one state to another. Any sentence in the
class under discussion will succeed in driving the system through its
states until the last word leaves it in the terminal state. For any other
input, either a point will come when the system cannot proceed
(because the next word does not occur as a label on any of the transitions leaving the current state), or else the system will be in a non-
terminal state when it runs out of input.

In a very simple network like this one, the only condition that has
to be met in order to take a particular transition is occurrence in the
input of the word labelling the transition; and the only action taken
if that condition is fulfilled is to move to the next state. If all the transitions are as simple as that, there are severe limits on what kind of

grammatical structures the network can cope with, and in fact the system would be little use in practice. But, in an ATN, many transitions have extra complications associated with them. Alongside the network itself, we can imagine there being a number of registers capable of storing different values: some registers may take simple yes or no values, others may have a greater range of possible contents. Then, in the network, certain transitions will be labelled with actions to be performed on the registers: 'If you take this transition, set the Gender register to the value Feminine', for instance; and certain transitions will be labelled with conditions (in addition to occurrence of the appropriate item in the input) that have to be fulfilled before they can be taken: for example, 'Don't take this transition unless the Tense register is set to the value Past'. These extra labels on transitions are the 'augmentations' in an Augmented Transition Network. Returning to our artificial example, suppose that, apart from *you* and *I*, the third person involved in the class of sentences we have been discussing is called *Mick*. Then we might want to allow for sentences like 'You know that Mick knows that I know that he knows'. We can refer to Mick as *he*, but only after we have already mentioned his name; we don't want to allow sentences like 'He knows that I know that Mick knows'. The easy way to set this up is to add a Pronoun register to the network, which will begin with the value 'negative' but change to 'positive' once Mick is mentioned. Then we can define the sentences we are interested in by the following network:

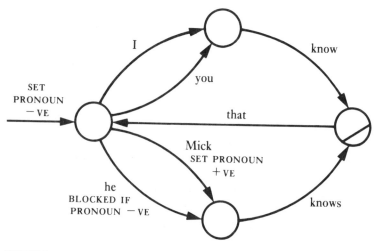

FIGURE 2

Taking the *Mick* transition sets the Pronoun register to positive, and the *he* transition can be taken only after that has happened.

For completeness I should mention one further subtlety of the ATN concept, namely 'recursion' (though as it happens my time-telling ATN did not need it). So far we have been assuming that all aspects of the bit of language we are interested in are represented in a single network, within which each transition corresponds to the occurrence of a single linguistic element. But frequently it is convenient (or even unavoidable) to use a *set* of networks. One of them is the 'master' network; within the master network, some of the transitions will correspond not to the occurrence of individual linguistic items but to traversals of other networks. Again the idea can be illustrated by extending our trivial example. The verbs in our sentences need not always be *know*; we might want to allow for sentences like 'I believe that Mick hopes that you believe that he knows'. Provided we are prepared to treat a word like *knows* as a sequence of a root followed by an ending -*s*, then the most economical way in network terms to handle this extension to the language is as shown in Figure 3:

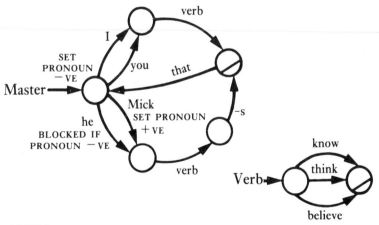

FIGURE 3

Whether after a third-person or a first- or second-person subject, the next transition in the master network requires a traversal of the subsidiary 'Verb' network. In more realistic and interesting cases, there may be many subsidiary networks, which may themselves be highly complex and which furthermore may in turn contain transitions requiring traversals of one another *or of the master network* (hence the term 'recursive').

To theoretical linguists, the ATN is a device of great significance. It is mathematically demonstrable that any grammatical phenomena which are clearcut enough to be defined in any format whatsoever are capable of being stated in terms of ATNs. The fact that transitions can be associated with output actions as well as with input conditions means that an ATN can be organized so as to accept sentences in their surface form and build up a representation of their underlying logic; ATNs can be seen as achieving the same theoretical goals as Noam Chomsky's 'transformational grammar', but in a more efficient and perspicacious fashion. Some cognitive psychologists go further and argue that ATNs offer a plausible model of language-processing mechanisms in the human mind (something that Chomsky expressly avoided claiming for his transformational theory), though others disagree. More practically, ATNs have been outstandingly successful in automatic systems for processing natural-language text.

The classic example is the LUNAR project of W. A. Woods, who invented the ATN concept in the late 1960s. After the first American expeditions to the Moon brought back samples of lunar soil and rock, a computerized database was established containing many scientifically-interesting measurements of these samples. At a geological congress in 1971 Woods set up an automatic question-answering system to which the scientists present were invited to pose whatever enquiries occurred to them concerning the lunar material. A large ATN system was used to extract the logical structure of the users' requests, in order to calculate the appropriate answer from the contents of the database. The users were given no special instructions about how to phrase their requests – they simply used whatever English turns of phrase they found natural; nevertheless, most of their queries were understood and correctly answered.

I do not suggest that systems as ambitious as this are practical possibilities in the CALL context. Woods's ATN system was too large, I think, to be accommodated in the memory of currect micros (it had a vocabulary of several thousand words), and the quantity of human research effort that went into designing the networks was far in excess of what seems feasible in the CALL domain. But this glance at what ATNs can in principle do may serve to whet the appetite to see how much mileage can be got out of transition networks at a more modest level. My time-telling network took, as far as I recall, no more than a couple of man-days to design, yet in its limited domain it is rather successful.

There are two important differences of kind, apart from sheer size and complexity, between my time-telling ATN and the sort of large-scale ATN involved in a project such as LUNAR.

One is that my ATN accepts input letter by letter rather than word by word. The networks illustrated above have transitions labelled with whole words; in my ATN, each individual transition is labelled with just a single character, and acceptance of a word involves moving through several states. Since input to the micro consists of key-presses representing individual characters, programming is rather simpler if this decision is made. However, provided one could rely on users including spaces to delimit words, it would not be difficult to implement a network which treated words as units; and designing the *network* (as opposed to designing the program which operates the network) would be very much easier if transitions were associated with whole words rather than individual characters. The reason I adopted the approach I did was that young children at the stage of learning to spell time-names cannot reasonably be expected to use the space-bar consistently to mark divisions between words, and there is no way that a network can be based on word units if words are not demarcated in the input. With software for older language learners this particular problem presumably would not arise.

The other major difference, which has nothing to do with users' maturity, is that I required my network to be 'deterministic'. That is, there are never alternative transitions with identical labels leaving the same state; in running through the network under the control of a given input there is always at most one possible next move. Often, allowing indeterminism simplifies the work of designing an ATN. Suppose, for instance, that we wished to expand the network of Figure 1 in order to allow sentences using *that* as a demonstrative, such as 'I know that old man, you know that boy': a straightforward way to do this would be to add states and transitions as in Figure 4:

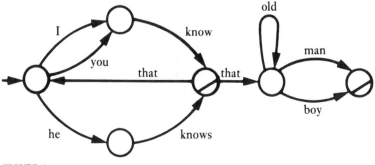

FIGURE 4

The network of Figure 4 is non-deterministic: alternative paths are available when *that* is input, and only after proceeding further through the input does it emerge which path was the right one to take. Woods's ATN-system has a great deal of this indeterminism. However, the extra programming complexity and memory required to implement a non-deterministic ATN is considerable, and I suspect that it would be impractical to use non-deterministic ATNs in a CALL context. Unfortunately, the price of the programming and memory saved by opting for determinism is that the network for any given area of language becomes more difficult to design.

Despite these problems, my eventual ATN is of quite manageable size: it has 113 states and 150 transitions. With these it is capable of recognizing correctly virtually every accepted way of naming a time in English (provided the time is a multiple of five minutes). Adult users have found it quite difficult to catch the system out, and although one or two out-of-the-way usages have cropped up which the system cannot handle as it stands (e.g. the American variant *quarter of* for *quarter to*) there would be little difficulty in modifying the network to incorporate them. A word-based ATN would need only a fraction as many states and transitions to achieve the same results.

Of the 150 transitions in the network, forty-odd include augmentations. A few of these relate to conditions on the availability of a transition (for instance, acceptance of the word *half* sets a register blocking the transition labelled *to*, since although we say, e.g. *quarter to four* and *twenty to four* we do not say *half to four*). Most of the work done by the augmentations, however, involves deriving a time-representation in a numerical form which the computer can understand, from the English expression keyed in by the user. The educational purpose of the system, after all, is not to check whether the user succeeds in keying in *some* time-name, but to compare the time-name keyed in with the time as displayed graphically on the clockface, noting what kind of errors the user is making (if any) and offering guidance to help improve performance. Thus, if the first characters in a time-name are *f-i-v-e* or *t-e-n*, an augmentation will cause the number 5 or 10 respectively to be stored in a temporary holding register. If, subsequently, the word *past* is encountered, another augmentation will shift the contents of the holding register to a register named 'Minutes' (while, if *to* is accepted, the difference between the holding-register contents and 60 will be placed in Minutes). If, on the other hand, another number-word such as *forty* follows, then the contents of the holding register are transferred to an 'Hours' register and 'Minutes' acquires the numerical value corresponding to the new word.

The network is held in the machine as two arrays. Each state and each transition is numbered, and the various transitions leaving any one state are always assigned a continuous sequence of numbers (e.g. the transitions from state 35 might be numbered 94, 95, 96, 97). The array 'states' has a row for each state and two columns, containing the number of the first and last transitions from the corresponding states: thus, in row 35 of 'states', column 0 would contain 94 and column 1 would contain 97. (If a state has no exits, i.e. it is compulsorily terminal, both columns in its row are assigned the value 0.) The array 'transitions' has a row for each transition and two columns, one for the character associated with the transition and the other for the state to which the transition leads; thus, if transition 94 runs from state 35 to state 102 and is labelled 'u', then transitions (94,0) would contain the code for 'u' and transitions (94,1) would contain 102.

The heart of the program is a procedure PROCtraversenetwork, defined as follows. At certain points where it would be irrelevant or confusing to quote detailed coding, I write ordinary English within square brackets; the rest is BBC BASIC. (Efficiency could be improved, e.g. by using resident integer rather than real variables, but this would have made the coding harder to follow.)

```
500 DEF PROCtraversenetwork
510    here=1: matched=TRUE
520    REPEAT
530       there=here
540       IF matched THEN [get a character from the
user and call it u$]: matched=FALSE
550       thisbranch=states(here,0):
lastbranch=states(here,1)
560       REPEAT
570          label=transitions(thisbranch,0)
580          IF thisbranch<>0 AND NOT
FNblock (thisbranch) AND (label=ASC u$ OR label=0) THEN LET
here=transitions(thisbranch,1): PROCdoaugment(thisbranch):
IF label=u$ THEN LET matched=TRUE
590          thisbranch=thisbranch+1
600       UNTIL matched OR thisbranch>lastbranch
610       IF matched THEN PRINT u$;
620    UNTIL NOT matched AND here=there
630    IF u$<>[the RETURN key] THEN PROCfai-
          lure:
ENDPROC
```

```
      640      IF FNterminal (here) THEN PROCsuccess
ELSE PROCincomplete
      650      ENDPROC
```

Each pass through the 520–620 loop represents a move from a state to an adjacent state. The state reached at any time is called 'here', and the previous state is called 'there'; line 510 initializes 'here' to 1, the number of the initial state. The variable 'matched' is false whenever a character input by the user is waiting to drive the system across a suitable transition, and it is true whenever the system is waiting for a new character to be keyed in by the user.

The inner loop between 560 and 600 checks each transition leaving 'here' in turn, seeking a transition labelled with the current unmatched character. If an appropriate transition is found, line 580 changes the value of 'here' to correspond to the state at the end of the transition and sets 'matched' to true, ready for the outer loop to be repeated for a new input character. This cycle continues until a character is input for which no corresponding transition is available. (If the input is in fact correct, the unmatched character will be the code representing the RETURN key.)

The function FNblock and the procedure PROCdoaugment between them handle the augmentations: FNblock checks whether a transition is conditional on the contents of one or more registers, and, if so, whether the registers do currently allow the transition to be taken, while PROCdoaugment carries out any operations on the registers required by the transition. (For most of the transitions, which lack augmentations, FNblock will return 'false' independently of the contents of any registers and PROCdoaugment will execute no action.)

The OR clause in line 580 is included to cope with the fact that, in designing an ATN, it is often convenient to include a transition labelled with no character at all, allowing movement from state to state in the network without moving further through the input string. For instance, in *Telling the Time*, the initial state 1 has transitions labelled 'h', 'q' in order to handle the possibility that the time expression may begin with the word *half* or *quarter*. If these and some other possibilities do not occur, the system jumps to state 50, which has transitions labelled with letters such as 'o' for *one*, 'e' for *eight* or *eleven* – words which may begin a time-expression as hour-names. It is necessary for state 50 to be separate from state 1, since hour-names can occur following, e.g. *past*, and we do not want to allow *quarter* or *half* to follow *past*; yet the transition from state 1 to state 50 requires no input from the user: state 50 simply allows some further possible initial characters, apart from those allowed directly by the initial state 1 (see Figure 5).

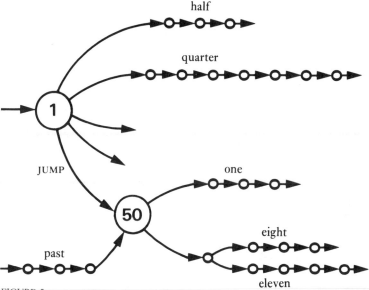

FIGURE 5

'Jumps' can easily be handled, provided a jump is always the highest-numbered transition from its source state and thus the last transition to be tested (otherwise a jump might wrongly be taken when in fact the current input character occurs as label on an alternative transition). Jump transitions are labelled with an arbitrarily-chosen code 0 (which does not correspond to any character), and line 580 allows a transition labelled in this way to be taken irrespective of the current unmatched character; the last IF clause in this line ensures that when a jump is taken the next cycle continues trying to match the same current character.

PROCsuccess, PROCfailure, and PROCincomplete provide the user with various responses to his input, and these can consist of whatever a teacher thinks most pedagogically appropriate. PROCsuccess is executed when the user has succeeded in producing a linguistically well-formed input. In *Telling the Time* PROCsuccess compares the final contents of the 'Hours' and 'Minutes' registers with the time as shown on the clock displayed, and reacts accordingly (if the time is not fully accurate it looks for a partial match, in order hint to the user what needs correcting). There is no need for the meaning-representation extracted from the user's sentence to be in numerical terms, as it is in *Telling the Time*; one could envisage another ATN-based CALL package inviting the user to construct statements about the events in a simple story, in which case PROC-success might produce comments on the truth or plausibility of the user's assertions. PROCfailure is executed when the user has input a sequence of characters which cannot possibly be completed to form any well-formed input; but it is not necessary to interrupt the user abruptly the moment he types his first incorrect character: one might prefer the system to go on accepting input up to the end of a word or until the user finally presses RETURN before commenting on the error, and either of these can easily be arranged by suitable coding within PROCfailure. These components are essentially independent of the network mechanism, so I shall not discuss them further here.

Advantages of ATNs

The ATN has several virtues as a component of an interactive educational software package. I have already drawn attention to its speed of response. In what I called the 'brute-force' approach, which invites the user to enter a string via an INPUT statement, analysis of the string does not begin until the user has finished keying it in and presses the RETURN key; even a mature learner may grow bored waiting for a response. With an ATN, analysis occurs *as the input is keyed in* (just as a human hearer follows an utterance while it is in progress, rather than waiting for the end before beginning to make sense of it). The occasional barely-detectable delay which I mentioned above referred to time taken by the system to cycle from line 540 to line 610; a rapid typist will sometimes notice a slight hesitation between pressing a key and appearance of the corresponding character on the screen, and this hesitation represents the time taken by the system to recognize how the user is moving through the network. Once the last key is pressed, analysis is complete and the machine responds immediately. In a word-based ATN the delay would occur only between words, where human typists make longer pauses anyway.

The fact that analysis is concurrent with input means that what appears on the screen need not always be identical with what the user is keying in, even if his input is acceptable. This can be very useful pedagogically. For instance, it was clear to me that the young users of *Telling the Time* ought not to be required to get punctuation right,

even if they were good at reading clocks and spelling the corresponding words. Adult users of English hesitate between *twentyfive*
and *twenty-five*, and will accept *twenty five* as two words with a space
between. Most adults know that *o'clock* has an apostrophe, but it
would be a shame to pick up a young child for omitting it if the child
was otherwise getting things right. Nevertheless, presumably it is
desirable for the child learner to *see* orthographically-standard forms
so that he gradually learns to produce them himself. With an ATN
this is easy to arrange. Normally, any character input at line 540
which succeeds in causing the system to make a transition at line 580
will lead to the same character being sent to the screen at line 610,
so that the user sees his own input echoed on the screen; but an
individual transition can carry an augmentation which suppresses the
printing of a character, or causes a different or an additional
character to be printed. Thus, in my system, spaces appear between
words on screen whether or not spaces are keyed in, and the word
twenty-five always appears hyphenated irrespective of whether a
hyphen, a space, or nothing is keyed in between the two elements.
With adult learners, too, there should be value in this ability silently
to normalize irrelevant linguistic peccadillos rather than using the big
gun of overt correction on every error, no matter how trivial.

Conversely, some errors deserve showy treatment. If a user of
Telling the Time reads the clock correctly but makes a random, unpredictable error in keying in the time-name, movement through the
network halts and the user is asked to try again. But some linguistic
errors are very predictable. If an error is predictable it can be built
into the network and dealt with individually when it occurs. Thus,
a common spelling error with English number-words is *fourty* for *forty*.
My ATN accepts the spelling *fourty* – but includes an augmentation
designed to help the user remember that it is wrong. (Question marks
flash, the offending letter 'drops' out of the word and tumbles slowly
down the screen, and the gap is closed up to produce *forty*.) Again,
there is surely scope for ATN-based software for mature language
learners to include augmentations that cope actively with regular
patterns of grammatical error.

Finally, the ATN approach has the major virtue of *modularity*. That
is to say, the design of a network to handle some particular area of
language (in this case, the area of English time-names) is one thing;
the design of a program to implement any such network on a micro
is another and separate thing, and changes to the former do not
require changes to the latter. Now that a program has been written
which implements a deterministic ATN on a BBC micro, I (or anyone

else) can design a network for some quite different area of English, or of another language; the network will be entirely different in structure, but the same program can be used to run it. Indeed, the ATN concept could be explained to someone who was familiar with an area of language material to be taught but who knew nothing about computers or BASIC, and they could design a network which would allow the computer to 'understand' the range of sentences in question even though that person could not read the program. If linguistic material is analysed by the 'brute-force' approach, on the other hand, the same person must master both the linguistic problems and the programming language with which they are handled; this is yet another way in which the brute-force approach is impractical.

Conclusion

Let me not appear to make unrealistic claims for what can be done with ATNs. Particularly as implemented on a micro, they have clear limitations. They can be made to accept a range of linguistic inputs much wider than the set of possibilities offered by a multiple-choice question, but the range of inputs accepted by any given ATN must nevertheless be fixed and limited. There is no hope of designing a system that will allow the user an open-ended choice of input and still succeed in responding appropriately. This constraint lies in the nature of the computer as a mechanical device, and it is surely foolish to imagine that it can ever be overcome. That implies a severe limit on the extent to which computers can ever be useful to the language teacher. This accepted, though, ATNs offer the chance of pushing about as far towards that limit as is practical in current technological and professional circumstances.

Finally, the other word of caution that needs to be spoken is that drawing transition networks, even for restricted, cut-and-dried areas of natural language, is quite a challenging task! Word-based networks are simpler than the letter-based network I have been describing, but they do require serious thought. However, the thinking involved is thinking about the linguistic material that the network is meant to deal with, rather than about problems created by the quirks of computers and their programming languages, so it may be less frustrating for the language teacher. If it is difficult to get an ATN for some piece of language right, that is because the language involved is genuinely complicated. There is something to be said in favour of activities which make us more aware of the complexity of the knowledge we impart to others.

Introduction to Chapter 12

Although, as Eric Atwell points out, the computing power required by workers in artificial intelligence or computer science in general far outstrips what can be expected to be at hand for language teachers in school interested in CALL, it is important not to be dismissive of the facilities presently available to the latter, especially given the rapid increase of power even in microcomputers. From this more optimistic position, then, Atwell provides readers of this collection with a very valuable service indeed. He documents and illustrates for the user concerned with language education how already available systems and programs can be put to use by the teacher, by the applied linguist, and, in principle, by the learner.

Atwell begins by exploring operating systems (VMS and UNIX), showing how they can be used to accommodate several users simultaneously, handling a series of complex tasks. There is obvious value here for the educational institution wanting to overcome the problem of accessibility and varied learning tasks. Associated with his discussion of operating systems, Atwell provides a glossary to a range of programs useful to the language teacher and learner, focusing especially on text editors, spelling checkers and style 'improvers'. One very valuable suite of programs discussed here is *The Writer's Workbench*, with language analysis facilities as immediately useful in the classroom as they have proved to be for independent authors. Once again we detect the growing move towards enabling learner autonomy with the aid of available software not necessarily conceived with the language learner in mind.

Finally, in this paper, Atwell tackles one of the problems heralded in earlier papers in the collection, that of the need to augment BASIC as the main programming language for micro users. As he points out, the usefulness and increasing availability of ADA, LISP, PROLOG, POP-11 and POPLOG should greatly increase the range of languages which can be made use of in the near future, even in relatively limited computing environments, by researchers into language analysis and language learning.

12 Beyond the micro: advanced software for research and teaching from computer science and artificial intelligence

Eric Atwell

Lecturers and researchers in British university and polytechnic computer studies departments generally have access to rather greater computing power than most linguists or English language teachers. As well as a range of micros, the computer scientist can use powerful multi-user *mainframes* and single-user *workstations* with very fast program execution speeds, a megabyte or more of main memory, hundreds or thousands of megabytes of disk memory, and correspondingly sophisticated software. However, because of the phenomenal rate of progress in computing, the computer science and artificial intelligence research and teaching tools of today may well be within the reach of other researchers and teachers tomorrow, or at least in a couple of years' time. This chapter looks at some of this software, concentrating on facilities which seem particularly relevant to English language teaching and research.

Sophisticated operating systems

The operating system is the main program resident in a computer, which schedules and organizes the use of processing resources in such a way that the user is unaware of the 'nitty gritty' of how the hardware actually works at a low level. For a micro user, the operating system is used mainly for file-handling: for instance, the user can load a file from a disk by issuing a simple command, without having to know anything about how blocks of binary code are read and interpreted, or about the detailed sequence of signals sent between the processing unit and the disk drive. On a modern mainframe, the operating system has to be much more sophisticated, to cater for a large number of users with widely varying requirements. Deitel (1983) explains this in more detail; here, we look at some of the most relevant aspects of advanced operating systems.

VMS and UNIX

VMS and UNIX are two of the most widely available and popular operating systems in British universities and polytechnics today. VMS is available on VAX mini and mainframe computers; its great attraction is that, although a sophisticated multi-user operating system with a very wide range of facilities, it is very user-friendly to beginners and casual users. Wherever possible, commands are English words, e.g. PRINT to print out a file on the printer; SHOW TIME to display the current date and time on the terminal; SET PASSWORD to allow the user to set (or change) his or her password. As more experienced users wish to save keystrokes, all commands can be abbreviated to their first few letters, so long as this remains unambiguous (e.g. PRINT can be abbreviated to PRIN, PRI, or PR, but not P alone as other commands also start with P).

UNIX is also available on VAX computers, and on a wide range of other machines as well. UNIX was originally developed at Bell Laboratories; at the time, most operating systems were built round specific computers, and Bell researchers decided to develop a 'machine-independent' operating system tailored for the user rather than the machine. Bell still hold the trademark rights for UNIX, but the system was so good that UNIX-look-alike systems have been or are being developed by most other computer manufacturers. UNIX has the reputation of appearing rather strange to the beginner, mainly because many commands are short mnemonics whose meanings are far from obvious to the newcomer; for example, 'wc' (short for Word Count) counts the number of words and/or letters and/or lines in a document; 'mv' (MoVe) is used to change the name of a file; 'who' displays a list of all users currently logged-in to the system. However, once the user has learnt a basic vocabulary (a task which should not particularly daunt the linguist, armed with a UNIX primer such as Miller and Boyle (1984) or Bourne (1982)), UNIX turns out to be an ideal environment for developing software, as it has a particularly rich set of 'tools' and facilities to aid the developer.

Concurrency

With a multi-user operating system, many users can interact with the computer apparently simultaneously. For this to be possible, the operating system must be able to organize a large number of processes running *concurrently*. This is actually achieved by a technique called *interleaving*: the system maintains a list of processes currently running 'simultaneously'; each process on the list can take a turn at getting the system's full attention for a few milliseconds, and then it must stop and wait until the system cycles round to its next turn. The problems of concurrent programming are dealt with in more detail in Ben-Ari (1982). Of course, the details of concurrency are kept hidden from users, so that an individual logging-in appears to have a *virtual machine* all to himself or herself. However, there are times when a single user would like to be able to run more than one process at a time, and UNIX makes this particularly easy. Firstly, adding '&' to the end of a command line causes the command to be run as a second process, concurrently with the main log-in process. For example, if a user has a program SLOWPROG which takes a long time to run, and he or she also wants to do some interactive work such as editing files, etc., then in most operating systems he or she will just have to wait until SLOWPROG has finished before typing any more commands; but in UNIX, the line

slowprog &

will cause SLOWPROG to be run as a separate process, leaving the terminal free for issuing other commands. Another use of concurrency is when a complex task is broken down into several programs, each passing their results on as input to the next program. For example, if a user wanted to count the number of spelling errors in a file MYTEXT, then he or she could run a spelling-check program over MYTEXT to produce an output file TEMP containing a list of errors, and then run a word-counting program over TEMP to output the number of words in this file. Under UNIX, there is no need for a temporary file between each process: programs can be *pipelined* to run concurrently and pass results directly from one process to the next, e.g.

spell mytext 1 wc

This means that quite complex tasks can be performed simply by pipelining the appropriate tools together; this facility is not available on other operating systems.

General-purpose tools

Even in widely varying applications areas, there are a number of comparatively simple tasks that many users will carry out repeatedly;

and so an advanced operating system like VMS or UNIX will include a number of general-purpose *tools* or *utilities* for such tasks. For example, often users may need to *sort* a list of numbers into ascending or descending order, or *sort* a list of words into alphabetical order; rather than have to write their own sorting program, they can use the SORT command to sort the file containing the list. Another useful tool is a command to list the *differences* between two files; for example, if a user writes a program which produces an output file OUTPUT1, and later amends the program and runs it again to produce an output file OUTPUT2, then he or she could straightforwardly uncover any differences between the files caused by the change in the program. A third commonly-available tool is a command to COUNT the number of lines and/or words and/or characters in a file.

Text editors

These simple tools simply take one or more files as input, do some standardized processing, and produce the appropriate output file. More sophisticated tools allow the user interactive control over the processing. For example, all operating systems have at least one *editor* for editing the contents of files (many systems have several alternative editors!). The simplest type of editor is a *line editor*: the user edits the file by typing a sequence of editing commands, effectively a 'program' which is interpreted and executed interactively. Unfortunately, the file itself is *not* directly visible to the user unless he or she explicitly displays lines using the appropriate command; this of course is not particularly helpful, so nowadays many operating systems also offer a *screen editor* as an alternative to line editors. With a screen editor, the text of the file itself is displayed on the terminal screen, and the user can 'move around' in the file by positioning the cursor with special arrow keys; mainframe screen editors are much closer than line editors to the text editors available on home micros and word-processors.

Help

Another very important tool is the *help* system. On most mainframe operating systems, it is possible to find out how to use a command by typing HELP followed by the command, e.g.

HELP SORT

This will cause information on the SORT command to be displayed. With a good help system, a beginner can use the facilities of an operating system without constantly having to refer to printed documentation and reference manuals to check the exact spelling and usage of commands; as the reference manuals accompanying a modern operating system can fill a large bookcase, this is particularly important!

UNIX tools for language analysis

The UNIX operating system is particularly well-endowed with tools which could be very useful to English language teachers and researchers. Apart from the general-purpose tools mentioned above which could be adapted for linguistic applications, UNIX includes a number of tools specifically designed for analysis of English language text files. In this section we examine these in detail. Of course, other operating systems may well have utilities roughly equivalent to some of the UNIX tools below (in particular, several alternative 'spelling-checkers' are available), but none that I know of have all of them.

GREP

GREP prints out all lines in a file containing a specified string, e.g.

grep 'spell' myfile

This will print out all lines in the file MYFILE containing the string *spell* (including, e.g. *spellbound* and *misspelling*, but not *spelt*). In fact, the files searched by GREP need not be English text files, but this application is obviously the most relevant for the English language teacher or researcher.

The string searched for can contain various wildcards, e.g. a period '.' matches any character, a carat '∧' matches the beginning of a line, and a dollar-sign '$' matches the end of a line. For more complicated searches, a variant of grep, EGREP, allows extended regular expressions as patterns to be searched for, e.g.

egrep '(any|some)(one|body)' myfile

This searches for all lines containing *anyone, anybody, someone,* or *somebody.*

SPELL

SPELL takes as input an English text, and produces a list of probable misspellings.

The program collects words from a named English text file, and looks up each textword in its spelling list. If an exact match cannot be found for a textword, then an attempt is made to strip off any inflections, prefixes, and suffixes, and the putative root is looked up again; if a match still cannot be found, the textword is added to the output file of misspellings.

The user can choose between two standard wordlists, one for British English, and the other for American English. Alternatively, the user can nominate another list to be used – in practice, what usually happens is that users want to add more words to the standard list. So that the spelling-checker can look up each textword quickly, the spelling list is not stored as a straightforward textfile: the information is restructured into a *hash table*, a form that allows particular words to be found rapidly. If the user wishes to update a hashed wordlist, there is another tool, SPELLIN, which merges the list of additions into the hashed wordlist.

Of course, a 'spelling-checker' that simply checks each textword against a spelling list can never be perfect. To begin with, the system will continually throw up proper names, technical terms, etc., as misspellings. A user can compensate for this by adding these new words to the spelling list, but the spelling list will never be complete, and adding many rare words can cause other problems. For example, if a user wanted to write a paper on the problems of castrated male sheep, he or she might be tempted to add the word *wether* to the spelling list; but thereafter, misspellings of *weather* or *whether* would not be recognized!

Another problem arises with inflected and derived forms of words. To save space (and hence speed up searches), most derived and inflected forms are not stored explicitly in the spelling list: instead, if a textword is not found straightforwardly, affixes are stripped off, and an attempt is made to find the 'root'. Unfortunately, SPELL places very few restrictions on which affixes can occur with which roots, and this allows some misspellings (such as '*unboy*', '*intoing*', '*intoly*') to slip through the net. Because of this potential problem, users have the option of getting SPELL to output all words not literally in the spelling list; in this list, words which might plausibly be derived from roots in the spelling list have their putative morphological structure indicated. Also, SPELL uses a STOPLIST of common misspellings which might otherwise go unnoticed because they could plausibly be derived from words in the spelling list (e.g. '*thier*' = '*thy*' − '*y*' + '*ier*'); users can use their own versions of this too.

Note that this allowance for users to provide their own wordlists means that SPELL can be readily adapted to other tasks. For example, teaching texts are often written using a limited controlled vocabulary; if the list of words in this controlled vocabulary is used as the spelling list, a writer can readily check that his or her text conforms to the limitations.

DICTION

DICTION performs a similar task to that of SPELL, but at the level of phrases rather than just single words – it searches a specified English text file for phrases which are often indicative of bad or wordy diction. Whereas SPELL produces a list of possible misspellings without context, DICTION prints out whole sentences, with the dubious phrase(s) highlighted by square brackets..

Of course, the choice of which phrases are to be pinpointed as objectionable is rather more subjective than the decision about what to put in the spelling list, and users are free to supply their own list of pet hates in addition to or instead of the standard file. As with SPELL, this means DICTION can be adapted to other applications; for instance, Cherry, who originally developed the DICTION program, has produced a variant SEXIST, which scours a document for potentially sexist phrases.

EXPLAIN

DICTION merely produces a list of sentences with dubious phrases marked, leaving it up to the user to decide what corrections or changes to make to the original text. EXPLAIN is an interactive thesaurus which can be used to elicit suggested corrections for the phrases marked by DICTION. In fact, both DICTION and EXPLAIN use the same file of dubious phrases; in this file, each phrase is paired with a suggested correction, but DICTION ignores this second part to each entry. When users provide their own list of phrases to be searched for, they can provide suggested substitutions as well (although this is not essential).

STYLE

STYLE reads an English text file, and prints out a summary of readability indices, sentence length and type, word usage, and sentence openers; in other words, STYLE attempts an analysis of the surface

characteristics of the writing style of a document. The following is
STYLE's analysis of this chapter:
readability grades:
>   (Kincaid) 16.4 (auto) 18.3 (Coleman-Liau) 12.7 (Flesch) 15.2
>   (35.4)

sentence info:
>   no. sent 167 no. wds 5431
>   av sent leng 32.5 av word leng 4.99
>   no. questions 2 no. imperatives 0
>   no. nonfunc wds 3420 63.0% av leng 6.32
>   short sent (<28) 46% (76) long sent (>43) 22% (37)
>   longest sent 127 wds at sent 164; shortest sent 3
>   wds at sent 125

sentence types:
>   simple 30% (50) complex 21% (35)
>   compound 18% (30) compound-complex 31% (52)

word usage:
>   verb types as % of total verbs
>   to be 38% (199) aux 18% (96) inf 18% (94)
>   passives as % of non-inf verbs 19% (83)
>   types as % of total
>   prep 11.0% (598) conj 4.0% (216) adv 5.5% (299)
>   noun 29.3% (1591) adj 20.3% (1100) pron 3.4% (183)
>   nominalizations 1% (73)

sentence beginnings:
>   subject opener: noun (48) pron (6) pos (0) adj (31)
>   art (24) tot 65%
>   prep 16% (26) adv 10% (16)
>   verb 1% (2) subconj 7% (12) conj 0% (0)
>   expletives 1% (2)

To produce this analysis, STYLE has to analyse the text in a fairly
'intelligent' way. First, the text has to be divided up into sentences.
This is not a trivial task, as

1. not all full stops mark sentence breaks (e.g. *3.14, Mr. E. Atwell*);
2. the text may not all be straightforward running prose – there may
   be 'non-sentences', like section headings, lists, or tables.

The next step is a simple surface syntactic analysis of each
sentence; STYLE does this by running another program, PARTS.
PARTS first assigns a set of possible parts of speech to every word
in a sentence: each textword is looked up in a short wordlist of 350
common words. If it is not found there, an attempt is made to match
the word against one of 51 suffixes indicative of specific word classes.

Finally, if this fails too, the textword is provisionally assigned the class UNK ('unknown'). PARTS then disambiguates words with more than one possible part of speech (e.g. *little*: adjective/adverb), and assigns a proper part of speech to words marked UNK. This is done, not by conventional parsing techniques, but by an algorithm which uses various heuristics about the expected local contexts of each part of speech. The designer herself stated that 'the method chosen for PARTS is best described as seat-of-the-pants' (Cherry 1980, p. 2), but it is surprisingly successful! Besides, the statistics output are only meant to be a rough guide, since style cannot be quantified precisely; so 100% accuracy is not required.

Having divided the text into sentences, it is fairly straightforward to calculate the various figures shown in the above example. The four readability grades are calculated using the formulae:

Kincaid: $(11.8*\text{sylperwd}) + (0.39*\text{wdpersent}) - 15.59$

Automated Readability Index (auto):

$(4.71*\text{letperwd}) + (0.5*\text{wdpersent}) - 21.43$

Coleman-Liau: $(5.89*\text{letperwd}) - (0.3*\text{sentper100wds}) - 15.8$

Flesch: $206.835 - (84.6*\text{sylperwd}) - (1.015*\text{wdpersent})$

The relative merits of these grades, and the details behind the other measures of style shown in the example above, are discussed in Cherry and Vesterman (1981). Users of STYLE can additionally ask for any or all of the following to be appended to the summary STYLE report:

1. a printout of the length and readability index of each individual sentence;
2. a printout of the text with each word on a separate line, with the part of speech assigned by PARTS next to it;
3. a list of all sentences that begin with an 'expletive', i.e. *There is*, *It is* (these sentence-openers tend to be overused in technical documents);
4. a list of sentences containing a passive verb;
5. a list of all sentences longer than a specified maximum;
6. a list of all sentences whose Automated Readability Index is greater than a specified limit.

Note that some of the above lists are liable to errors, since the linguistic analysis routines of STYLE and PARTS are necessarily crude and oversimplistic. Nevertheless, STYLE clearly has great potential for the English language teacher or researcher!

The Writer's Workbench

This is a user-friendly package of English language text analysis programs , including SPELL, DICTION, SEXIST, and STYLE as well as several others. The package is not available as standard on UNIX systems; it is an 'add-on extra' for commercial word-processing applications, but obviously it would also be useful in English language teaching and research. More details of *The Writer's Workbench* are included in Cherry and Macdonald (1983); Cherry *et al.* (1983); and Macdonald *et al.* (1982).

Programming languages

Most English language teachers and researchers who have some experience of programming have tended to stick to BASIC, probably because for them this is the most readily accessible language. Home micros come with some version of BASIC built in, and nearly all university computing services offer BASIC on their mainframes, so there may seem little point in attempting to program in another language. However, this may well be a rather short-sighted attitude for any linguist who aims to eventually progress beyond toy programs. The short-term overheads of having to learn a new programming language may be more than made up for by the time saved by programming short cuts available in the new language but not in BASIC; and besides, linguists may well relish the challenge of learning a new language! This section outlines some of the alternatives to BASIC currently available on mainframes, concentrating on what they have to offer the English language teacher and researcher. Horowitz (1984) gives a fuller overview of programming languages currently available.

Note that most of the software discussed so far is specific to UNIX, but the languages and subsystems mentioned in the rest of this chapter are available on a wide variety of machines and operating systems (including some personal computers and micros).

Old favourites: COBOL, FORTRAN, PASCAL

The three alternatives to BASIC most widely available on mainframes are COBOL, FORTRAN, and PASCAL. COBOL (see, e.g. Parkin 1982; McCracken 1976) has sophisticated facilities to deal with the complex structured files and databases used in business environments; furthermore, the language was designed to have an 'English-like' syntax. A program consists of a sequence of *sentences*, grouped into *paragraphs*, and each sentence must start with a *verb* (as all sentences are imperatives) and end in a full stop. FORTRAN (see, e.g. McCracken 1974) is well-suited to highly-efficient numerical computations, as required, for instance, in advanced computer graphics, or speech understanding or production systems. PASCAL (see, e.g. Cooper and Clancy 1982; Jensen and Wirth 1975) is the youngest of the three languages, and it has been adopted by most computer studies departments as the first programming language to teach students, as it encourages the design of efficient, well-structured programs.

These languages all have the advantage that there is usually plenty of available expertise to help with software design and debugging problems. Also, existing software can be incorporated into any new programs. For example, if a PASCAL or FORTRAN program involves statistical calculations, then it can use the standard subroutines or procedures provided in the system *library*, such as the NAG library of mathematical routines.

The main disadvantage of these languages from the linguist's point of view is the very poor facilities these languages have for manipulating strings or tree-structures. Although the users of COBOL, FORTRAN and PASCAL may sometimes look down on BASIC as a beginner's language, the advanced features offered by these alternatives may well prove poor compensation for the linguist.

ADA

ADA is a comparatively new language, so not all operating systems will have an ADA compiler – yet! ADA was designed to combine the best features of a number of other languages, including COBOL, FORTRAN, and PASCAL; it is backed by the US Defence Department (and also by other NATO partners) as an eventual replacement for all other programming languages on their computers, so it is bound to catch on! As shown, e.g. in Price (1984) or Pyle (1981), ADA has better string-handling facilities than the three previous languages, and programs can access *packages* of additional functions (such as string-handling functions) which effectively extend the language in any desired direction. Another innovation is that ADA programs can include subprograms called *tasks* which will run concurrently. In fact, ADA's chief drawback is that, as it has so many advanced features that have no straightforward equivalent in BASIC, COBOL, etc., it takes a great deal longer to learn to use the language to its full potential! This initial learning effort is clearly worthwhile when engineering complex systems involving thousands (or even millions) of instructions, but it is offputting to the casual computer user.

LISP

LISP was the original language designed specifically for *list processing*. An *array* in BASIC or other languages is a structure containing a number of more basic elements; the number of elements must be fixed at the outset by a DIMENSION statement (or its equivalent), and all elements must be of the same type. A *list* is a much less constrained structure: the number of elements can change during the program run, and the elements can be of differing types – numbers, strings, or even other lists. This makes lists ideal for representing tree-structures, e.g.

(Sent (Subj the cat) (V ate) (Obj the mouse))

In LISP, *everything* is treated as a list; even the program itself is a list of function calls, each of which is a list of function names and arguments or parameters. The following function definition is a short example of this *functional* style of programming:

(define (printdouble x (print (plus x x)))

LISP has been described as 'the machine code of artificial intelligence'. Some beginners are put off by its strange notation (particularly the proliferation of brackets), but it is extremely versatile; Winston and Horn (1981) and Siklossy (1976) give fuller introductions aimed specifically at the non-mathematician.

PROLOG

PROLOG is an acronym for PROgramming in LOGic. A PROLOG program is not a series of instructions to be obeyed in sequence, but rather a set of facts and inference rules stated in a notation based on Predicate Logic. As an example, the following denote the facts that Tom is the father of Harry and Harry is the father of Jim, and a rule defining what a grandfather is:

father(tom,harry).
father(harry,jim).
grandfather(X,Z) :- father(X,Y), father(Y,Z).

When using the PROLOG language, the user starts by *asserting* a number of facts and rules, which are added to a *database*. The user can then ask 'questions', which the PROLOG system will try to answer by making inferences based on the facts and rules in the database; for example, to the question:

    ?–father(tom,harry).

the PROLOG system will reply 'yes'; and to the question:

    ?–grandfather(X,jim).

the PROLOG system will reply 'X=tom'.

PROLOG is widely used in artificial intelligence research, as it is particularly well-suited for encapsulating 'knowledge' that can be stated as a formal rule-system, such as a grammar of English. Clocksin and Mellish (1984) is the definitive introduction to PROLOG; and a version of PROLOG available under CP/M for micros, called micro-PROLOG, is described in Clark and McCabe (1984).

POP-11

Much is made of the distinction between *interpreted* and *compiled* languages. Programs in interpreted languages such as BASIC run comparatively slowly because each BASIC instruction must be trans-lated to machine code before it can be obeyed during a program run; however, programs can be developed *interactively* in small steps, with frequent test runs between changes. POP-11 achieves the best of both worlds with an *incremental compiler*: programs can be developed interactively, but every new procedure or function is automatically compiled as soon as its definition is complete, so that all subsequent procedure calls actually activate fast, compiled machine code. POP-11 programs are thus a series of procedure and function definitions, each one using previously-defined procedures as 'building blocks'. The language syntax itself is also incremental: not only can new procedures and functions be defined, but even new syntax words, e.g. *infix operators*. In general, the language is very powerful, with exten-sive facilities for string and list processing, pattern matching, database querying, etc.

A third 'incremental' feature of the language is that it is very easy for the beginner to learn the basics, and later develop his or her skills in more advanced features as and when they prove useful. POP-11 is embedded in the POPLOG teaching and research environment (see p. 182), which includes a powerful screen editor and numerous library packages. Most of the reference material on POP-11 is only available with this POPLOG system, but an overview is included in O'Shea and Eisenstadt (1984).

Packages and subsystems

Some pieces of software available on an operating system such as VMS or UNIX cannot really be classified as general-purpose programming languages, but they are more sophisticated than most tools. For example, Heidorn *et al.* (1982) are developing an experimental text analysis system called EPISTLE which will include spelling, grammatical, and stylistic analysis all in one program; this program is so complex that currently it only runs on a large IBM mainframe. This section looks at some currently available examples of *packages* or *subsystems*.

MINITAB

Several packages are available to help linguists and others with little computing background to use the computer without having to learn a programming language. MINITAB is a good example; it helps users to analyse statistical data, but users do not have to learn a complicated command language. In MINITAB, the user issues commands in pseudo-English, such as

READ THE FOLLOWING DATA INTO COLUMNS C1 AND C2
81 6
84 7
90 10
75 2
89 11
PLOT C1 AGAINST C2

and the MINITAB program responds by displaying graphs, plots, etc., to order. The syntax of MINITAB has very few restrictions: each command line must start with a verb like READ, PLOT, or ADD, and include the relevant column numbers C1, C2, etc.; but all other words are simply ignored, leaving users free to issue commands in almost any format they choose. Ryan, Joiner and Ryan (1982) give more details of MINITAB.

Programming environments

Many older programming languages are catered for by an operating system simply with the addition of a *compiler*. For example, a PASCAL programmer uses the standard operating system editor to create a file containing the text of a PASCAL program, and then runs the

PASCAL compiler, which takes as input his PASCAL program file (the *source program*), and outputs a machine code equivalent program (the *object program*). BASIC and some other languages require something more, so that programs can be built up interactively. On most operating systems, typing the command BASIC will invoke a BASIC 'subsystem' – a mini-operating system including most of the file-handling and other commands found in a home micro BASIC system, such as NEW, SAVE, etc. There is a trend to develop similar *programming support environments* for other languages, including many more sophisticated aids to program development. For example, an Ada Programming Support Environment (APSE) will be available soon with facilities for keeping track of the numerous subprograms which may be written by different individuals collaborating on a large software engineering project.

The POPLOG teaching and research environment

POPLOG is one such environment, built around the powerful programming language POP-11 (see above). It was originally developed at Sussex University, for teaching Arts undergraduates on the Cognitive Science programme, and it is particularly user-friendly for beginners. Users can ask for HELP on any command, and in addition there is an extensive TEACH facility. For example, if a student types TEACH GRAMMAR, a tutorial text on English grammar is displayed on the screen, interspersed with invitations to the student to try out some example programs which demonstrate phrase structure rules, sentence generation, parsing, etc. For the more advanced user, the POP 11 code of any of the demonstration programs can be examined using the SHOWLIB command; and detailed documentation and references can be examined using the DOC or REF commands. An overview of the POPLOG system is included in O'Shea and Eisenstadt (1984); although originally developed for teaching and research in cognitive science and artificial intelligence, the general POPLOG framework could readily be adapted for English and linguistics research and teaching.

Conclusions

Most of the software discussed in this chapter is currently only available on university mainframe computers, but with the rapid increases in hardware technology, personal computers will soon be powerful enough to support at least some of it. In particular, UNIX (or scaled-down versions of it) is available on a growing range of personal computers and workstations, allowing linguists to access a wide range of tools and programming languages, and so to develop advanced software for English language teaching and research.

Introduction to Chapter 13

Although Knowles's and Sampson's papers on phonetics teaching and the use of ATNs identify two valuable research fields of use to CALL, it is in the two well-established domains of lexical and grammatical research that we can already see major advances for the language educator. The two final papers in this collection, by John Sinclair and Geoffrey Leech, reporting respectively on work at the Universities of Birmingham and Lancaster, substantiate that claim.

John Sinclair's paper tackles the issue of handling long texts, identifying a range of lexical operations which can be accessed by researchers, teachers and, in principle, by learners. The paper starts by glossing a set of basic techniques for language data processing, setting the operations out in an ordered list of actions: identifying word-forms, representing texts, frequency listing, collocational environments, concordancing and producing text analysis statistics for a range of varieties and styles. More than only being of value to lexicography, however, Sinclair's research reported here offers insights into the adequacy of descriptions in text linguistics as well as in semantics. In addition, for the language teacher and learner, the techniques offer ways of achieving stylistic coherence in the writing process and, following Alderson's suggestions about CBELT, ways of assessing the nativeness of advanced second language learners' usage. As an aid to the reader of the paper, each of the techniques listed above is provided with example data in a helpful set of tables.

13 Basic computer processing of long texts[1]

John Sinclair

Introduction

The basic techniques for processing texts by computer were developed some years ago in the investigation of vocabulary patterns (Jones and Sinclair 1974; Reed 1977). However, they were not readily available to most researchers because they required access to mainframe computers, and often considerable expertise in computing, because early systems were not user-friendly. Also, despite the apparent power of big computers, in practice there have been many problems in achieving ease and reliability in carrying out basic processing, when the text is more than a few thousand words long.

Now computers are much more accessible, both small ones with ever more impressive specifications, and large ones with sophisticated interactive operating systems, and networks of increasing versatility to link them up. Many text stores exist, and it is becoming easier to make text stores with the rapid growth of information technology. So the opportunity to process long texts is within the grasp of most serious researchers.

It is, therefore, a good moment to review the basic techniques of language data processing, and to assess their value in linguistic research. At the very least, the quality of linguistic evidence is going to be improved out of all recognition, because of the power of the computer in data-management. But it is more than likely that the coordinated resources of man and machine will lead to new postulates in theory.

The computer is incurably and pedantically data-orientated. For a linguist, there are no shortcuts to his or her abstractions. The first stage of adaptation is to resign oneself to plodding through the detail. Then some aspects of the detail begin to look rather fuzzy, and in need of a tighter specification. It now seems likely that the relation between data and abstractions, so painfully exposed by the computer, is going to become a major research area.

Input

Once a text has been selected for study, the first decision is in what way it is to be re-created inside the computer. It may seem a simple enough process, to reproduce a text inside the machine, but in practice not all the features of a text are coded. Different features are picked out according to the needs of the work. For most general processing the text is kept to a very simple format – usually a single long string of letters, spaces and punctuation marks. The letters of the alphabet, punctuation marks and the word-space are called *characters:* the distinction between upper and lower case is preserved. Page and line numbers are kept only for reference purposes, and other layout, setting and typeface information is discarded.

That is all, then, that the computer 'knows' about text – a long succession of nondescript characters marked off in pages and lines.

Words and word-forms

There has been some research based purely on counting the characters, but most students move quickly to some simple notion of a word. The one used here is a *word-form*, and that is an unbroken succession of letters (the hyphen and apostrophe need special attention, but I shall not go into such detail here).

Note that a word-form is close to but not identical to the usual idea of a word. In particular, several different word-forms may all be regarded as instances of the same word. So *drive, drives, driving, drove, driven*, and perhaps *driver, drivers, drivers', driver's, drive's* make up ten different word-forms, all related to the word '*drive*'. It is usual in defining a word-form to ignore the distinction between upper and lower case, so *SHAPE, Shape* and *shape* will all be taken as instances of the same word-form. This convention no doubt blurs a few hundred useful distinctions, like *polish* and *Polish*, but obliterates many thousands of word-forms which have an initial capital letter merely because they begin a sentence. For other purposes this distinction is valuable, but on balance, for studying word-forms, it is best ignored.

The computer can find, sort and count word-forms fairly easily; it finds the conventional notion of a word much more vague and complicated, and there is no standard procedure for converting word-forms to words. For example should *meanest* and *meaning* be related together, as forms of the word '*mean*'? There are thousands of such problems, and new research of this kind will be better founded if the greatest use is made of the simplest categories.

Already it is clear that, in the absence of standardization, the ad hoc decisions of one researcher do not suit the next, and much of the laborious work of gathering and presenting basic information has to be done afresh in each project. The best way to keep this wastage to a minimum is to work for as long as possible with data in a form close to its physical occurrence, and only to introduce abstractions where these are unavoidable. Most linguistics works with more abstract categories, with words rather than word-forms, because human beings can appreciate that kind of concept; but in computing such concepts are indeterminate. Hence it is good policy to defer them for as long as possible.

Text and vocabulary

Using the simple notion of a word-form, we can now represent a text as a succession of word-forms. The word-forms can be counted, so that the length of the text, measured in word-forms, can be calculated. Next, the word-forms can be compared with each other, and it will be found that there are many repetitions of the same word-form. So another count can be made of the number of different word-forms, which is called the *vocabulary* of the text.

In this paper I shall frequently refer to a short sample passage which is printed as Appendix A on page 203. Its length in word-forms is 189. This is often called the number of 'running words' in the text. Such a short passage is only of use in illustrating the processes: in actual research texts are thousands or millions of running words in length. But by using a short text it is possible for the reader to follow exactly what the computer does, which to explain discursively would be impracticable.

Frequency lists

First occurrence

The simplest operation on a text is to turn it into a list of the word-forms in the order of their first occurrence, noting the frequency of each. Each successive word-form is compared with each previous one.

If it is a new word-form it is provided with a counter set at *1*; if it has occurred before it is deleted from the text and *1* is added to the counter at the place of first occurrence of the word-form.

> *Example*
> If the text is the ridiculously short *The cat sat on the mat*, this operation would give the result:
>
> | | |
> |---|---|
> | the | 2 |
> | cat | 1 |
> | sat | 1 |
> | on | 1 |
> | mat | 1 |

See Figure 1 for a longer example taken from the sample text (Appendix A).

This kind of a list is helpful as a quick guide to distribution in a text, and for a number of more specific purposes. If two word-forms have about the same frequency, but one occurs early in the text and the other doesn't occur until late, then this is possibly an important difference between them. If, in a technical text, there is very little technical vocabulary for some time and then a rush of it, that is a clue to a high-level structural boundary in the text, perhaps the end of a general, layman's introduction to a technical subject. Even in the sample text, Figure 1 shows how *human* and *language* open up a new topic. Such observations can help a lot in the selection of texts for English teaching. At present selections are made on an intuitive basis, and there is no guarantee that a fragment of text is representative of the book or paper it came from. Quite often what appears to be introductory matter is offered as typical technical text.

A frequency list of word-forms is never more than a set of hints or clues to the nature of a text. By examining a list, one can get an idea of what further information would be worth acquiring. Or one can make guesses about the structure of the text, and so focus an investigation.

Alphabetical order

The information that is now available in the frequency list can be rendered in several ways. The most common are alphabetical order (Figure 2) and frequency order (Figure 3). Both these lists can of course be placed in ascending or descending order. In Figure 3, word-forms of the same frequency are arranged alphabetically.

The main use of alphabetical lists is for reference, but they are occasionally useful as objects of study. They are often helpful in

word	freq	word	freq	word	freq
there	2	earphones	1	anything	1
are	2	may	1	too	1
many	2	seem	1	human	3
kinds	2	fairly	1	language	2
of	10	static	1	small	1
activity	6	but	2	sub-section	1
and	8	in	5	important	1
communication	5	we	3	attempts	1
is	11	see	1	set	1
only	3	stage	1	out	1
one	1	where	1	special	1
them	1	halted	1	characteristics	1
although	2	time	1	have	1
often	1	if	2	become	1
it	4	consider	1	quite	1
does	1	whole	1	sophisticated	1
not	1	process	1	research	1
look	2	obvious	1	workers	1
much	1	enough	1	now	1
like	2	nervous	1	recreated	1
the	8	authors	1	most	1
shelves	1	legendary	1	aspects	1
a	5	silent	1	verbal	1
library	2	reader	1	animals	1
can	1	armchair	1	machines	1
very	2	making	1	perhaps	1
inactive	1	continuous	1	mankind's	1
indeed	1	fast	1	remaining	1
someone	1	precise	1	boast	1
sitting	1	eye	1	that	1
with	1	movements	1	thought	1
his	3	radio	1	first	1
eyes	1	listener	1	certainly	1
shut	1	brain	1	an	1
listening	1	highly	1	intricate	1
to	2	active	1	distinctive	1
transistor	1	he	1	kind	1
through	2	taking	1		

FIGURE 1 The first order word list

formulating hypotheses to be tested, and checking assumptions that have been made. For example where rough estimates are to be made they are sometimes used (e.g. in Kjellmer 1984 which uses the reverse order lists of Brown 1963). Mostly, however, they play a secondary role, available when there is a need to check the frequency of a particular word-form.

5	a	2	if	1	radio
1	active	1	important	1	reader
6	activity	5	in	1	recreated
2	although	1	inactive	1	remaining
1	an	1	indeed	1	research
8	and	1	intricate	1	see
1	animals	11	is	1	seem
1	anything	4	it	1	set
2	are	1	kind	1	shelves
1	armchair	2	kinds	1	shut
1	aspects	2	language	1	silent
1	attempts	1	legendary	1	sitting
1	authors	2	library	1	small
1	become	2	like	1	someone
1	boast	1	listener	1	sophisticated
1	brain	1	listening	1	special
2	but	2	look	1	stage
1	can	1	machines	1	static
1	certainly	1	making	1	sub-section
1	characteristics	1	mankind's	1	taking
5	communication	2	many	1	that
1	consider	1	may	8	the
1	continuous	1	most	1	them
1	distinctive	1	movements	2	there
1	does	1	much	1	thought
1	earphones	1	nervous	2	through
1	enough	1	not	1	time
1	eye	1	now	2	to
1	eyes	1	obvious	1	too
1	fairly	10	of	1	transistor
1	fast	1	often	1	verbal
1	first	1	one	2	very
1	halted	3	only	3	we
1	have	1	out	1	where
1	he	1	perhaps	1	whole
1	highly	1	precise	1	with
3	his	1	process	1	workers
3	human	1	quite		

FIGURE 2 Alphabetical order word list

Frequency order

The same information can be sorted again so that the list begins with the most frequent item, and continues down to the single occurrences (Figure 3). In a text of any length, this is a document worth studying – in a short text of course the reasons for word-frequency are too local to be very interesting.

11	is	1	brain	1	one
10	of	1	can	1	out
8	and	1	certainly	1	perhaps
8	the	1	characteristics	1	precise
6	activity	1	consider	1	process
5	a	1	continuous	1	quite
5	communication	1	distinctive	1	radio
5	in	1	does	1	reader
4	it	1	earphones	1	recreated
3	his	1	enough	1	remaining
3	human	1	eye	1	research
3	only	1	eyes	1	see
3	we	1	fairly	1	seem
2	although	1	fast	1	set
2	are	1	first	1	shelves
2	but	1	halted	1	shut
2	have	1	he	1	silent
2	if	1	highly	1	sitting
2	kinds	1	important	1	small
2	language	1	inactive	1	someone
2	library	1	indeed	1	sophisticated
2	like	1	intricate	1	special
2	look	1	kind	1	stage
2	many	1	legendary	1	static
2	there	1	listener	1	sub-section
2	through	1	listening	1	taking
2	to	1	machines	1	that
2	very	1	making	1	them
1	active	1	mankind's	1	thought
1	an	1	may	1	time
1	animals	1	most	1	too
1	anything	1	movements	1	transistor
1	armchair	1	much	1	verbal
1	aspects	1	nervous	1	where
1	attempts	1	not	1	whole
1	authors	1	now	1	with
1	become	1	obvious	1	workers
1	boast	1	often		

FIGURE 3 Frequency order word list

The listing for a particular text can be compared to that of other texts or to large collections of language. The most frequent items tend to keep a stable distribution, and so any marked change in their order can be significant. Figure 4 shows the top of a frequency list of 7.3 million words.

the	309497	were	18547	only	8889
of	155044	which	18344	it's	8848
and	153801	an	17446	will	8834
to	137056	so	17433	than	8315
a	129928	what	16434	yes	8234
in	100138	their	16160	just	8190
that	67042	if	16008	because	8128
I	64849	would	14687	two	7334
it	61379	about	14547	over	7285
was	54722	no	14386	don't	7253
is	49186	said	14163	get	7241
he	42057	up	13552	see	7216
for	40857	when	13501	any	7029
you	37477	been	13417	much	6795
on	35951	out	13361	way	6791
with	35844	them	13322	these	6791
as	34755	do	12943	how	6758
'	30952	my	12761	down	6755
be	29799	more	12718	even	6609
had	29592	who	12708	first	6410
but	29572	me	11697	did	6220
they	29512	like	11564	back	6201
at	28958	very	11483	got	6190
his	26491	can	11271	our	6189
have	26113	has	11241	new	6127
not	25419	him	11110	go	6029
this	25185	some	10537	most	5893
are	23372	into	10414	where	5920
or	22445	then	10265	after	5797
by	21916	now	10246	your	5740
we	20964	think	10007	say	5636
she	20958	well	9654	man	5339
from	20933	know	9549	er	5277
one	20354	time	9481	little	5260
all	20022	could	9214	too	5210
-	19736	people	9083	many	5182
there	19145	its	9061	good	5180
her	18916	other	8904		

FIGURE 4 COBUILD frequency count — the top 113 forms

Word frequency profiles

The examination of frequency lists can be aided by simple statistical information such as is provided in Figures 5 and 6. To explain these, let us examine line 3 in Figure 5. This line deals with word-forms which occur three times. Column 2 tells us that there are four of them, and Column 3 keeps a running total of the number of different word-

Word-form count	Number such	Vocabulary total	Perc. of vocabulary	Word-form total	Perc. of text
1	85	85	75.22	85	44.97
2	15	100	88.50	115	60.85
3	4	104	92.04	127	67.20
4	1	105	92.92	131	69.31
5	3	108	95.58	146	77.25
6	1	109	96.46	152	80.42
8	2	111	98.23	168	88.89
10	1	112	99.12	178	94.18
11	1	113	100.00	189	100.00

FIGURE 5 Word frequency profile (1)

forms that have been reported (totalling 113 – for more detail see Figure 14). Column 4 relates the number in Column 3 with the total of 113, expressed as a percentage. So the word-forms that occur no more than three times constitute 92.04% of the 'vocabulary' – the number of different word-forms.

Column 5 considers the running text, where the total number of word-forms is 189. If there are four word-forms which occur three times each, then 12 must be added to the previous total in Column 5. Column 6 relates the number in Column 5 with the total of 189, and reports that the word-forms which occur no more than three times occupy 67.2% of the text. This figure will drop as the text size increases. In longer texts the most frequent word-form, *the*, itself occupies about 7% of text.

Figure 6 is similar to Figure 5 but presents the information the other

Word-form count	Number such	Vocabulary total	Perc. of vocabulary	Word-form total	Perc. of text
11	1	1	0.88	11	5.82
10	1	2	1.77	21	11.11
8	2	4	3.54	37	19.58
6	1	5	4.42	43	22.75
5	3	8	7.08	58	30.69
4	1	9	7.96	62	32.80
3	4	13	11.50	74	39.15
2	15	28	24.78	104	55.03
1	85	113	100.00	189	100.00

FIGURE 6 Word frequency profile (2)

way round. If we follow the line beginning with 3 again, Column 2 is the same, but Column 3 gives a total, out of 113, of the number of different word-forms with an occurrence of three or more. Column 4 reports this as only 11.5% of the total, Column 5 shows that these more frequent words account for 74 word-forms in the text, and Column 6 points out that 74 is 39.15% of the total of 189 separate word-forms in the text.

Collocation

Once the frequency of word-forms has been studied, the next stage is to examine the environments within which the word-forms occur. The objective is to discover ways in which words affect each other's occurrence. We know that there are thousands of phrases in a language (like *red herring, kith and kin, depend on, at loggerheads*) where the component words influence each other. How red is a red herring? Why do we not say *depend at*, or *of*, or *through*? Where else would you find *kith, loggerheads* except in these phrases? As well as these obvious influences, there are many thousand less obvious, but significant, *collocations*. A collocation is the regular co-occurrence of two or more words or word-forms, within a given extent of text.

Concordances

Index

The computer presents us with co-occurrence information in the basic form of a *concordance*. A concordance is a collection of all the occurrences of a word-form, each in its own textual environment. In its simplest form, it is an index. Each word-form is indexed, and a reference is given to the place of each occurrence of it in a text. Figure 7 is an example of this type.

KWIC

For many years now the KWIC (key word in context) format has been widely used in data-processing; it saves the researcher looking up each occurrence. The word-form under examination appears in the centre of each line, with extra space on either side of it. The length of the context is specified for different purposes. Here is a concord-

Blood	AE12	1050	Blood	AU	415	Bloom	SAA	1120
	AE12	1209		AU	608		T27	10
	AE12	1216		AU	609		NS	1
	AE12	1254		WB	91		G4	211
	AE12	1309		WB	382		AE10	450
	AE12	1376		WB	402		AE11	41
	OAL	271		WB	439		KT3	83
	OAL	404		M15	101		HIF	47
	AF	79		M15	114		HIF	169
	DO	29		M15	120		WB	532
	DO	68		M15	202		AS	51
	DO	136		M15	631	Bloomed	M12	526
	KT1	19		M15	685	Blooming	HP	40
	KT1	145		M15	710		SAA	562
	KT1	468		GP	111		T23	61
	KT2	96		CI	41		AK	149
	KT2	127		CI	603		J3	191
	KT2	189		ETP	29		SLT2	13
	KT2	199		STP	24		MC	31
	KT2	317		AS	40		G2	99
	KT2	329	Bloodier	ET	9		AE3	440
	KT2	572	Bloodily	ESH	1		AE4	43
	KT2	583	Bloodless	HAP	1565		AE5	386
	KT3	138		AE2	739		AE5	449
	KT3	346		AE11	651		AE7	78
	KT3	499		M11	480		AE7	658
	KT3	527	Bloodshot	M15	285		AE12	37
	KT3	604	Bloody	AM	220		AE12	578
	KT3	629		EM	17		OAL	64
	KT3	706		SCD2	3		OAE1	24
	KT3	753		SCD2	24		AF	10
	KT3	824		PAR	7		MG	15
	KT3	989		DA	122		B	51
	TJD	89		AA	1014		CAM	159
	TJD	110		SAA	770		AS	59
	TJD	159		EDGA	16		G1	273
	M8	22		PD	59		G4	269
	M8	39		HAP	35		FL	14
	M8	119		HAP	1368		FL	105
	M8	154		HAP	1675	Bloomy	BR	13
	M8	178		HAP	1952		AE9	276
	M8	195		HAP	1986		FL	343
	M8	209		HAP	2365	Blossom	PC1	4
	M8	241		J3	67		BR	16
	M8	286		J3	399	Blossomed	ETG	7
	M8	298		J6	857	Blossoms	SMA	30
	M8	309		J10	268		HAP	1847

Montgomery (1967)

FIGURE 7

ance to *The cat sat on the mat* with just one word-form printed on either side (±1):

the *cat* sat

the *mat*

sat *on* the

cat *sat* on

   the cat

on *the* mat

Figure 8 shows a concordance to the word-form *is* in the sample text, with four word-forms printed on either side (±4).

The full KWIC format prints a whole line of text, with the word under study in the middle. Such concordances are the foundation of the COBUILD project at Birmingham University. This is an extensive study of contemporary English using a basic corpus of 7.3 million words, so the total concordance is 7.3 million lines long.

of activity and communication	is	only one of them
communication where the activity	is	halted in time if
whole process the activity	is	obvious enough the nervous
nervous activity of authors	is	legendary and the silent
reader in his armchair	is	making continuous fast and
radio listener his brain	is	highly active if he
highly active if he	is	taking anything in there
human communication through language	is	only a small sub-section
small sub-section although it	is	very important attempts to
mankind's only remaining boast	is	that we thought of
of it first it	is	certainly an intricate and

FIGURE 8 Concordance to *is*: eleven occurrences

Longer environments

Figure 8 shows an environment of four word-forms on either side of the word-form in the centre. This pattern can be varied according to need, though the visual convenience is lost if the citation exceeds one line. Figure 9 shows the same concordance for *is*, but with an environment of a whole sentence in each case. For some words like *finally* or *so*, it may be necessary to cite more than a paragraph.

Ordering within concordance

The basic concordance at Figure 8 lists occurrences in text order,

There are many kinds of activity, and communication	is	only one of them, although often it does not look much like activity.
But in a library we see a stage of communication where the activity	is	halted in time.
If we consider the whole process, the activity	is	obvious enough.
The nervous activity of authors	is	legendary, and the silent reader in his armchair is making continuous, fast, and precise eye movements.
The nervous activity of authors is legendary, and the silent reader in his armchair	is	making continuous, fast, and precise eye movements.
And, like the radio listener, his brain	is	highly active if he is taking anything in.
And, like the radio listener, his brain is highly active if he	is	taking anything in.
There are many kinds of communication, too, and human communication through language	is	only a small sub-section, although it is very important.
There are many kinds of communication, too, and human communication through language is only a small sub-section, although it	is	very important.
Perhaps mankind's only remaining boast	is	that we thought of it first!
It	is	certainly an intricate and distinctive kind of activity.

FIGURE 9 Concordance to *is*: sentences

just as the basic word-list is in order of occurrence. However, within the concordance to a particular word-form, it is easy to arrange for other orderings. The one which is most generally helpful is alphabetical ordering to the right of the central word-form. (Figure 10) This ordering highlights phrases and other patterns that begin with the central word. In the tiny example, the word-form *only* shows up immediately.

Another presentation of interest is reverse alphabetization to the left of the central form. (Figure 11) This shows up *it* and *the activity*. *The activity* refers to *communication*, and *it* refers to *human verbal communication*, which is stated to be a small sub-section of communication. This is a useful clue to the topic of the passage, in that four

of it first it	is	certainly an intricate and
communication where the activity	is	halted in time if
radio listener his brain	is	highly active if he
nervous activity of authors	is	legendary and the silent
reader in his armchair	is	making continuous fast and
whole process the activity	is	obvious enough the nervous
human communication through language	is	only a small sub-section
of activity and communication	is	only one of them
highly active if he	is	taking anything in there
mankind's only remaining boast	is	that we thought of
small sub-section although it	is	very important attempts to

FIGURE 10

human communication through language	is	only a small sub-section
highly active if he	is	taking anything in there
radio listener his brain	is	highly active if he
of activity and communication	is	only one of them
reader in his armchair	is	making continuous fast and
nervous activity of authors	is	legendary and the silent
small sub-section although it	is	very important attempts to
of it first it	is	certainly an intricate and
mankind's only remaining boast	is	that we thought of
communication where the activity	is	halted in time if
whole process the activity	is	obvious enough the nervous

FIGURE 11

of the cited clauses have a similar subject. Closer examination shows that clauses 1 and 4 also have subjects centring on *communication*; that all the others except clause 9 show another type of subject; and that 9 (*boast*) is different again, and on its own.

From this brief example it can be seen how, with appropriate systems of analysis and reference, a computer-supported investigation can be quick, efficient and useful.

Concordance processing

It is valuable to think of a concordance as a text in itself, and to examine the frequencies of word-forms in the environment of the central word-form. Some very common words, like *the, and* and *of* will show a frequency that is much the same as their overall frequency

a	1	highly	2	radio	1
active	2	his	2	reader	1
activity	4	human	1	remaining	1
although	1	if	3	silent	1
an	1	important	1	small	2
and	4	in	3	sub-section	2
anything	1	intricate	1	taking	1
armchair	1	it	3	that	1
attempts	1	language	1	the	4
authors	1	legendary	1	them	1
boast	1	listener	1	there	1
brain	1	mankind's	1	thought	1
certainly	1	making	1	through	1
communication	3	nervous	2	time	1
continuous	1	obvious	1	to	1
enough	1	of	5	very	1
fast	1	one	1	we	1
first	1	only	3	where	1
halted	1	process	1	whole	1
he	2				

FIGURE 12 Concordance to *is* (± four words): alphabetical list

of	5	although	1	making	1
		an	1	obvious	1
activity	4	anything	1	out	1
and	4	armchair	1	process	1
the	4	attempts	1	radio	1
		authors	1	reader	1
communication	3	boast	1	remaining	1
if	3	brain	1	silent	1
in	3	certainly	1	taking	1
it	3	continuous	1	that	1
only	3	enough	1	them	1
		fast	1	there	1
active	2	first	1	thought	1
he	2	halted	1	through	1
highly	2	human	1	time	1
his	2	important	1	to	1
nervous	2	intricate	1	very	1
small	2	language	1	we	1
sub-section	2	legendary	1	where	1
		listener	1	whole	1
a	1	mankind's	1		

FIGURE 13 Concordance to *is* (± four words): frequency list

in the language, but others will show a strong influence from being close to the central word-form in the concordance.

Let us prepare an alphabetical list and a frequency list of the concordance 'text' shown in Figure 8 – see Figures 12 and 13. (Note that where two occurrences of *is* are close together, the same text word-form can occur more than once in the environment and so its frequency in the concordance 'text' can be greater than its frequency in the original text.)

In such a short text we cannot expect the linguistically important patterns to be distinguishable from all the other statistical effects of the process. The word-form *is* in any case is unlikely to have strong lexical collocations of a conventional nature. But the method is clear from these examples.

Text analysis statistics

As soon as the computer has been trained to identify characters, word-forms and sentences, it can produce figures for a number of relationships – see Figure 14. This can be very useful in comparing texts, or searching for texts with particular characteristics.

Length of the text in word-forms	= 189	
No. of different word-forms	= 113	
Length of the text in characters	= 940	
Average word length	= 4.97	
Longest word	= 15	
Length of the text in sentences	= 11	
Average sentence length in word-forms	= 17.18	
The longest sentence	= 28	
No. of sentences with less than 10 word-forms	= 0	0.00%
No. of sentences with 11 to 20 word-forms	= 7	63.64%
No. of sentences with 21 to 30 word-forms	= 4	36.36%
No. of sentences with 31 to 40 word-forms	= 0	0.00%
No. of sentences with more than 41 word-forms	= 0	0.00%

FIGURE 14 Text analysis statistics

Selective information

When a text is very long, the word lists will also be very long and the concordances will be very very long. Not all this information is needed every time, hence it is important to be able to select. Selections can be made as follows:

a) by frequency. If we omit from a frequency list word-forms which only occur once, it shrinks to about half its size. Also for some purposes we only require a list of very frequent words (e.g. Figure 4). It is commonplace to distinguish roughly between grammatical and lexical items by this means. At other times it is useful to divide the vocabulary of a text into frequency bands.

b) by form. It is possible to specify words by their alphabetical make-up, or by the number of letters in them, or a combination of both, like 'three-letter words beginning with *t*'. It will be found that formal constraints can be devised which approximate to several word-classes, e.g. present participle, regular adverbs.

These two types of selection can also be combined to make sensitive analytical instruments.

Intermediate categories

When a researcher has easy access to the processing described so far, it is possible to formulate objectives in linguistic description, and devise procedures for pursuing these objectives. A considerable amount of research on specific topics can be launched – in stylistics, for example, and in English language teaching. In cases where rather simple categories like *word-form* are adequate, there is no need to pursue more abstract categories, and indeed good reason not to.

For many purposes, however, and for research into language structure in general, it is desirable to establish intermediate categories like *word*, word-classes like *adverb* or *adjective*, larger syntactic categories like *phrase* or *clause*, and *lexical items*, which are lexical units comprising one or more morphemes (see, e.g., Yang 1985).

The specification of categories of this kind is a purely practical matter; the researcher has to devise a selection procedure which matches his intuition, and is consistent with authoritative published descriptions. In all probability there will be some rules, formulated in terms of the physical data, to capture surface regularities. Then there will be exclusion lists and additional lists. Even then it must be recognized that the procedure will be prone to a small measure of discrepancy.

Many such procedures exist as programs in CALL (computer-assisted language learning), in automatic analysis (Leech *et al.* 1983) and in machine translation. The move from word-form to word, for example, is called *lemmatization*, and there are many different ways of doing it, and many different levels of sophistication. At one extreme, Harris (research in progress, University of Birmingham) takes the view that it is worth actually listing and classifying the commonest 30,000 word-forms of English, and sorting out ambiguities like *mean* one by one. This leads to a very accurate and powerful system, and the remaining word-forms of English will either be clearly marked for word-class, because derived from words in the central list, or unusual words, probably foreign borrowings, which would have to be treated uniquely by any method.

At the other extreme, the document processing programs within the latest version of the UNIX operating system offers as many rules as possible, a few lists of frequent and irregular word-forms, and a default category so that anything which cannot be placed is called a noun. Tim Johns (1982) has a program which offers to pluralize English nouns, but which has to fit into 1k of storage and so is very heavily dependent on efficient rules.

New approaches

The most exciting aspect of long text data-processing, however, is not the mirroring of intuitive categories of description. It is the possibility of new approaches, new kinds of evidence and new kinds of description. Here the objectivity and surface validity of computer techniques become an asset rather than a liability. Without, of course, relinquishing our intuitions, we try to find explanations that fit the evidence, rather than adjusting the evidence to fit a pre-set explanation.

It is clear that the early stages of computer processing give results which conflict with our intuitions. In addition to problems in identifying word-classes, the notion of *collocation* turns out to be not nearly as simple as it looks. Current work in lexicography shows that, for many common words, the most frequent meaning is not the one that first comes to mind and takes pride of place in the run of dictionaries.

Progress will be made by trying to relate these conflicting positions. No one would wish to give priority to either at the expense of the other. The computer is not a device which will produce sensible categories without guidance, but on the other hand a linguistic description which is not supported by the evidence of the language has no credibility.

New evidence from long texts, where the computer does little more than clerical work, will challenge our current linguistic descriptions quite fundamentally. Such evidence has not been available before and its assimilation should contribute to the maturation of linguistics as a discipline.

Appendix A: Sample text

There are many kinds of activity, and communication is only one of them, although often it does not look much like activity. The shelves of a library can look very inactive indeed, and someone sitting with his eyes shut listening to a transistor through earphones may seem fairly static. But in a library we see a stage of communication where the activity is halted in time. If we consider the whole process, the activity is obvious enough. The nervous activity of authors is legendary, and the silent reader in his armchair is making continuous, fast, and precise eye movements. And, like the radio listener his brain is highly active if he is taking anything in.

There are many kinds of communication, too, and human communication through language is only a small sub-section, although it is very important. Attempts to set out the special characteristics of human language have become quite sophisticated. But research workers have now created most aspects of human verbal communication in animals and machines. Perhaps mankind's only remaining boast is that we thought of it first! It is certainly an intricate and distinctive kind of activity.

Notes

1. This paper adopts much of the structure of a Demonstration Program on text processing which was written by Professor Yang Huizhong during his attachment to Birmingham University in 1983–84. Several of the figures are taken directly from the displays of his program, written in BASIC, which is obtainable from English Language Research, University of Birmingham.
   I would like to acknowledge the help of Jeremy Clear in the preparation of this paper.

Introduction to Chapter 14

Geoffrey Leech offers an account of the potential of research into computer-based grammatical analysis for the CALL practitioner. He thus provides not only a counterpoint to Sinclair's paper on lexical analysis, as we noted, but also a warrant for the thesis of the book as a whole, namely that the twin endeavours of computer-based linguistic research and educational applications like CALL ought to be interdependent within a continuum of applied linguistic research and practice.

However, Leech cautions against those who would ask computers in education to be ready now to stimulate those human processing capacities which we take for granted in any classroom. It is important to dispel this myth, both when strongly advocating CALL and also when equally depreciating it for its clear limitations. There is a distinction, which Leech identifies, between modelling cognitive processes, and providing the kind of rapid and flexible reaction to learner input characterized in this volume by Sampson's suggestions. Turning to language processing, Leech offers an account of work at Lancaster in the establishment of the LOB Corpus and its subsequent utilization in the field of grammatical analysis. He outlines steps in the ideal analysis of spoken input to the computer (acoustic analysis, phonetic analysis, phonological analysis, morphological analysis, parsing, semantic analysis, and pragmatic analysis) and then offers analysis of the necessarily limited parsing (grammatical analysis) programs currently in use. The implications of this research for language educators ought to be clear: we can make use of them for analysing learner input and for its subsequent evaluation, and we can offer to the learner grammatically controlled responses which are sensitive to the input of the learner, in the adaptive way suggested by Alderson's contribution to this volume. Most excitingly for learners and teachers anxious to develop their own classroom autonomy, Leech's research identifies ways in which the results of computer-based linguistic analysis can be put to the service of the practitioner. In return, as it were, these techniques can be drawn upon to increase our own knowledge of learners' interlanguage, offering a new database for linguistic and psycholinguistic research.

14 Automatic grammatical analysis and its educational applications

Geoffrey Leech

Introduction: background issues

My main task in this paper is to explain some current research in automatic grammatical analysis, and what purposes it can serve in educational applications such as CALL.

In order to do this, however, I feel I have to deal more generally with the whole question of using computers for automatically analysing or processing English language text. The mention of automatic grammatical analysis raises a question: how far is it possible to teach computers to simulate human linguistic abilities, e.g. the ability to analyse or generate acceptable and appropriate English sentences? The answer to this question may be of two opposite kinds.

On the one hand, if our experience of computers is limited to CALL programs written for the present generation of micros in educational use, we will probably reply that computers are 'dumb' machines incapable of analysing language in any way other than crude character-based matchings and manipulations. Any appearance of human-like linguistic behaviour on the part of the computer is a mere hoax by clever programmers, such as Weizenbaum, the inventor of ELIZA (see Davies, this volume, p. 23).

On the other hand, if we are influenced by the more optimistic prognostications from research in artificial intelligence and information technology, we shall probably claim that the era of 'intelligent' computer systems – capable, among other things, of understanding human language – is just round the corner. It is with this expectation that many governments, with the USA and Japan in the lead, are putting vast sums of money into research and development of *fifth generation* computer systems capable of imitating intelligent human behaviour in such areas as logical inference, sensory perception, manipulation, and not least, in linguistic behaviour, which computer scientists like to call *natural language processing*.

A realistic view, it is clear to me, lies somewhere between these two assessments, which we may call the 'dumb machine' view and the 'intelligent machine' view of the linguistic powers of computers. Research in natural language processing is making considerable advances after being rather neglected in the 1960s and 1970s. Currently available are fairly crude and limited, but serviceable systems in such areas as question-answering front ends to databases (cf. Woods 1973); machine translation (cf. Hutchins 1978); and text critiquing (Heidorn *et al.* 1983). But we are still light years away from the ultimate achievement of natural language processing – that human beings should be able to engage in linguistic interaction with a computer without being able to tell that they are communicating with a machine rather than another human being!

For educational users working with small micros, even this degree of progress, however, may seem hopelessly remote from real life. There has seemed to be a large gulf separating CALL software written in BASIC for small machines, and natural language processing software written in such languages as LISP and PROLOG for large university mainframe computers. How could one begin to make use of such sophisticated software on an APPLE or BBC micro?

The answer, at present, is that one could not. But hardware capabilities are increasing so rapidly (see Atwell, this volume, p. 168) that processing which five years ago could be carried out only on the most powerful mainframe machine will shortly be possible on an average micro. At the same time, the power of a single-site university mainframe will be surpassed by the power of a network to which various interacting kinds of equipment can be attached, such that a micro as part of a network will be able to summon up powerful storage and processing facilities. Thus the present gulf between large machines and small machines, and between natural language processing research and its educational applications, is likely to diminish or disappear in the future.

In this 'moving staircase' situation, it is reasonable to explore what may lie ahead within the next five years or so, rather than restrict one's attention to the limited possibilities of today. It is in this spirit that I wish to examine the educational potential of some natural language processing research.

There is, however, a problem of realism to be faced up to before we proceed. CALL by aspiration identifies itself with the most sophisticated and ambitious areas of artificial intelligence research. Perhaps the computer's most obvious advantage over other language-learning technologies is its ability to respond appropriately and linguistically to the learner's input. Thus, to realize its full potential, the computer should become a truly communicative machine, able to carry out intelligent interactive conversation with the learner.

This is an attractive ideal, but I believe we must reject its reality, just as we should reject the ideal of the computer as an intelligent language processor of truly human ability. The error which attributes flesh-and-blood properties to technological inventions is a powerful one which has persisted since the times of ancient Greece, and today influences both artificial intelligence research and CALL. This error may be called the 'Daedalus myth' after the legendary Greek inventor for whom the solution to the problem of human flight was to attach wings made of feathers to the human frame – with fatal consequences for his son Icarus. The Daedalus myth would lead us to favour bicycles with horses' tails or with feet instead of wheels; submarines with scales and fins; and anthropoid robots with fingers, toes and hair. In practice, such curiosities have never survived the Darwinian struggle of technological progress. But strangely, the myth is deepseated, and is particularly difficult to eradicate when we come to machines (computers) which are technological extensions of the human mind, rather than of the human body. Whereas bicycles with feet are merely comic, computers which pretend to behave just like human minds are a serious goal of research. This is because cognitive science finds it valuable, as a research strategy, to 'model' aspects of human psychological behaviour by computer. But such modelling should not be confused with a more limited and practical educational goal of enabling computers to respond flexibly and appropriately to the input of language learners.

If we are to steer clear of the Daedalus myth in its modern form, we should not suppose that in the next few years, it will be possible for learners to hold meaningful human-like interactions with computers. (For this to be possible, the computer would not only have to possess human-like knowledge of language, but would also have to contain a human-like model of the real world: something of phenomenal complexity.) But we can examine the developments now taking place in natural language processing, and consider how they can be adapted in the fairly near future to the educational sphere. A computer capable of using at least *some* degree of linguistic knowledge is better than one which has no such knowledge at all. In other words, we should aim at making the best of a 'semi-dumb, semi-intelligent' computer.

Two present approaches to natural language processing

In the present state of the art, there are two very different routes along which to advance towards the goal of successful automatic language processing. The first route is to program the computer with sufficient linguistic and real-world knowledge to enable it to communicate about a limited domain of discourse. Such a domain may, for example, be restricted to a 'toy world' such as a spatio-temporal world consisting of certain geometrically-shaped objects, like the table-top world of Winograd (1972). Most language processing systems which exist today are limited in this way: a miniature example is the 'telling the time' world described by Sampson (this volume, pp. 152–64. (For further details of such limited-domain systems, see Winograd 1983, Chapter 7.) Progress along this route may be measured in terms of the increasing size of the domain for which the system may be used. We may imagine a gradual extension towards the goal of successful processing of unrestricted discourse, e.g. from a machine translation system which can translate weather forecasts from French into English to a machine translation system which can deal with any kind of French text.

The second route is to deal with unrestricted discourse from the beginning, but to restrict one's goal initially to a partial processing of language, and/or to a processing which contains a proportion of errors. This approach typically relies upon information gathered from a large corpus of English texts (spoken or written) (see Sinclair, this volume, pp. 185–203), and can be illustrated by the work with which my colleagues and I in UCREL (Unit for Computer Research on the English Language) at Lancaster have been associated. In our case, the first objective (following the work of Francis and Kučera (1982) on the Brown Corpus) was to undertake a *grammatical tagging* of the Lancaster-Oslo-Bergen (LOB) Corpus of written British English texts (Leech *et al.* 1983a, 1983b). This meant that every one of 1,000,000+ running words in the Corpus had to be associated with its appropriate grammatical category label, such as 'preposition', 'past participle', 'modal auxiliary'. Although this was no more than a first stage of grammatical analysis, 'teaching' the computer to undertake this limited task to a 96+% level of accuracy was by no means an easy task, which took over two years and which relied on the research of co-workers in Norway (see Johansson 1982). (One prerequisite for such processing, for example, is that the computer should contain a fairly large lexicon of English words together with their possible grammatical classes.)

We are now undertaking a second stage of automatic processing, in which every sentence in the Corpus will be *parsed*, i.e. analysed in terms of phrase and clause structure. The idea is to develop parsing programs which will deal with any kind of text – including texts containing errors, 'bad grammar', etc. The parser will make the best prediction it can about the correct analysis of each sentence, but it may well get the answer wrong. It is nevertheless useful to have such fallible analyses, since it is easier to correct a fallible analysis than to attempt to do the whole job by hand; particularly if (as we hope) the percentage of error is low, as was the case with the grammatical tagging.

This second approach to natural language processing relies on the expectations that (a) by 'recycling' of information from completed analyses, the errors produced by the system can gradually be reduced to a minimal level, and that (b) an analysis at a lower level will provide a foundation for the development of analysis at a higher level. Hence it is assumed that, just as grammatical tagging will help parsing, so parsing will eventually help semantic analysis, so that eventually a total integrated general-purpose language analysis system will be developed.

The level-by-level approach builds on the view of language as a multi-levelled phenomenon. The levels interact differently according to which of the following four processes are being considered:

Analysis	*Synthesis (or Generation)*
A. spoken input	C. spoken output
B. written input	D. written output

For example, the problem of analysing spoken input to the computer (*speech recognition*) may be subdivided into the stages of acoustic analysis, phonetic analysis, phonological analysis, morphological analysis (or grammatical tagging), syntactic analysis (or parsing), semantic analysis, and pragmatic or discoursal analysis. The opposite ordering is appropriate to speech synthesis. The same order is appropriate to the analysis of spoken and written texts, except that orthographic analysis (instead of phonetic and phonological analysis) precedes the level of grammatical tagging. It is unfortunate for CALL that computers have priorities, in respect of these four processes, which are the opposite of those typical of the human learner. For the computer, processing of speech (A and C) lags behind that of writing (B and D). Also, analysis for the machine is more difficult than synthesis. A consequence of this is that much of the energy of researchers in natural language processing has gone into the automatic analysis of written input. The work on the LOB Corpus I shall briefly describe is of this kind. But looking at CALL in a longer-term perspective, all four processes are important for learners' interaction with computers.

Although a level-by-level progression from the 'lowest level' to the 'highest level' is a rational research strategy for the present, it must be borne in mind that in an integrated natural language processing system, there will be advantages in being able to interleave the different levels, or to process them in parallel.

Examples of grammatical tagging and parsing

Before we come to the educational applications of automatic grammatical analysis, here are some illustrations to show what is meant by grammatical tagging and parsing. In Version 1, I have taken the first sentence of the first text used by Scott Windeatt for his cloze experiment (this volume, p. 95), adding grammatical tags according to the Lancaster tagging system. The tagging system (known as CLAWS) uses a set of 134 grammatical category labels, or tags. The tags are normally assigned automatically (any corrections being made by hand), but in this illustrative example the whole thing has been done manually:

Version 1

    For more than three centuries readers in   all   countries
    IN   AP   IN   CD   NNS   NNS IN ABN   NNS

    have been delighted by the adventures of   an   absurd
    HV BEN   VBN   IN   ATI   NNS   IN AT JJ

    gentleman named Don   Quixote and his   squire Sancho Panza.
     NN   VBN NPT NP   CC PP\$ NN   NP   NP

    Key to tags:
    ABN = predeterminer; AP = postdeterminer; AT(I) = determiner; HV = *have*; BEN = *been*; CC = coordinating conjunction; CD = cardinal numeral; IN = preposition; JJ = adjective; NN = singular common noun; NNS = plural common noun; NP = proper noun; NPT = titular noun; PP\$ = possessive pronoun.

In Version 2, I have taken the same passage, and added to the text and the line of tags a further line representing the syntactic structure of each sentence. The structure is represented as a labelled bracketing: each higher constituent is represented by a single upper case letter (followed by one or more subscripts), and is delimited by an opening and closing square bracket. The same structure could be alternatively represented as a tree diagram, of the kind associated with phrase structure grammars:

Version 2

```
For  more than three centuries readers in    all     countries
IN   AP   IN   CD   NNS         NNS    IN   ABN   NNS
[S[P [N   [P   [N   N]P]N]P]    [N     [P   [N    N]P]N]
```

```
have been delighted by  the adventures of  an   absurd
HV   BEN  VBN      IN   ATI NNS      IN   AT   JJ
[V        V]       [P   [N           [P   [N&
```

```
gentleman named   Don Quixote and  his squire Sancho Panza.
NN        VBN     NPT NP      CC   PP$ NN     NP     NP
          [Tn[Vn] [N   N]Tn] [N+      [N   N]N+]N&]P]N]P]S]
```

Key to parsing symbols:
S = sentence; P = prepositional phrase; N = noun phrase; N&
= coordinate noun phrase; N+ = non-initial part of a coordinate
noun phrase; Tn = past participle construction; Vn = past participle phrase; brackets indicate the opening and closing of
constituents.

The present state of affairs is this. We can already produce output
of the kind illustrated by Version 1 with over 96% accuracy. The
project on which we are engaged at the moment[1] has as two of its
objectives the development of parsing programs for the automatic
parsing of the LOB Corpus, and the improvement of the grammatical
tagging system CLAWS, so as to achieve a significantly higher degree
of tagging success. Thus, by the time the project is due to finish in
December 1986, we should be able to offer both an enhanced grammatical tagger and a parser. One may look ahead a little further to the
end of the five-year period I mentioned in my Introduction as a period
of great change, and expect that by that time natural language
processing systems of this kind will be reasonably available and
successful.

I have focused on our own research at Lancaster, but of course
many other language processing systems are reaching a comparable
degree of development (see the survey article, Leech and Beale 1984).
There is a general trend towards natural language processing systems
which are advanced enough to be useful for CALL.

Educational applications

Suppose, not implausibly, that a computer for CALL in 1990 can make
use of the type of 'limited intelligence' grammatical capability outlined
above. Suppose further that this capability can be adapted for text
synthesis, as well as text analysis. What advantages would this give
over the CALL software available today?

First, we can distinguish three main types of processing for CALL:
1. grammatical analysis of stored texts;
2. grammatical analysis of learners' input;
3. grammatically-controlled synthesis of responses to the learner.
Let us consider these separately.

1. Grammatical analysis of stored texts

We may assume that CALL in the future will have access to a large amount of disk storage, which will enable a 'bank' of many texts, classified according to level, topic, vocabulary, etc., to be available for a given program or authoring package. These texts can be stored together with their grammatical analyses (tags or parses), so that the text processing does not have to take place within the time-scale of a learning session.

A number of applications of this facility suggest themselves:
a) It will be possible to retrieve from the text corpus examples of a given grammatical feature (e.g. progressive aspect, passive, particular modal auxiliaries, phrasal verbs), so that the CALL session can focus on that topic.
b) It will be possible to perform various grammatically-determined 'deformations' of texts, in order to provide suitable material for CALL procedures. For example, it will be possible to delete all words of specified classes (e.g. prepositions or modals), thus generating modified cloze procedures for particular purposes.
c) It will be possible to provide a 'profile' of each text in terms of its suitability for illustrating given grammatical topics.
d) It will be possible to evaluate, grade, or select texts according to measures of stylistic difficulty in terms of grammatical structure.

2. Grammatical analysis of learners' input

Although the problem of response time (see Sampson, this volume, p. 153) is bound to limit the feasibility of grammatical processing of learners' input, we may suppose that some kinds of grammatical analysis of a word, phrase, sentence, or text produced by the learner will be practicable. This will be a great advantage over the present situation in which the computer can generally only produce an accept-or-reject response to the user's input. For example, in a cloze exercise, it will be possible to accept a word as grammatically appropriate, even if it is not the exact word required. For other grammatically-defined procedures, it will be possible to accept a grammatical structure as correct, even if it does not match a specified sequence of words. Hence the target behaviour of the learner will be permitted a degree of linguistic creativity.

This ability of the computer to evaluate learners' productions grammatically can be extended beyond CALL to CBELT (computer-based English language testing: see Alderson, this volume, pp. 99–110). Another important possibility is learners' self-evaluation, which is a function of text-critiquing systems such as EPISTLE and *The Writer's Workbench* (see Atwell, this volume, p. 177). The simplest kind of text-critiquing system is the spelling-checker which comes with commercial word-processors: such a checker merely attempts to match a text word with an entry in a stored lexicon, and flags it as a possible error if no entry is found. A more advanced spelling-checker (of a kind currently being developed at Lancaster – see Atwell 1983) would take account of grammatical context, thus identifying as a possible error a word which, although matching a word in the lexicon, appears in an improbable context (e.g. the mistyping of *if* for *is* in *Seeing if believing*). Such a facility is obviously not restricted to a learning situation, but may be available as an 'extra' in word-processing software. In principle, it is only a small step from this to the type of error detector which would be designed for the EFL market, and which would spot errors of grammar, as well as of spelling. Similarly, such systems could be modified to deal with stylistically unacceptable or inappropriate grammar.

3. Grammatically-controlled synthesis of responses to the learner

At present the type of language produced by the computer in response to the learner is largely 'canned language' triggered by a restricted range of input. Any input outside the expected range is likely to produce an offputting negative or 'try again'. It will be an obvious advantage if computers can respond to the creativity· of the learner (as foreseen in 2 above) by their own form of creativity: a response which takes account of the variability of the learner's own behaviour. Such a response could, for example, be a substitution frame, or template, in which certain grammatical slots are filled by random selection from grammatically-appropriate words. This would mean turning the lexicon which is necessary for grammatical tagging (see 2 above) into a productive, rather than analytic device.

It is worth commenting at this point that a natural language analysis system depends on various language databases, such as a lexicon, a list of productive affixes, or a grammar. Such databases can equally well be applied to text synthesis as to text analysis. We can therefore envisage the combination of a lexicon and a grammar being used to generate random sentences according to specified patterns. This kind of facility is essential in CALL for what has been called 'conjectural learning' (Higgins, this volume, p. 38), where the object is to enable learners to explore the language for themselves, arriving at their own hypotheses about what is grammatical or ungrammatical. According to Higgins, part of the challenge of such software for the learner is in trying to 'beat the computer', finding out where the rules which are programmed into it fail. From this point of view, there is actually some advantage in a limited or defective grammar!

Conclusion: longer-term perspective

In the preceding sections, I have had occasion to refer to the connections betwen linguistic databases (such as a grammar and a lexicon), CALL, and CBELT. This leads me to a somewhat specu-lative conclusion about the kind of educational computing environment which may be attainable in (say) ten years from now.

An *Integrated Language Education Network* will contain a bank of CALL software for self-access or for classroom use. Each work station will also have access to a bank of CBELT tests and test items, such facilities being available for the learner's self-evaluation, as well as for testing purposes. The CALL and CBELT programs will be able to make use of corpora of graded and classified English language texts, and language databases in the form of a grammar and a lexicon. The grammar and the lexicon will also be available as reference tools for teachers or students who wish to retrieve explicit knowledge about the language. All these components will be capable of interacting with one another, and with a natural language processing system. In this paper I have restricted attention to lexical and grammatical processing, but we may also hope, at least in the longer term, for components which will handle the processing of speech and of meaning.

Note
1. A project under Research Grant GR/C/47700 of the Science and Engineering Research Council.

Software index

Bibliography

Adams, E N, Morrison, H W and Reddy, J M 1968 Conversation with a computer as a technique of language instruction. *Modern Language Journal* **52** (1): 3–16

Ahl, D H 1976 Learning, innovation and animals. *The Best of Creative Computing* **1**: 196–201

Ahl, D H 1978 *Basic computer games*. Creative Computing Press, Morristown, New Jersey

Alderson, J C 1978 *A study of the cloze procedure with native and non-native speakers of English*. Unpublished Ph.D. dissertation, University of Edinburgh

Alderson, J C 1979 The cloze procedure and proficiency in English as a foreign language. *TESOL Quarterly* **13**: 219–28

Atwell, E S 1983 Constituent-likelihood grammar. *ICAME News* **7**: 34–67, Bergen

Avner, R A 1979 Longitudinal studies in computer-based authoring. In O'Neill, H F Jr. (ed.) *Issues in instructional system development*. Academic Press, New York

Ben-Ari, M 1982 *Principles of concurrent programming*. Prentice-Hall

Blum-Kulka, S and Olshtain, E 1984 *Applied Linguistics* **5** (3): 196–213

Bourne, S 1982 *The Unix system*. Addison-Wesley, Reading, Massachusetts

Breen, M P 1983 How would we recognize a communicative classroom? *Proceedings of 1983 British Council staff seminar at Dunford House*. British Council

Breen, M P 1984 Processes in syllabus design and classroom language learning. In Brumfit, C (ed.) *General English syllabus design. ELT Documents* **11**, British Council and Pergamon Press

Breen, M P, Candlin, C N and Waters, A 1979 Communicative materials design: some basic principles. *RELC Journal* **10** (2): 1–13

Brown A F (ed.) 1963 *Normal and reverse English word list 1–8*. University of Pennsylvania Press, Philadelphia

Bruton, J G 1964 *The English verb in context*. Cambridge University Press

Byers, R A 1983 *dBase II for every business*. Ashton-Tate, Culver City

Canale, M 1984 *An overview of adaptive language testing*. Paper presented at 6th Annual Colloquium in Research in Language Testing, TESOL Convention, Houston, Texas

Canale, M and Barker, G 1984 *LOGO and computer-assisted language learning*. Handout TESOL 1984

Candlin, C N 1984 Syllabus design as a critical process. In Brumfit, C (ed.) *General English syllabus design. ELT Documents* **11**, British Council and Pergamon Press

Carrier, M 1983 Computer games in EFL. *Report of IATEFL Conference, Twickenham, April 1983*: 47–9

Chandler, D (ed.) 1983 *Exploring English with microcomputers*. MEP Readers 1 Published in association with the National Association of Teachers of English for the Microelectronics Education Programme by Council for Educational Technology, London

Chapelle, C and Jamieson, J 1983a Language lessons on the PLATO IV system. In Wyatt D H (ed.) *Computer-assisted language instruction. System* **11** (1): 13–20

Chapelle, C and Jamieson, J 1983b Using informative feedback messages in CALL courseware. *TESOL Newsletter* **27** (4): 26–7

Cherry, L 1980 PARTS – a system for assigning word classes to English text. *Computing Science Technical Report* **81**, Bell Laboratories

Cherry, L and Vesterman, W 1981 Writing tools – the STYLE and DICTION programs. *Computing Science Technical Report* **91**, Bell Laboratories

Cherry, L, Fox, M, Frase, L, Gingrich, P, Keenan, S and Macdonald, N 1983 Computer aids for text analysis. *Bell Laboratories Records*, May/June: 10–16

Cherry, L and Macdonald, N 1983 the UNIX Writer's Workbench software. *BYTE*, October: 241–48

Clark, K and McCabe, F 1984 *Micro-Prolog: programming in Logic*. Prentice-Hall

Clarke, D and Fox, J 1984 *Computer-assisted reading*. Mimeo. University of East Anglia

Clocksin, W and Mellish, C 1984 *Programming in Prolog*. (2nd edition) Springer-Verlag

Cook, V J 1984 Communication games with a microcomputer. *World Language English* **3** (2): 119–23

Cook, V J and Hamilton, T 1984 *CHATTERBOX: program for the BBC Micro*. British Council

Cooper, D and Clancy, M 1982 *'Oh! Pascal'* Norton

Cousin, W D 1983 *Computer clozentropy: phase one. Report*. Mimeo. Moray House Centre for Computer Education/Scottish Centre for Education Overseas

Davies, A 1983 *Computer-assisted language testing*. Mimeo (written as a report to British Council's English Teaching Advisory Committee, July 1983)

Davies, G 1980 New technologies for linguists. *Computer Age* **9**: 23–6

Davies, G 1982 Micros in modern languages. *Educational Computing* **3** (8): 30

Davies, G 1985 *Talking BASIC*. Cassell

Davies, G and Higgins, J 1982a *Computers, language and language learning*. CILT, London

Davies, G and Higgins, J 1982b Computers, language learning and teaching. *CILT Information Guide* **22**

Deakin, R 1984 *dBase II explored: a simple guide to building your own database*. Century Communications Ltd, London

Deitel, H 1983 *An introduction to operating systems*. Addison-Wesley, Reading, Massachusetts

Dinerstein, N T 1984 *dBase II for the programmer.* Scott, Foresman and Co., Glenview, Illinois

Doroff, S and Doroff, L 1983 *dBase II in English 1.* English Computer Tutorials, Inc., Chicago

Farrington, B 1982 Computer-based exercises for language learning at university level. *Computers in Education* 6: 113–16

Fortescue, S 1983 Hands on experience! *ARELS Journal* 4: (4): 138

Fox, J 1982 Computer-assisted learning and language teachers. *British Journal of Language Teaching* 20 (2): 89–92

Fox, J 1984 Computer-assisted vocabulary learning. *ELT Journal* 38 (1): 27–32

Francis, W N and Kučera, H 1982 *Frequency analysis of English usage: lexicon and grammar.* Houghton Mifflin, Boston

Freedman, A 1984 *dBase II for the first-time user.* Ashton-Tate, Culver City

Freeman, D and Tagg, W 1985 Databases in the classroom. *Journal of Computer Assisted Learning* 1 (1): 2–11

Gardner, R C 1979 Social psychological aspects of second language acquisition. In Giles, H and St. Clair, R N (eds.) *Language and social psychology.* Blackwell

Harrison, C 1983a English teaching and computer-assisted simulations. In Chandler, D (ed.) 1983

Harrison, C 1983b *Software evaluation* and *Testing a CALL program.* Mimeo. CILT, London

Hayes, B 1984 Computer recreations. *Scientific American* 250 (2): 12–16

Heckhausen, H and Weiner, B 1972 The emergence of a cognitive theory of motivation. In Dodwell, P (ed.) *New horizons in psychology 2.* Penguin

Heidorn, G, Jensen, K, Miller, L, Byrd, R and Chodorow, M 1982 The EPISTLE text critiquing system. *IBM Systems Journal* 21 (3): 305–26

Hendrix, G C and Sacerdoti, E D 1981 Natural language processing: the field in perspective. *BYTE* 6 (9): 304–52

Higgins, J 1982a How real is a computer simulation? *ELT Documents* 113: 102–9

Higgins, J 1982b *GRAMMARLAND: a non-directive use of the computer in language learning.* Mimeo. British Council

Higgins, J 1983a *John and Mary: the pleasures of manipulation.* Paper presented at IATEFL Conference, Twickenham, April 1983

Higgins, J 1983b Can computers teach? *Calico Journal* 1 (2) September 1983

Higgins, J 1983c Computer-assisted language learning. *Language Teaching* 16 (2): 102–14

Higgins, J 1983d The computer as a communicative environment. *TESOL Newsletter* 17 (4): 9

Higgins, J 1984a The computer and text. *Media in Education and Development* 17 (3): 173–76

Higgins, J 1984b *Learning with a computer.* Paper presented to the Bologna Conference, April 1984. Mimeo. To appear in Holden, S (ed.) *Proceedings of the Third Bologna Conference*

Higgins, J 1984c Reading and risk taking: a role for the computer. *ELT Journal* 38 (3): 192–8

Higgins, J 1984d *The computer and grammar teaching.* Mimeo. To appear in

Stevens, V (ed.) *Readings in CALL.* Newbury House, Rowley, Massachusetts

Higgins, J and Johns, T 1983 Approaches to CALL for English as a Foreign Language. *Journal of English Language Teaching* (India) **17** (5): 151–5

Higgins, J and Johns, T 1984 *Computers in language learning.* Collins

Holmes, G 1984 *Creating CAL courseware: some possibilities.* In Wyatt, D H (ed.) 1984: 21–32

Horowitz, E 1984 *Fundamentals of programming languages* (2nd edition) Springer-Verlag

Hosenfeld, C 1976 Learning about learning: discovering our students' strategies. *Foreign Language Annals* **9**: 117–29

Howatt, A 1969 *Programmed learning and the language teacher.* Longman

Hutchins, W J 1978 Machine translation and machine-aided translation. *Journal of Documentation* **34** (2): 119–57

Introstat: a microcomputer statistics package for the behavioural sciences 1982 Ideal Systems, P.O. Box 681, Fairfield, Iowa

Jensen, K and Wirth, N 1975 *Pascal-user manual and reports* (2nd edition) Springer-Verlag

Johansson, S (ed.) 1982 *Computer corpora in English Language Research.* Norwegian Computing Centre for the Humanities, Bergen

Johns, T 1982a The uses of an analytic generator: the computer as teacher of English for specific purposes. *ELT Documents* **112**: 96–105

Johns, T 1982b Exploring CAL: an alternative use of the computer. In Roe, P (ed.) 1982

Jones, C 1981 Computer-assisted language learning: testing or teaching? *ELT Journal* **37** (4): 247–50

Jones, C 1983 *Clozemaster: a reading skills program.* Wida Software, London

Jones, C and Sinclair, J 1974 English lexical collocations. *Cahiers de Lexicologie* **24**: 15–61

Kemmis, S, Atkin, R and Wright, E 1977 *How do students learn?* Working papers on computer-assisted learning: UNCAL evaluation studies. *Occasional Publications* **5**, Centre for Applied Research in Education, University of East Anglia

Kenning, M-M 1981 Computer-assisted language teaching made easy. *British Journal of Language Teaching* **19**: 119–23

Kenning, M J and Kenning, M-M 1983 *An introduction to CAL teaching.* Oxford University Press

Kjellmer, G 1984 Why *great: greatly* but not *big: bigly? Studia Linguistica* **38**(1): 1–19

Krashen, S D 1982 *Principles and practice in second language acquisition.* Pergamon Press

Krutch, J 1981 *Experiments in artificial intelligence for small computers.* Howard W. Sams, Indianapolis

Last, R 1979 The role of computer-assisted language learning in modern language teaching. *ALLC Bulletin* **7** (2): 165–71

Last, R 1980 Computer-assisted learning: single element in total teaching process. *Educational Computing* **1** (8): 25–7

Last, R 1981 *TES/T Manual.* Hutton Press, Driffield, Yorkshire

Last, R 1984 *Language teaching and the microcomputer.* Blackwell

Leech, G N 1983 *Principles of pragmatics.* Longman

Leech, G N, Garside, R G and Atwell, E S 1983a The automatic tagging of the LOB corpus. *ICAME News* **7**: 13–33

Leech, G N, Garside, R G and Atwell, E S 1983b Recent developments in the use of computer corpora in English language research. *Transactions of the Philological Society*: 23–40

Leech, G N and Beale, A D 1984 Computers in English language research. *Language Teaching* **17**: 216–29

Lewis, R 1981 Pedagogical issues in designing programs. In Howe and Ross (eds.) *Microcomputers in secondary education*. Logan Page, London

Lewis, R and Harris, J 1980 Physics with or without computers. *Computers and Education* **4** (1)

Lewis, R and Tagg, E D (eds.) 1980 *Computer-assisted learning: scope, progress and limits*. North Holland Publishing Co., Amsterdam

Lewis, R and Tagg, E D (eds.) 1981 *Computers in education, part 1 and part 2*. North Holland Publishing Co., Amsterdam

Littlewood, W T 1981 *Communicative language teaching: an introduction*. Cambridge University Press

Macdonald, N, Frase, L, Gingrich, P and Keenan, S 1982 The Writer's Workbench: computer aids for text analysis. *IEEE Transactions on Communications* **30** (1): 105–10

Maddison, A 1982 *Microcomputers in the classroom*. Hodder and Stoughton

McCracken, D 1974 *A simplified guide to Fortran programming*. Wiley, New York

McCracken, D 1976 *A simplified guide to structured Cobol programming*. Wiley, New York

Megarry, J, Walker, D K F, Nisbett and Hoyle, E (eds.) 1983 Computers in education. *World year book of education*. Kogan Press, London

Miller, C D F and Boyle, R D 1984 *UNIX for users*. Blackwell, Oxford

Montgomery, G (ed.) 1957 (rept 1967) *Concordance to the poetical works of John Dryden*.

Murphy, D 1982 Computers: a revolution in language teaching? *Practical English Teaching*, December 1982: 41–2

Odendaal, M 1982 Second language learning and computer-assisted language instruction (CALI). *INTUS News* **6** (1): 37–45, Stellenbosch University

Olson, D R and Bruner, J S 1974 Learning through experience and learning through media. In Olson D R (ed.) 1974 *Media and symbols: the forms of expression*. University of Chicago Press

O'Shea, T and Self, J 1983 *Learning and teaching with computers*. Harvester Press, Brighton

O'Shea, T and Eisenstadt, M 1984 *Artificial intelligence: tools, techniques and applications*. Harper and Row

Papert, S 1980 *Mindstorms. children, computers and powerful ideas*. Harvester Press, Brighton

Parkin, A 1982 *Cobol for students* (2nd edition) Edward Arnold

Phillips M 1983 *Intelligent CALL and the QWERTY phenomenon: a rationale*. Paper presented to the 16th annual meeting of the British Association of Applied Linguistics, September 1983. Mimeo. CILT, London

Prabhu, N 1983 *Procedural syllabuses*. Paper presented at the 18th RELC conference, Singapore, April 1983

Price, D 1984 *Introduction to ADA*. Prentice-Hall

Pyle, I 1981 *The Ada programming language*. Prentice-Hall

Reed, A 1977 CLOC: a collocation package *ALLC Bulletin* 5

Roberts, G E 1981 The use of microcomputers for the teaching of modern languages. *British Journal of Language Teaching* 19 (3): 125–29

Roe, P (ed.) 1982 *Exploring CAL: an alternative use of the computer in teaching foreign languages.*

Roe, P 1985 Making IT available. In Quirk, R and Widdowson, H G (eds.) *English in the world: teaching and learning the language and literatures*: 68–81, Cambridge University Press

Rushby, N J 1979 *An introduction to educational computing*. Croom Helm, London

Ryan, T, Joiner, B and Ryan, B 1982 *Minitab reference manual*. Statistics department, Pennsylvania State University

Self, J 1985 *Microcomputers in education*. Harvester Press, Brighton

Sharples, M 1983 A construction kit for language. In Chandler, D (ed.) 1983: 51–8

Shaw, T 1984 *dBase II: developing applications*. Addison-Wesley, London

Siklossy, L 1976 *Let's talk Lisp*. Prentice-Hall

Skehan, P 1982 ESP teachers, computers and research. *ELT Documents* 112: 106–19

Smith, F 1978 *Reading*. Cambridge University Press

Smith, P R 1981 *Computer-assisted learning*. Pergamon Press

S.P.S.S. *Statistical package for the social sciences.*

Stei, G 1983 Format for the evaluation of courseware used in CALL. *Calico Journal* 1 (2)

Stevens, V 1984 *Escaping the stigma of programmed learning*. Paper presented at the TESOL convention, Houston, March 1984

Strachan, R M 1983 *Guide to evaluating methods*. National Extension College, Cambridge

Stultz, R A 1984 *The illustrated dBase II book*. Wordware Publishing Inc., Plano, Texas

Taylor, R P (ed.) 1980 *The computer in the school: tutor, tool, tutee*. Teacher's College Press, Columbia University

Tung, P 1984 *Some considerations of CAT system design*. Paper presented at the TESOL convention, Houston, March 1984

Underwood, J H 1984 *Linguistics, computers and the language teacher: a communicative approach*. Newbury House, Rowley, Massachusetts

Unistat 1984 Statistical package. Unisoft Ltd., London

Van Campen, J, Markosian, L and Seropian, H 1980 *A computer-based language instruction system with initial application to Armenian*. Technical report 303, Institute for Mathematical Studies in the Social Sciences, Stanford University

Van Ek, J A and Alexander, L G 1985 *Threshold level English*. Pergamon Press

Van Lier, L 1982 *Analysing interaction in the second language classroom*. Unpublished Ph.D. thesis, University of Lancaster

Wainer, H 1983 On item response theory and computerized adaptive tests. *The Journal of College Admissions* 28 (4): 6–9

Ward, R with Phillips, R, Sewell, D and Rostron, A 1983 *Language and thought*. Acornsoft

Ward, R with Phillips, R, Sewell, D and Rostron, A 1983 *Hidden shapes and sizes*. Acornsoft

Watson, D (ed.) 1984 *Exploring geography with microcomputers*. CET, London
Weischedel, R M, Voge, W M and James, M 1978 An artificial intelligence approach to language instruction. *Artificial Intelligence* 10: 225–40
Weizenbaum, J 1984 *Computer power and human reason*. Penguin
Wilks, Y A 1972 *Grammar, meaning and the machine analysis of language*. Routledge and Kegan Paul
Williams, J and Davies, G 1982 *Questionmaster* Hutchinson
Windeatt, S 1980 A project in self-access learning for English language and study skills. *Practical Papers in English Language Education* 3: 43–82, University of Lancaster
Winograd, T 1972 *Understanding natural language*. University of Edinburgh Press
Winograd, T 1983 *Language as a cognitive process. Volume 1: Syntax*. Addison-Wesley, Reading, Massachusetts
Winston, P and Horn, B 1981 *Lisp*. Addison-Wesley
Woods, W A 1973 Progress in natural language understanding: an application in lunar geology. *AFIPS conference proceedings* 42: 441–50
Wyatt, D H (ed.) 1982 Computer-assisted instruction. Special issue of *English for Specific Purposes* (Oregon) 58/59
Wyatt, D H (ed.) 1984 *Computer-assisted language instruction*. Pergamon Press
Wyatt, D H and Post, N E 1982 *A practical guide to further study in microcomputer-based DAI for language teaching*. American Language Academy
Yang, H 1985 Automatic identification of technical terms. *ALLC Journal* (forthcoming)

Index

DATE DUE

The Library Store   #47-0103